T.

PRACTICAL PSYCHIC SELF-DEFENSE HANDBOOK

A SURVIVAL GUIDE

Combat Psychic Attacks, Evil Spirits & Possession

ROBERT BRUCE

HAMPTON ROADS
PUBLISHING COMPANY, INC.

Cover design by **Adrian Morgan**
Illustrations by Robert Jesse Olaithe

Hampton Roads Publishing Company, Inc.
Charlottesville, VA 22906
www.hrpub.com

Library of Congress Cataloging-in-Publication Data available upon request

ISBN : 978-1-57174-639-9
10 9 8 7 6 5 4 3
Printed on acid-free paper in Canada
MP

This book is dedicated to Benjamin Bruce.
"May the good light of truth always find you, my son."

Acknowledgments

I would like to acknowledge the following people who supported or assisted me, or contributed in some way, big or small, with the creation of this book: Ben, Jesse, James, Kathlene, Patricia, Wynne Bruce, Ginny and David Eldridge, John T. Turner, M. D., Romero Lourenço da Cunha, Donni Hackanson, Errol Drane, Michael Ross, Mitch Kibblewhite, Donald McGlinn, Fiona Clark, Karim, Gerik, and Rob Blanch.

A big thank you to all my Internet friends and volunteers.

Many thanks go to the management and staff of Hampton Roads and Red Wheel/Weiser.

A huge thank you goes to Frank DeMarco

A special thanks to Keith Alderslade—for the sanity breaks.

Contents

Introduction

Core Affirmation: "I am loved and I am worthy. I am safe and I am free. I am powerfully protected. I am master of my body and ruler of my mind."

Welcome to *The Practical Psychic Self-Defense Handbook.* This second edition offers a whole new level of accessibility and understanding, along with new countermeasures and practical advice to help with a broad variety of weird and sometimes dangerous real-life paranormal situations. Knowing how to spot negative problems early and take effective action prevents ongoing problems and suffering in the long term.

This book is every bit a survival guide. You can think of it as something like a fire axe, kept under glass with big red letters that say, "In case of paranormal weirdness—break glass!" It is wise, though, to digest the contents of this book before you tackle any paranormal fires.

People suffering from psychic attack or other paranormal troubles are frequently blamed for attracting or creating their own problems, for having done something wrong, or for having bad karma. This attitude is unfair and largely based on ignorance concerning how things actually work in the greater spiritual reality.

I was in this situation myself around 1990. I was unsupported, judged, blamed, avoided, and, in general, let down. When the teachers and healers I approached for help saw I had serious paranormal problems, I was not helped, but avoided. I am sure a lot of people wanted to help, but very little is known about the how and why of such dark problems. Even less is known of what to do about them.

A lot of things that look good on paper fall down in practice. Many people pretend or persuade themselves that they have the higher knowledge and skill and faith to deal with real evil spirits, demonic attacks, and possession problems, but they are usually just as clueless and afraid as are the victims of these dark maladies. "Just surround yourself with white light" I was so often told, but when this did not work I was openly blamed for not doing it right. The teachers walked away one by one, shaking their heads and telling me I was being difficult. They knew the truth with a capital T. So it must be my fault.

The real truth down here on planet earth is that a serious paranormal problem can be likened to a gang of armed criminals busting into your home and tying you to a kitchen sink. You manage to sneak out your cell phone and start dialing and whispering quietly.

You call a neighbor: "Tell them to go into the light." *Click.*

You call a New Age friend: "Ask your guides to take them away." *Click.*

You call your mom: "Have you been drinking again?" *Click.*

You call the police: "Have your medication checked." *Click.*

You call the hospital: "Take two aspirin and drink plenty of water." *Click.*

Your cell phone battery dies.

With no other options available, you have a good think about your problem and come up with a plan yourself. You sneakily set fire to the garbage under the sink and smoke the place out. The bad guys choke and run from the building. Wet soap gets your hands free. A wet towel helps you breathe. You lock all the doors and windows, dive into the basement, and dig out Grandpappy's old shotgun. Then you put out the fire under the sink and review the situation.

By taking decisive action and doing a few simple things, you have placed yourself in a much better position. It may not be perfect—the bad guys are still outside—but life is definitely looking up for you. This is much like the advice offered in this book. It is based on the maxim of "What works, works."

This is not to say that no one out there can help with serious paranormal problems. There are some, but they are few and far between. It's the same with books on this subject. There is little that offers much by way of practical advice and help. Most books on this subject are not useful to the average person. One generally has to read a wheelbarrow full of books just to get a few snippets that work.

Because of the general lack of information on these matters and a lot of popular but unrealistic beliefs, when I first experienced serious paranormal problems, I was faced with working it out for myself the hard way. I made just about every mistake possible. I was almost killed several times. I barely survived. I suffered and I experimented and I observed and I grew and I learned. After a couple of decades of helping myself and many others, I eventually learned enough to make a difference.

The actual reasons for paranormal problems are generally beyond human understanding. These reasons can involve unhealthy lifestyle choices, occult dabbling, conflicts, and making enemies. The opposite can also apply, in that Neg interference can be a test or a response to spiritual development. But paranormal problems just happen to some people for no apparent reason. Often, people are just in the wrong place at the wrong time.

"What you resist, persists," said Carl Jung. This maxim is frequently cited as a reason not to do anything beyond positive thinking to resist or defend yourself against paranormal problems. It is also used as criticism, accusing people of causing their own problems by focusing on negative things. But would any reasonable person apply this maxim to things like sunburn, termites, burglars, and addictions? That would, of course, be ridiculous! So why should this principle apply to the evil spirits invading your mind and your home? They'll just go away if you ignore them, right? This maxim was obviously never meant to be used as a reason to not do anything to help yourself in any given situation. Other maxims that do apply here are "God helps those who help themselves" and "Trust in God, but keep your powder dry." While there are times when it is best to do nothing but think positive, in real-life paranormal situations, positive action must be taken, or things can get decidedly worse.

Early detection and action are crucial factors when dealing with negative forces and beings. This book addresses the most common types of negative psychic influences, attacks, and problems and how to deal with them. By and large, dealing with them does not require anything too outlandish.

The book begins with a quick-start guide for people who don't have time to read the whole book and need to take action immediately.

In Chapter 1 I provide context for what is to come by discussing the unseen environment. This discussion includes a quick rundown on the astral dimension, which is the environment from which most paranormal activity is based. I also discuss some natural sleep-related factors, including sleep paralysis, astral and psychic senses, and the mind-split effect, that can occur during sleep. These things can be exploited by negative forces. They can also cause problems in and of themselves, if you do not know what is happening.

I introduce the involvement of the physical body, the mind, and the higher self, along with issues of free will, choice, and permission. These are integral to the life equation concerning paranormal issues and spiritual problems. They control natural shielding and safeguards and are central to the mechanics of spiritual problems and paranormal activity, including overshadowing and possession.

I then explain the most common types of psychic interference and attacks and discuss exposure issues and the main symptoms of negative interference. I discuss energy-body attachments and ways to utilize the abilities of the energy body to counter negative interference and to remove attachments. Then we look at the structure of the human energy body and its major energy centers (commonly called Chakras), including the relationship of the outer energy-body sheath (the outer skin of the aura) and how attachments by negative beings can cause skin blemishes and lumps to appear in the physical body. I also provide methods for removing skin blemishes.

Then I introduce core images, explaining how the mind is involved with psychic attacks and negative attachments, including natural and false trauma memories, and giving procedures for discovering and removing hidden core-image attachments.

Next is the main countermeasures section, which contains many different methods of dealing with paranormal issues—methods to suit most situations. I then discuss children's paranormal problems, along with specific methods for handling them.

A discussion about overshadowing and possession issues is followed by simple, but effective pentagram banishment and cleansing methods that anyone can use.

All the procedures given in this book are based on the maxim "What works, works." These are things that I do myself and that I teach others with similar problems. These methods have been repeatedly tested and used in real-life field conditions and found to be broadly effective.

Enjoy the book.

The Core Affirmation

I am loved and I am worthy.
I am safe and I am free.
I am powerfully protected.
I am master of my body and ruler of my mind.

The Core Affirmation is a set of seven spiritually charged statements that express the perfection of your life without any negative influences. These statements are filled with positive intention. Your higher self will respond and work towards bringing about this perfect state of being in your life.

The Core Affirmation heads every chapter and is extensively used throughout this book. It is shown frequently so it sinks into your mind and thus becomes easy to remember. Please use it as much as possible. Print it out and place it on walls around your home. Give it to your friends. Add it to your email signature. Record it and play it on repeat. Say it aloud when you are alone or driving. Saturate your mind with it. This is powerful magic. The more you say it and think it and see it, the stronger will be its effects on your life.

Quick-Start Guide

Core Affirmation: "I am loved and I am worthy. I am safe and I am free. I am powerfully protected. I am master of my body and ruler of my mind."

The quick-start guide provides simple instructions and countermeasures that can be applied immediately. After you gain a little peace of mind, you can read and do more.

Do These Things First

Start repeating the Core Affirmation. Say it aloud as much as possible. Repeat it silently as you are falling asleep.

Turn on all the overhead lights. Make your environment as bright as possible. Sleep with the lights on while there is a problem. (Placing a dark cloth over the eyes makes it easier to sleep.)

Take a long shower as soon as possible. Imagine you are being washed inside and out with electric violet or white light. Repeat this shower as often as necessary. The running water of a shower is your primary EMF (electromagnetic-force) defense against direct attack. Notice that you feel more peaceful under the shower. Use that peace to recite the Core Affirmation aloud and often.

After showering, rub Tiger Balm or Tee Tree oil into your feet and anywhere that is feeling weird sensations. Add more as necessary.

Use plenty of incense or essential oils in every room—white sage, dragon's blood, frankincense, or whatever you have. Keep the incense burning. Have plenty on hand.

Start playing music—loudly, if the situation is bad.

Slice garlic cloves and place them around the room on plates or tissues. Replace them daily.

Sleep electrically grounded, or earthed (see Chapter 7). Get automobile jumper leads and an antistatic computer wrist strap. Connect one end to a metal tap, water pipe, or grounded steel and the other end to your bare skin during sleep.

Place a power extension cord on the floor, coiled to form a perimeter around your bed. Plug in a small lamp or clock so its cord runs current.

Play music through headphones to occupy your mind and drown out invasive thoughts. Play the music louder while you're awake and softer while sleeping.

Soak your feet in an earthed (electrically grounded) bucket of warm heavily salted water. Imagine murky bad energy is being sucked out of your feet. Use automobile jumper leads or salty wet cloth to connect the water to a metal tap or pipe, which will electrically ground the water in the bucket. If this is not possible, stand in or on top of running water of any kind (e.g., water running through a garden hose, bathtub tap, water-main pipe, or natural stream or creek—anything electrically grounded).

Get as much light and sunlight as possible. Avoid dark, quiet places.

Essential Guidelines

Break or minimize contact with potential sources of attack.

If possible, make peace with sources of attack and defuse the situation.

You *must* get adequate food and sleep every day. Seek medical advice if you need help. Lack of food and sleep will increase exposure to psychic attacks and worsen symptoms. Again, sleep and food are priorities.

Avoid alcohol and recreational drugs. These will make things worse.

If your bedroom or home atmosphere is disturbed, fix it with light and incense, or sleep elsewhere. Try sleeping on the couch or in another room, for example, or sleep in a motel or at a friend's home, or camp out on your back lawn.

Develop a businesslike attitude and, as far as possible, do not talk about the problem, particularly to people who might be critical or unsympathetic. Refer to the problem only indirectly ("That *thing* is happening again" or similar).

Keep your mind *off* the disturbance and disturbing thoughts. Use the Core Affirmation and other positive thoughts and statements, mantras, and prayers. Watch lots of happy movies. Listen to happy, uplifting music.

Get a Q-Link. (See "Further References.")

Legal Disclaimer

CHAPTER ONE

The Unseen Environment

Core Affirmation: "I am loved and I am worthy. I am safe and I am free. I am powerfully protected. I am master of my body and ruler of my mind."

A great range of positive and negative inorganic beings—unseen spiritual forces—affect humanity in many often-unsuspected ways. I have spent much of my life searching for explanations and practical ways to counter the negative influences. In my early days, this was a matter of personal survival. Later, it became a healer's quest to help the many helpless people with similar problems who were led to me.

I class all spiritual forces and beings that have unwholesome effects upon human life as Negatives—Negs for short—regardless of what type of spirit or energy is actually involved. This helps simplify and desensationalize an otherwise complex, fear-inducing subject. There are many types of Negs. They are known by many names. Negs can be thought of as misguided or mischievous spirits, deranged ghosts, demons or jinn, toxic thought forms, whatever you like. What matters most is dealing with them.

The effects of Negatives on human life form a part of the underlying workings of life. Negative forces are just as necessary for spiritual growth as the positives are. These are unseen aspects of natural selection and spiritual evolutionary processes. Beyond this, there are times when they need to be dealt with. Think of this book as a spiritual first-aid course. It is wise to learn basic medical first aid well before an accident happens, just in case. It is also wise to learn what is in this book, just in case.

Negs spread misery, disease, and spiritual corruption. They interfere with human life on every level, far more frequently than one might suspect. Psychic influences and paranormal issues are natural parts of human life and society. But the negative aspects do not have to be endured meekly. All Negs have natural weaknesses and much can be done to avoid or counteract Neg-related problems. By and large, this does not involve doing anything too outlandish.

Neg-related paranormal activity needs to be put into context. So following are brief explanations of some of the most important factors.

Unseen Environments: The physical universe is only part of a reality spectrum that includes unseen energies and dimensions that permeate our physical reality. Quantum physics shows the existence of other dimensions that most people cannot directly perceive. If you lack personal experience with such things, this science provides a good basis from which to approach nonphysical realities, forces, and beings.

Unseen environments can be said to exist at higher frequencies than that of the physical universe. They exist at angles of perception outside of 3D reality that we cannot normally perceive. This makes them invisible and undetectable to our five senses and to scientific instruments. Just as different types of energies—such as light, gravity, x-ray, heat, microwave—can occupy the same space at the same time, so unseen environments coexist with the physical universe.

The Astral Real-Time Zone: The closest unseen environment to the physical universe is what I call the astral real-time zone. This subtle environment shares some properties of the physical universe (it is a direct and objective real-time reflection of reality) and some properties of the astral dimension (it is a fluid, nonphysical environment). The astral real-time zone permeates the physical universe and contains a perfect reflection of reality, as reality happens.

An astral projector in the real-time zone is like a ghost in the real world. All Negs utilize the real-time zone to be close enough to the physical universe to affect its inhabitants.

Computer Analogy: A good analogy here is to imagine the physical universe to be a vast computer called Source, with an operating system called the Collective Unconscious. All conscious beings are discrete programs that exist and function within this operating system. In this sense, Negs can be likened to computer viruses and malware. They infect and alter, invade and damage how these living conscious programs (people) function.

Your Higher Self and You

Your higher self has many names and aspects. My conception of higher self includes the conscious and unconscious mind, and the physical body's innate intelligence on the cellular level. It controls your natural shields (your default antivirus/anti-Neg protection), which is obviously breached during any type of Neg invasion. These breaches are allowed to happen because of free will, choices, and permission factors, or because Negs find ways around your natural defenses. Either way, your higher self holds the keys to whether or not you are susceptible to Neg problems. The actions of your higher self are often attributed to the divine or to the actions of spiritual beings. To help to conceptualize this, consider your higher self to be connected with Source through a gradient of consciousness, which runs from you to Source.

Iceberg Analogy: Imagine that you are an iceberg floating on a great ocean. The conscious aspect of you, the part reading my words, floats above the ocean. Under the waves rests 90 percent of you, which is your unconscious mind and higher self. The iceberg that is you floats in a vast ocean, along with countless other icebergs—other living beings. The ocean represents the collective unconscious. The icebergs all perceive themselves to be separate individuals, although all are composed of and are floating in seawater. Frozen or liquid, it's still seawater. In this analogy, Source would be the subatomic particles and elements from which the seawater and icebergs are composed.

Source is universal consciousness and energy. You are an integral part of the universe. There is no actual separation between you and the rest of the universe—only perceived and believed separateness. You are an integral part of everything and everyone else. This is what Eckhart Tolle means when he says in his book *The Power of Now,* "You are the *now.*" He is saying, "You are Source."

The following exercise demonstrates this relationship between you and Source.

Take your index finger and point to Source.

Next, point to where Source is not.

You actually cannot point to either. Source is everywhere and in everything, including you and your higher self. You are composed of Source. You and Source are, therefore, indivisible aspects of each other.

A further analogy may help: Consider the fingertip of your index finger. Imagine that this is you and that the rest of your body is the universe and everything else in it. You cannot separate your fingertip from your body. Your fingertip is not a separate and discrete being. It is connected to every part of you on the cellular level. But you, as a fingertip, do not realize that you are a part of the whole. In this sense, you are Source and your fingertip is you. This is the truth of nondual existence and of universal consciousness. You feel and believe yourself as separate from everything. For you to exist and function as a physical being, this sense of separateness is necessary. But on a deeper spiritual level, you are a part of everything, and everything is a part of you. The more you embrace your nondual nature, the more connected you become to everything. This connectedness causes your higher spiritual aspects to draw closer to you and to take a more active part in your life.

Permission and Agreement Issues

What Negs can do to a person is limited by the level of permission they have obtained. Permission and agreements relate to the free will of individuals. The higher self will sometimes adjust a person's natural shields and defenses to allow a Neg influence or invasion, if this has been requested by that person or is required by that person's higher self.

Permission can take many forms. Agreements are like legal contracts, where, for example, on a higher level of consciousness, a person may agree to allow a negative influence into his/her life in exchange for something. This something usually involves a test or an opportunity to grow by experiencing and/or overcoming difficulties. Affirmations and positive statements of intention can be used to revoke permission and agreements or to reduce their effects in real life.

Permission for negative interference is commonly given when spiritual advancement and abilities are greatly desired. This permission can manifest a series of real-life trials and negative interference whereby spiritual growth and advancement can be achieved.

Paranormal, Medical, or Psychological?

Paranormal phenomena cannot easily be explained by modern science. Consequently, all Neg problems are, from a scientific and medical standpoint, considered to be hallucinations or manifestations of mental illness. Neg-related problems have not been scientifically researched to any great extent and are largely misunderstood today. Consequentially, little practical help is available, and even less common knowledge. The truth is that many physical and psychological disorders are caused and spread by negative spiritual influences.

The Human Energy Body and Aura

The human energy body, along with the mind, is the vehicle through which Negs interact with people. Every cell of your body is alive with bioelectrical activity. Beneath this activity exist layers of subtle spiritual energy fields that comprise the human energy body. This subtle body is every bit as complex and essential to life as its physical counterpart. The human energy body permeates the physical body and extends beyond the human skin in an egg-shaped field called the aura.

The energy body has multiple layers; it also has multiple energy centers, called chakras. Chakras are like the vital organs of the energy body. There are seven primary energy centers (major chakras), hundreds of secondary energy centers, three main energy-storage centers, and dense areas of tertiary centers (tiny energy-exchange pores). There is also a central channel (called *Sushumna*, in Eastern terms) running up through the center of the body and two major energy conduits (called *Ida* and *Pingala* in Eastern terms), winding up either side of the central channel.

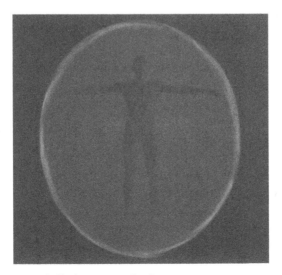

Figure 1: The human aura sheath

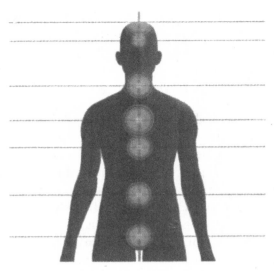

Figure 2: The human energy body and its chakras

In order to significantly affect humans, Negs need to broach the natural defenses of the human energy body and gain access to its chakra system. When they do, they gain access to the mind, and through the mind, the brain and the physical body. We will be revisiting this subject in more depth further on in this book.

Sleep and Astral Issues

A number of factors involving the mind, energy body, and sleep can be related to Neg activities. But some natural sleep-related phenomena can also be mistaken for Neg attacks, due to a poor understanding of what can happen during presleep and sleep.

Lack of sleep: Lack of sleep will cause the energy body's natural defenses to weaken and its chakras to activate. This can be a primary factor in Neg problems. Negs will not only take advantage of this situation, but will also use various means to deny people sleep as a way of further weakening natural defenses. These means can include telepathically manipulating dreams and causing nightmares and nocturnal phenomena that will induce fear and deprive persons of sleep. For these reasons, it is important to get healthy amounts of regular sleep. Healthy sleep is crucial when Neg activity and interference are noticeable. Please do not hesitate to see a health professional if sleeping becomes a problem.

Sleep projection: During sleep, the body, mind, and energy body undergo some major natural changes. The physical body slows into a state of deep relaxation as the brain moves through a range of altered states of consciousness and cycles of dreaming. The energy body expands and generates a subtle astral copy of the physical body and its mind, called the astral body. The astral body is automatically projected just outside the physical body, where it rests, often mimicking the position of its sleeping physical counterpart. The astral body is connected to the physical body and energy body by unbreakable energy filaments, most often called the Silver Cord. This sleep projection of the astral body is a natural, automatic process. If it happens while the mind is held awake, it is called astral projection. If the dreaming mind awakens during this process, it is called lucid dreaming.

THE MIND-SPLIT EFFECT

Natural sleep projection generally goes unnoticed and is rarely remembered. However, occasionally glitches can occur during this process, causing problems ranging from mild confusion to extreme fear.

The *mind-split effect* is my term for what happens during sleep, sleep projection, and astral projection. The original copy of the mind and memory never leave the physical body while it lives. The projected astral double contains a full copy of the mind and memory of the sleeper/projector, up to the moment of separation and while it is held out of body. Three identical copies of the same mind can exist and function simultaneously: the physical body/mind, the astral body/mind, and the dream body/mind. These three aspects are integrated while people are fully awake.

The dream mind is the most noticeable other aspect of mind beyond the normal awake state of consciousness. The dream mind will sometimes become active when overtired persons are resting or trying to fall asleep. It can also become active during meditation sessions. When the dream mind becomes active, the eyelids flicker noticeably. This odd sensation, called rapid eye movement, or REM, indicates that the mind is dreaming. It is sometimes possible to catch glimpses of what is happening in the dream mind.

Because REM and dream activity can happen while persons are still awake, it is obvious that the dream mind is a separate aspect of the mind, capable of functioning independently. The astral body/mind is just another aspect of mind. Under the right circumstances, as said, two or even three of these aspects are capable of operating simultaneously.

The dream mind and astral mind gather experience memories independently from the moment they become active, the moment the mind-split effect occurs, to the moment awake consciousness is restored. Most of these memories disappear into uncharted areas of the unconscious mind upon waking. Occasionally, though, dream and astral memories will be recalled, often mixed.

Problems can occur when the physical body's copy of mind regains consciousness while its other aspects are also conscious. This can cause a variety of sleep-related phenomena, including sleep paralysis (the physical body is awake, but cannot move) and senses like astral sight and hearing, and more rarely, touch and smell and taste.

Astral Sight and Hearing

Astral sight is the phenomenon of seeing through closed eyelids during sleep or in the preludes to sleeping or awakening. The quality of astral sight can range from seeing vague, shadowy shapes, images, and colors to seeing as if your eyes were open and the overhead light were lit.

Sounds heard through astral hearing can range from bell tones (tuning-fork sounds) and buzzing or humming electrical noises to peculiar sounds and voices. Some astral noises (e.g., a train roaring past close to your head, a lawnmower starting up in your bedroom) can be frighteningly loud—as loud as they would be in real life.

Astral sight and hearing happen when the physical body is asleep, but the mind is still awake. This is also called a trance state or an altered state of consciousness. In this state, psychic abilities will often manifest that allow seeing and hearing into the astral dimension. Spirits and astral projectors can also sometimes be seen and heard in this way. These abilities can also become activated by overtiredness, when the physical body falls asleep while the mind is held awake.

Sleep Paralysis

Sleep paralysis is something that most people will experience at some time in their lives. When it happens, persons wake up physically paralyzed, unable to move a muscle or even blink. This can also happen while you are trying to fall asleep or while just relaxing. It most commonly occurs when persons are overtired. Although this condition usually only lasts a minute or two, it can be terrifying, especially if its cause is unknown. This condition is often misinterpreted as something sinister. Astral sight and hearing will often occur during episodes of sleep paralysis, which can make the situation even more fear inducing.

I suspect that unknown subtle mechanisms relating to the nature of sleep and how the mind animates the physical body are involved with sleep paralysis. This condition is well known to be associated with out-of-body experiences (OBE, or astral projection). Natural astral projectors usually suffer frequent bouts of sleep paralysis during their lives.

The physical body is not truly paralyzed during sleep paralysis. Nerve connections between the physical brain and body remain intact. The mind simply becomes disassociated from its physical body during sleep and is unable to animate the body for a short time. This dissociation is said to be caused by a temporary glitch in the mechanism that deactivates the physical body during sleep, to stop the body from copying what it is doing in its dreams.

Sleep-paralysis episodes will occasionally be accompanied by unexplainable feelings of dread. There is often a tangible presence sensed as coming from a particular direction. This feeling of a disturbing presence is caused by the mind-split effect that happens when an unsuspected astral projection is in progress. In this case, the astral double is awake and active, and possibly the dream mind is as well. This activity is using all of the physical body/mind's available consciousness energy, which is causing the paralysis. The sense of tangible presence is caused by subtle energy interactions between a person's paralyzed physical body/mind and his/her own astral projected double. This effect is strongest at close range.

(Please see my book *Astral Dynamics* for more detailed information concerning the mind-split effect and other sleep- and astral-related phenomena.)

Core Images

Core images are combined energy-body and mental devices used by Negs to infiltrate and manipulate people. Natural core images are powerful memories formed by real-life traumas. These memories are the first targets for Negs during psychic invasion. After these are compromised, false core images are implanted through telepathic dream manipulation. In time, networks of controls are created in the minds and energy bodies of victims. These networks attempt to circumvent natural shielding to give

Negs varying degrees of access and control. (More information on core images is provided further on in this book.)

Workable Neg Profile

Over thirty years of observing Negs and experimenting with counter-measures, I have developed a workable profile that fits the majority of troublesome Neg types. While there are many different types and levels of spirit beings, only a few are troublesome to humans. To help clarify these things and avoid confusion, following is a list of statements concerning this Neg profile. I will be elaborating on these statements throughout the book to provide more specific context.

This Neg profile includes some types of ex-human ghosts, as well as various types of nonhuman spirits. The nonhuman types of Negs can be thought of as earth-type spirits. (Other types of Negs, including air, fire, and water spirits, rarely interact with humans and, thus, cause fewer problems. This lack of interaction makes them difficult to observe, so Negs of these types are not included in this profile.) The observations and countermeasures given here, by and large, concern only Negs that are manifesting close enough to the physical dimension to affect people.

For all intents and purposes, Negs have no physical substance. Their reactions to some countermeasures suggest they are two-dimensional energy beings that are bound to the surface of the earth. These are like shadows we cannot see. Negs may project images that can be seen above the surface, but they do so while remaining firmly attached to the surface.

Negs appear to exist in a thin layer of energy that covers the entire surface of our planet. This energy layer appears to follow the contours of the earth, including the surfaces of buildings, walls and ceilings, inside and out. Lightning appears to be responsible for generating such a field. Several thousand lightning strikes per minute occur around the world. This continual electrical onslaught dissipates uniformly over the surface the whole planet, which is conductive, and creates what can be called a perpetually dissipating surface energy field.

Some Negs appear to exist in electromagnetic fields of the upper atmosphere. This type of Neg seems to extend or drop down on webs, or threads of energy, that can attach to the head area of people. Some people with this condition report feeling wires inside their heads. This type of Neg does not respond as well to running-water countermeasures, although no Neg is invulnerable to strong levels of EMF grounding. Fortunately, this type of Neg is less common than others and accounts for only a small percentage of troublesome Negs.

By and large, most types of free-roaming Negs do not appear to perceive the world in the same way as we humans do. While all Negs are psychic and telepathic, it appears they gain human senses, like sight and hearing, only while overshadowing or possessing living people. Negs do not have eyes and ears per se. If free-roaming Negs could see independently, as we do, then a garden hose gushing water on the ground would not form an effective barrier to them—which it does. They would see the end of the hose and simply go around it, but they never do. Why?

Negs cannot cross running water unaided. Water has a powerful electrical-grounding effect on Negs when water is connected to the earth. Tap water flows through pipes from a dam that is heavily electrically grounded. Running water also generates an electromagnetic (EM) field of its own, which repels Negs. This sensitivity to electrical grounding and EM fields also explains why power cables and some electrical devices cause Negs problems.

Analogy: the effect running water has on Negs can be likened to frequency. Running water can be said to produce a high frequency, and Negs are composed of a low frequency. These frequencies do not mix, and so Negs are repelled by the water. Add some incense, strong light, and beautiful sounds, all of which affect Negs adversely, and you create a strong anti-Neg environment.

People suffering panic attacks, acute depression, or psychosis will often take very long showers. Some will spend many hours at a time under a shower. They say that they feel better and more in control while under running water. When they are away from the shower, the debilitating problems quickly return. I suggest that people take showers instinctively, in much the same way as some animals head for water when frightened. Also, when hospital patients shower regularly, they rest easier and require less medication. There are no scientific explanations for these well-known phenomena. The common factor here is, of course, direct physical exposure to electrically grounded running water and the frequencies it generates. This has positive effects on the human energy body, and on the physical body and mind.

Apart from air spirits, Negs cannot fly, contrary to what is commonly assumed. If they could, then running water would not affect them. I have proven this through countless field tests in real-life situations. For example,

I have a garden hose on the ground, gushing water. I lead or carry a person who is under a new and severe Neg attack over the hose. The attack stops *instantly*. If we recross the hose, the attack usually begins again, also instantly. If we recross the hose, again the attack stops instantly. If we stay on the safe side of the hose, there are no more Neg attack symptoms. So why doesn't the Neg just move a few feet and go around the end of the hose to continue its attack? But this never happens. Therefore, logic says that free-roaming Negs do not have visual sight that is comparable to human sight.

Negs can use sensitive living beings (human or animal) as vehicles to carry them across running water. This appears to shield them from the effects of running water.

Negs are sensitive to fire, which can be used in similar ways as running water. If persons under Neg attack cross a small fire burning on the ground, the attack will usually be broken. I say "usually," because more research is needed to ascertain the effectiveness of fire as a countermeasure. Running water is safer and more widely accessible and should always be used first.

Negs are sensitive to strong light, particularly sunlight. I have not encountered a single Neg attack in full sunlight, out in the open. Daylight attacks will happen inside buildings, but not in the open. Negs appear to hitchhike with sensitive living beings, human and animal, in order to move about in daylight. Light—either sunlight or strong artificial light—is detrimental to Neg attachments and appears to damage them. The strength and color of light is important. White light has a stronger effect on Negs than other colors. Flashlights, when placed directly over an area of the body where Neg interference is being felt, will ease such problems. Sleeping with the overhead light on significantly reduces Neg problems. The stronger the light, the stronger the effect.

Negs contain or can produce electromagnetic fields and are sensitive to some types of magnetic and electromagnetic fields. Some electromagnetic devices affect Negs. More experimentation is needed to ascertain specific frequencies that are detrimental to Negs. Negs can also interfere with some types of electrical and electronic devices. I have, for example, seen Negs damage computer and TV screens, as if a magnet were being passed over the screens. I have also seen Neg faces burned into screens in this way.

Negs are sensitive to certain scents, smokes, and chemicals. They are repelled by sulfur, garlic, and certain incenses and essential oils. Negs are also attracted to certain scents, such as the smell of alcohol, garbage, and decay. In this sense, cleanliness of body, clothing, and the home environment are important. Some scented soaps, shampoos, and lotions are also helpful as repellents to Negs.

Negs are affected by certain words, symbols, and rituals. Words and symbols express ideas and intentions. Some words appear to connect with powerful ancient forces in the collective consciousness of humankind. Some words gain intention power through belief and repeated use. Some are believed to be powerful by millions of people over centuries, and so they become powerful.

Negs are sensitive to loud noises, particularly to sudden loud noises, like those made by firecrackers, gongs, bells, or banging pots and pans together. This noise appears to distract them or weaken them, often causing them to leave the area entirely.

Negs have the ability to shield their true energies and identities. This masking is like a glamor. Glamor is a field of intention energy that hides the truth. Glamor around a living human changes how they are perceived by others. Glamor can make an old and unattractive person look young and desirable. It can also cause nice, young, attractive persons to appear as being old and unattractive, or repulsive. Negs use glamor extensively to fool human psychics. A Neg spirit will often, for example, present itself as a sweet lost child. Psychics and clairvoyants will perceive the Neg as such and feel sympathetic towards the spirit. Negs are notorious deceivers and liars. People overshadowed or possessed by Negs will also often have a glamor around them. Negs also punish and isolate people by projecting around them a field of glamor that irritates and repels other people.

The above profile is constantly being updated. There are many unknown factors concerning Negs. No single countermeasure provides a total solution to Neg problems, unfortunately. Combinations of countermeasures are needed, along with some experimentation to find what works best in any given situation. The best outcome is to make Negs so uncomfortable that they detach and go elsewhere.

Plumbing and Neg Concentrations

Cities and towns in our modern world are heavily crisscrossed with underground plumbing; pipes full of running water line every street and run around and through every building. Since running water has properties that repel and/or demanifest Negs, modern plumbing severely limits their freedom to travel and, thus, causes Negs to become concentrated in towns and buildings. Negs would naturally disperse from buildings and populated areas at a much faster and healthier rate if it were not for our underground water pipes. The larger the city or building is, and the older it is, the heavier the Neg concentration within it can become. Earthbound Neg types can become trapped inside city blocks or buildings. In time, old buildings can become heavily contaminated with Negs, including earthbound ex-humans (ghosts) from people who die there, that do not move on into the hereafter.

Power cables also affect Negs, as do sewers, rivers and streams (including underground streams), lakes, and oceans.

Some Negs never seem to work out how to move beyond these limitations, whereas others overcome them by hitching rides with susceptible people and animals. These people and animals are used as shields to carry Negs over running water and other barriers.

Types of Negs

Some types of Negs bear further explanation. The following discussions provide information on some of the more well-known Neg types and some other oddities I have observed.

HEREDITARY ATTACHMENTS

A great many Neg problems result from hereditary attachments. This type of Neg moves down through the generations, from parent to child. Some will follow only one gender, and others will follow whomever is available. Some family Neg problems appear to go back many hundreds of years. The original attachments may have resulted from curses, or they were attachments picked up by ancestors and passed down through the generations. For example, an alcoholic ex-human spirit may move from parent to child and will continue doing so until it is somehow banished or evicted.

Some hereditary attachments follow only the surname of a family. A name change through marriage or legal action will often break a family Neg attachment.

Hereditary Neg problems will usually become noticeable in early childhood, if you know what to look for. They typically start with a series of nightmares and night terrors when a child is around three to five years of age. These problems usually ease once the Neg(s) involved have developed sufficient energy and psychological (core-image) attachments to the child. These attachments can result in noticeable personality changes. More on children's problems later.

EARTHBOUND SPIRITS AND GHOSTS

After death, most deceased people exist in the astral real-time zone as ghosts for a time, from a few days to a few weeks. The duration of this interim between life and the afterlife is variable. The deceased appear to be held in the astral real-time zone by residual vital life energy. During this time, they will typically frequent areas, homes, and people they were familiar with during their lives. When this vitality is used up, spirits fade away and move on to the next stage of existence. When this happens, they fall asleep on the astral real-time level and begin processing their lives at a higher level. This can be likened to how living people fall asleep at night and dream; the physical body stays in the bed, while the mind exists on another level.

Most deceased people do not seem to realize that they have died. Beyond some minor poltergeist activity and an occasional apparition, the vast majority of recently deceased humans do not cause any serious problems for the living.

Energy vampirism is a common factor shared by all ex-human earthbound types and the majority of troublesome Negs. It seems to be a matter of necessity for spirits, but particularly for earthbound ex-humans, existing for any length of time close to the physical plane to replenish their vital energies regularly. Accidental vampirism can also happen through close contact between spirits and humans. In the typical scenario, recently deceased spirits try to hug or get close to loved ones and unintentionally absorb vital energy through osmosis—like a dry sponge absorbing fluid. The living humans involved are usually unaware they are losing energy, because the amount of energy seems insignificant. If it's understood that close contact can cause problems, the possibility of a spirit becoming accidentally earthbound can be avoided.

The above situation suggests that the real problem with energy vampirism is not that the living humans involved are losing energy, but that some spirits become accidentally earthbound in the process. There are, however, notable exceptions, where deceased spirits realize what they are doing and actively feed off the living. Intentional energy vampirism can cause debilitating health problems in the living, as far more vital energy is drained to empower deceased spirits. In severe cases, victims will experience severe fatigue and a loss of body heat.

Earthbound ex-human ghosts appear to share some limitations with nonhuman Negs. Ghosts are also sensitive to EM fields and electrical grounding and cannot cross running water unaided. I think that once an ex-human spirit's connection to its physical body is lost, if it becomes earthbound, it automatically connects to the same energy field on the surface of the earth as other Negs do. To cross running water, earthbound ex-human spirits must attach themselves to susceptible living beings (human or animal) and piggyback a ride, as other types of Negs do. As the majority of ex-human ghosts are not aware of this factor—this is not common knowledge—they find themselves unexplainably stuck inside buildings and areas of land surrounded by water-main pipes. As already noted, a high concentration of water pipes and power lines can result in buildings or areas of land, like city cemeteries, accumulating ex-human earthbound spirits and becoming haunted.

ADDICTED AND DERANGED GHOSTS

Some ex-human spirits linger after physical death due to earthly addictions—addictions to sex, drugs, alcohol, smoking, or food, for example. These types of earthbound spirits tend to frequent areas and places where they can best feed their addictions. For example, alcoholic earthbound spirits will frequent bars. They soon learn to overshadow susceptible drinkers in order to experience alcohol again. This can lead to long-term overshadowing and even possession. New substance abusers can be created in this way, when susceptible people are exposed to addicted spirits in the long term. Intoxication through alcohol and recreational drug use increases susceptibility to Neg influences.

Anger, greed, revenge, and other negative human emotions can also hold ex-human spirits close to the earth.

It is unfortunate that ex-human earthbound spirits do not realize the nature of the afterlife, where all their needs would be met. Life in the afterlife is virtually indistinguishable from real life. So if, for example, a spirit has smoking and coffee addictions, these things are freely available in the afterlife.

Deranged earthbound spirits are far more troublesome. These are usually mentally ill, addictive types with strong negative emotions and needs. These will often cause mental and emotional problems in the living persons they overshadow. In time, as such spirits become less and less human, they can start to behave like nonhuman Neg types. This may, indeed, be the process whereby some apparently nonhuman Neg types are created.

Love for living persons can also hold ex-human spirits close to the earth. This type of extended earthbound existence does not usually cause significant problems for the living. This is more a process of the spirits and the living persons involved letting go and moving on rather than anything malicious or sinister.

INCUBI AND SUCCUBI

Stories of unseen lovers, traditionally called incubi or succubi, go back many thousands of years. An incubus is the male version, and the succubus is the female version, although both these terms describe the same being in different forms. These types prey on susceptible living humans and feed on their sexual energies. In the early stages of incubus approach, partial or full paralysis will often be induced. (Logically, such paralysis is produced by direct manipulation of the mechanisms relating to sleep and astral projection.) Often, a beautiful face and body will be seen and/or felt by the victim, as the spirit makes love to him/her. If victims succumb to the charms of an incubus and become enamored, they will often begin to deliberately summon the incubus each night by wishing it back. This desire gives the spirits involved all the permission they require to exploit people further.

There are different types of incubi. Some are sex-addicted ex-human earthbound spirits, some are wild nature spirits, and some are demonic. The demonic variety is the most powerful and dangerous—and addictive. Sex with a demonic incubus is far more energetically powerful than sex with another person. This is because the energy body and sex chakra of the victim is exploited to enhance the sex act.

Age does not appear to be a factor with incubi; attacks are just as likely to happen to people in their early teens as they are to people in their eighties. Younger persons are, however, more at risk of becoming addicted to this kind of attention.

ELEMENTALS AND NATURE SPIRITS

Pure elemental spirits relate to elements of nature—air, fire, water, and earth. Some elementals are related to more than one element. All elemental beings are dualistic by nature—positive and negative, good and bad aspects. The basic elemental spirit types are fire spirits (salamanders), earth spirits (gnomes), air spirits (sylphs), and water spirits (undines).

Nature spirits are best known as the fairy beings of Celtic mythology, as wild spirits involved with the processes of nature. Some nature spirits are intelligent—such as the leprechauns of Ireland.

While these are all powerful beings, problems with elementals and nature spirits are rare. If left undisturbed, these spirits actively avoid people unless their territory is disturbed. If problems are encountered, it is generally best to enlist the help of a local shaman who is familiar with the local nature spirits. The countermeasures given in this book will help, although it is often wise to just vacate the problem area.

ASTRAL WILDLIFE

Some of the most common types of Negs I call astral wildlife. These types of beings often have the appearance and nature of animals and insects. The most frequently encountered forms are of snakes and oversized spiders, scorpions, and various types of bugs. These can be observed clairvoyantly or with astral sight. They are often found in areas where other types of psychic and energy interference are ongoing, such as in haunted houses. People suffering psychic attacks or Neg interference will sometimes see snakes, spiders, and other oversized insects in their dreams and, with astral sight, in the room around them. These Neg types are often seen on the floors, walls, and ceilings.

Astral wildlife will often attempt to feed off people during sleep and the prelude to sleep. They require people to be deeply relaxed or sleeping in order to feed. People affected in this way will often feel sharp, sting-ing pains, most commonly in the feet and toes. These sensations can vary from annoying to very painful. Other parts of the body can also be affected. These types of Neg are not particularly intelligent or danger-ous. Astral wildlife can often be cleaned out of a house with fumigations, spring cleaning, and other simple countermeasures, which are coming up later in this book.

COLUMNS AND TWISTERS

Little is known about this type of Neg. These look like columns of thick black smoke or like a small twister, or upside down twister. They vary from several inches to a few feet in height, if seen clairvoyantly or with astral sight during presleep. This type is generally unfriendly and best avoided. If disturbed, they can strike like a snake, and there will be physi-cal swelling and infection in the bite area. Infections resulting from any kind of Neg-related injury are usually virulent. It is wise to seek medical attention promptly. This type of Neg can also usually be cleared away with fumigations, spring cleaning, and other countermeasures.

DEMONS

Every culture has names for evil spirits. The words *demon, djinn, jinn,* or *genie* are used to describe the higher orders of nonhuman spirit beings of negative persuasion. There are literally hundreds of types and subtypes in the vast amount of information available. Much of this information is ancient. When observed clairvoyantly, many demons appear with a form that is part animal and part human, such as a snake with a humanoid head, or a humanoid form with the head of a wild boar. Other common types look like the character Golum in *The Lord of the Rings* movies, but with short horns in the head.

Many common demon types have big eyes; long, skinny arms and legs; leathery, reptilian skins, often with colored spots here and there; and clawlike hands.

The word *demon* has all but been banned in the New Age world and is seldom used today. There is widespread disbelief that this type of spirit being even exits. This is part of the reason why I use the term *Neg* so widely. Using *Neg* instead of *demon* helps desensationalize and simplify an otherwise fear-inducing and emotional subject.

Demons are highly intelligent and extremely dangerous. They are best avoided where possible. By and large, demons have a stronger level of consciousness than a human. So it is impossible to go mind to mind with a demon and win through brute mental force. The countermeasures given in this book do work against demons, although they must be applied with more vigor and diligence than they are with other types of Negs. The banishment procedures given near the end of this book are necessary for effectively countering demons.

POLTERGEISTS

The word *poltergeist* means "noisy ghost." This is the most common spirit manifestation of all. While poltergeists have been observed for centuries and theories about them abound, little is actually known about them beyond their capacity for being noisy and for damaging property. It is known that a child or early teenager is usually present in the home that has a poltergeist problem. It is suspected that children may produce the energy that poltergeists use to manifest and cause problems.

You may have read about poltergeist activity, but you really have to experience it to believe it. It is quite something to behold. Poltergeist phenomena range from audible taps, knocks, and loud bangs on walls to the movement of physical objects. Electrical appliances can be interfered with and sometimes damaged. Spontaneous fires can also be attributed to some types of poltergeists. Reducing problems in homes and families infected with poltergeists generally takes consistent work and application of countermeasures. It is often easier to move house, as the house itself can be the problem. A poltergeist problem can sometimes be connected to plumbing and electrical-wiring issues, as discussed earlier. These things can attract, allow, or even trap poltergeists inside a building.

FLUTTERS

Flutters is my term for an unusual and apparently harmless type of small spirit entity I discovered in the early nineties. As far as I am aware, these have not been documented as independent spirit beings. Flutters take up residence in the human energy body. They cause occasional fluttering, pulsing sensations in the physical flesh wherever they are active. I suspect that flutters are a kind of discrete ectoplasmic entity.

Ectoplasm is a semisolid spiritual substance that can be produced by the human energy body in certain circumstances and by rare spiritual mediums; the act of producing ectoplasm is called physical mediumship. Ectoplasm has weight and can be seen and touched. It glows in the dark and feels cold and damp to the touch.

What I call flutters may be related to what are called astral larvae in the world of magic. Astral larvae can be described as immature Negs in larval form. Exactly what they are is difficult to ascertain, so I will continue to rely on my observations.

Flutters are usually active only enough to be observed when the physical body is deeply relaxed or asleep. This activity can happen during presleep or when persons are in altered states where the mind stays awake while the physical body sleeps. I spend many hours per day in this state, and this has allowed me to make observations.

Stimulation of the nerves of the physical body is involved, as there is physical movement of the flesh. The fluttering may be felt in peculiar places, such as in an elbow, a thigh, a bicep, or a small area of the chest.

Flutters can move around the body quite rapidly and noticeably. Activity is intermittent and appears to go through cycles.

Flutters appear to be transferable. They can spread from one person to another when two people sleep close together. When two people who each have flutters sleep together, both flutters will move to an area where their physical bodies are touching. If, say, the feet of both people are touching each other's feet, the flutters will begin pulsing together quite noticeably in that area, almost as if they were communicating. If physical contact at the feet is then broken, the flutters will immediately move to another area where there is physical contact, such as the hands, shoulders, hips, or stomach. When flutters move through the body, they can be felt flowing like a thread through the flesh from one place to another. This movement is painless, but noticeable. If seen with astral sight or other senses, flutters often have the form of a small eel.

Little if anything is known about flutters today. I originally thought they were a unique condition to myself, but over the years I have surveyed thousands of people at my lectures and workshops, and a small percentage of people in every group report similar symptoms. No one has reported flutters causing anything bad to happen. They are mostly just annoying.

I have tried everything I know to communicate with, to remove, or to destroy flutters. They do not respond to communication attempts. They do respond to body-awareness energy and visualized actions, like using a flaming blowtorch, and can be chased around the body. The only thing that works is embracing a healthy lifestyle and regular exposure to sunlight. These things progressively reduce flutter activity. Illness and overtiredness and getting physically run down will increase flutter activity. Flutters appear to be aware, and their activity will usually increase when they are discussed or focused on.

PSYCHIC VAMPIRES

Psychic vampires are living people who drain vital life energy from other living people. By and large, they do it accidentally. Psychic vampires drain people of vitality through any type of contact, in person or remotely, such as via telephone calls or live Internet communications.

We all know people like this. Spending even a short time with them is exhausting. Psychic vampires are not particularly aggressive people. Often they are quiet, timid types, but generally of a depressing and circular mindset. This is the type that carries the troubles of the world with them. They love to talk about their problems, but they are usually not solution oriented.

More rarely, some psychic vampires know what they are and deliberately feed off of other people. Many realized psychic vampires feed solely off of the ambient energies of crowds. Today there are organizations of psychic vampires, where likeminded people—including those who like to be drained of energy—get together.

Neg Interference: Potential Reasons

The question of why Negs interfere with or attack people, and how victims are selected, is complex. Not enough is known, given that this subject is generally avoided and widely disbelieved in the modern world. So I must rely on personal observations and logic. Let's look at some possibilities.

PSYCHIC SENSITIVITY

Victims of Neg abuse are generally intelligent, psychically and emotionally sensitive, and psychologically vulnerable. They can include adults and children of any age. People who are not psychically and emotionally sensitive, and who are more heavily grounded and shielded, can still be affected by Negs, but they will not usually feel the typical symptoms.

Psychic and emotional sensitivity appears to provide the connections and receptivity Negs need to approach and interfere with living people. If this sensitivity is not present, then Neg interference is less likely to happen. It is for these reasons that persons undergoing psychic or Neg attacks should stay grounded and try to shut down psychic abilities and sensitivities.

CURSES

A curse is a powerful, intentional *wish* that has been placed upon a person. It can relate to family hereditary attachments, which can follow family lines down through the ages. Curses can be performed by magical operations or naturally by persons with strong natural psychic abilities. Curses can involve thought forms or spirit entities, even demons, being ordered to attach to persons and punish them. The earthbound spirit of the person laying a curse, after his/her death, can also carry out the curse, passing this on from parent to child down through the generations.

Curses can be intended as devices of revenge and punishments. They can also be inflicted by opportunistic Negs. A type of death curse may, for example, come about simply because a resident Neg in the dying person urgently requires a new living host. So it attaches to whomever is available. If the dying person curses someone, this intention and direction can provide opportunities for a desperate Neg. There are countless reasons why a curse might be laid on a person or a family line.

The duration of a curse depends greatly upon the strength and natural psychic abilities of the person laying the curse and/or upon the Negs involved. Historically, some curses can last thousands of years. Curses can also be attached to places, buildings, and objects.

JUST FOR FUN

Some Negs appear to live vicarious lives, skipping from living host to living host, but forming no lasting attachments or relationships. This type of behavior is usually exhibited by addictive or deranged ex-human earthbound Negs. These types maintain their astral real-time zone presence by stealing life force from living humans and animals through energy vampirism. This type of Neg will survive as long as it has vulnerable living people available. Some Negs are ancient, and it can be difficult to tell whether they were once human or not.

Now we have a basic frame of reference to work with, let's build on it and take a look at some of the forces and issues involved.

CHAPTER TWO

Psychic Interference and Attack

Core Affirmation: "I am loved and I am worthy. I am safe and I am free. I am powerfully protected. I am master of my body and ruler of my mind."

M any types of psychic and subtle energy interference can be classed as psychic attack. This chapter discusses the most common types. In the simplest form, psychic influences and attacks are temporary maladies that cause no lasting harm. By and large, these influences are usually unintentional.

For instance, salesmanship can involve a level of psychic influence. A good salesperson connects with customers and exerts psychic influences to make deals. Ethical salespersons will use this influence to help their customers. Customers will experience the desire to buy something. If salespersons lack this ability, they do not stay in sales for very long. Some talented salespersons can exert very strong psychic influences. Susceptible (psychically sensitive) customers can be made to buy just about anything, regardless of whether or not they actually want or can afford the items. This type of sales power correlates to how Negs influence people to do things and to make decisions that they would not normally choose.

Most people would be shocked to learn they had negatively influenced or attacked another person by brooding over petty disagreements. Control issues are particularly common with parents, who become so used to micromanaging and making decisions for their children that they do not know when to stop. This attitude can pass down through the generations and causes a lot of heartbreak. Children of controlling parents often become controlling in their relationships and with their own children.

The human urge to control, manipulate, and dominate is a weakness that is heavily exploited by Negs. This characteristic is common to most living psychic attackers.

Some people have natural, often unrealized psychic abilities. They can inadvertently psychically influence or attack others. A good example is a parent or grandparent who is sad and brooding about the lack of phone calls and contact from children or grandchildren. This brooding focus will exert psychic pressure and may cause many problems for the recipients of this focus. There is no malice here, but psychic attacks still happen.

Symptoms and Severity of Psychic Attack

The intensity of psychic attacks varies considerably. Some or all of the following symptoms can be experienced in varying combinations: feelings of anxiety and pressure, depression, a sense of impending doom, an increase in the severity of any psychological conditions, shortness of breath, disturbed sleep, chakra sensations and pressures, bad dreams, sharp jabbing or pricking pains in the feet, jabbing pains and cramps in other parts of the body, pressure headaches and migraines, compulsions and obsessive thoughts and urges, and bad luck.

Sudden cramps and pains that come and go in a short time for no apparent reason is a fair indicator of psychic attack. More intense attacks can involve these same symptoms at a stronger level. Stronger symptoms can involve life-threatening health problems, including unusual virulent infections and severe muscular cramps that can tear muscles. For example, a severe infection might suddenly appear in an elbow where there is no broken skin, in a tooth with no sign of decay, or in a kneecap or shin. Stomach or back muscles may cramp, and hernias can occur. A leg muscle may cramp so severely that it tears and bleeds and requires urgent medical attention. When anything like this happens and psychic attack is suspected, please seek medical attention sooner than you would usually. Taking extra-good care of your health is an important countermeasure. When Negs are involved, take no chances with your health.

Beyond the mild influencing that you might experience in a sales situation or the uncomfortable atmosphere you might feel coming from an angry relative, Negs are usually involved somewhere in psychic interference and attack. The person initiating a psychic attack is usually unaware that Negs are involved. If the biological host of a Neg (the source of an attack) becomes angry at another person (the victim), a psychic connection is formed between the two people. The attacker's resident Neg(s) will then reach out and attempt to punish the target. Negs will always assist their biological hosts in this way. This is a part of the unwritten contract between a Neg and its living host—the fine print of the permission agreement. Negs are also opportunistic. They take advantage of situations for various reasons. They drain people of energy as a matter of course and will attempt to attach to any potential new biological hosts.

Full possession of humans by Negs does happen, but it is uncommon. By and large, Negs need their biological hosts to function in human society. Most Negs lack basic human emotions and social skills. They cannot hold jobs or maintain relationships. Most seem content to go along for the human ride, exerting influences to get what they want. In this way, they share the lives of their unsuspecting human hosts.

Types of Neg Problems

The following are some of the most common types of Neg problems and the ways that they can happen.

Energy Draining: During all Neg attacks, energy is drained from victims. Imagine an entity is a dry sponge and a human is a puddle of vital fluid. With any contact, vital fluid/energy is absorbed by the entity. Some Negs do nothing but feed. They will often develop a network of living humans (possibly even animals, too) from which they regularly feed. In this case, the people involved may experience intermittent sleep disturbances, bad dreams, and periods of exhaustion. These symptoms might happen only a few times a year, or more regularly in severe cases.

Direct Attacks: Direct Neg attacks will come on suddenly. Any of the symptoms given earlier can be involved, often at severe levels. Direct attacks can also cause strong fear-inducing atmospheres; cold-tingling, shivering waves up the back; loss of body heat; partial to full paralysis; muscular cramps; sharp, stabbing pains; and unnatural thoughts, fears and compulsions. Direct attacks are most likely to happen at night, between sunset and sunrise. Negs actively avoid sunlight and are strongest at night. Attacks are often strongest in the hour before dawn breaks.

Phenomena: Psychic attacks can involve various types of paranormal phenomena. These phenomena will be stronger if victims are psychically talented. Such talent and energy may not be realized, especially in children. Psychic talent and mediumistic abilities provide the raw energy to power phenomena, such as poltergeist activity, atmospheres, and apparitions.

Unusual Ailments: Psychic interference and overshadowing by Negs can cause a variety of unusual ailments, such as allergies, dietary intolerances, intestinal and bowel disorders, stomachaches, earaches, and vision problems. Unusual skin condition, including eczema, lumps, infections, inflammations, acne, rashes, and hives, can appear rapidly as a result of psychic attack and energy-body interference.

Preexisting Weaknesses: Neg attacks always include unhealthy or socially detrimental influences. Preexisting weaknesses will *always* be exploited and magnified by Negs, often to obsessive levels. For example, a mild drinking problem can quickly escalate to obsessive drunkenness. Normally gentle and tolerant persons can become aggressive and intolerant. Any psychological weakness will be magnified and used during psychic attacks.

Addictions: Addictions are often Neg related. Bad habits can be created and promoted by Negs in order to feed their own cravings. Addictions can also be used to punish and weaken people and make them more susceptible to Neg attachments and controls. During psychic attacks, addictive urges will be greatly increased, usually at the worst possible times.

Alcoholism and drug addictions are the most common Neg-enhanced maladies used to hinder or stop sensitive people from making significant spiritual progress and contributions in life. Over time, substance abuse erodes natural shielding and damages general health, reputations and relationships. Any addiction can be Neg-related, including food, pornography, and sex. In these ways, many people who could help the world to become a better place are rendered ineffective.

Psychic Attacks by Living Humans: The simplest psychic attacks are caused by the intrusive emotional energies exerted by strong personalities. This type of pressure is evident to emotionally and psychically sensitive persons when they are exposed to such people. Pressure is usually first sensed in the solar plexus and chest. It can be accompanied by mild confusion and a difficulty in organizing one's thoughts, sudden tiredness, sweating, head pressure, dizziness, and difficulty breathing. More severe forms can cause stomach cramps, vomiting, diarrhea, fainting, sudden attacks of belching and gas, and even partial physical paralysis. These more severe symptoms are caused by Negs interfering with the internal workings of the physical body.

People with strong Negs inside them are often very opinionated, controlling, single-minded, moody, and easily offended. They have big egos and reflect the intentions of their resident Negs. They are always trying to justify themselves and to further their authority over others. This type of person can be outspoken or quiet and moody. When such a person becomes moody or angry, a sensitive will often feel a cold and disturbing atmosphere surrounding that person. This atmosphere can have a specific border and be felt from several yards or more away. This is the type of person that most people tippy-toe around, trying not to trigger any upset.

Brooding-Malice Attacks: Conditions that can cause unintentional psychic attacks arise when one person (the aggressor) becomes annoyed with another person (the victim). If the aggressor broods or obsesses over this annoyance with malice, a psychic attack can result. While this attack can happen at any time, it will usually begin during the evening while the psychic aggressor is sitting and quietly obsessing. The aggressor may appear to be relaxing and watching TV, but in the back of his/her mind s/he is seething obsessively over the annoyance. Most people relax and shift into a light trance state while watching TV. If a psychic aggressor is obsessing and brooding about something at this time, psychic attack can occur. This attack will be worse if aggressors continue obsessing while falling asleep and while sleeping. Aggressors can also astral project and attack people in this way.

Neglike Behavior: Obsessive thinking and urges are common to most Neg-related situations. Have you ever argued with people who just won't let go of an idea or a problem or a hurt or an insult? Some people will lay awake all night worrying and obsessing about things. These are very Neglike behavior traits—meaning, the worry and obsession are often empowered by Negs. If you see this behavior in yourself, stop and recite the Core Affirmation many times until it stops. If you are trying to rest, use the Core Affirmation as a mantra to help you fall asleep.

Deliberate Attacks: Deliberate psychic attacks precipitated by living humans are uncommon, but they do happen. All psychic and magical practices can be used to harm others. Magical and psychic-energy practices are all two-edged swords. They can be used to help or to hinder, to heal or to harm, simply by changing the intentions with which they are used. There is no black magic or white magic; there is only magic and the intention with which it is used.

Circumstantial Attacks: Random attacks—being in the wrong place at the wrong time—can happen when circumstances bring susceptible persons into contact with Neg-carrying hosts or with free-roaming Negs. These types of attacks are usually of short duration, unless the Negs concerned manage to obtain hitchhiking status. Hitchhiking will enable random situations to continue and potentially turn into long-term problems. This is why early detection of a hitchhiking Neg and quick counteraction are so important.

Freaky Is Fascinating: For all the above-given reasons, sensitive people should actively avoid haunted buildings (any area with a disturbed atmosphere). It is particularly unsafe to party in haunted buildings, as alcohol and recreational drugs greatly increase psychic susceptibility. I see a disturbing trend today: tours are popularizing haunted buildings, and TV shows are sensationalizing haunted and disturbed buildings. Freaky may be fascinating, but these are not safe activities.

Single or Group Attacks: A powerful Neg can affect many people simultaneously. Often, a person under psychic attack is the only one in a family or group to experience any symptoms. However, some attacks have a wide focus that can affect whole families or large groups of people. Often, Negs will use their controls to turn people against each other and thus affect many people. When any group or crowd behaves badly, there are usually Negs at work.

Pregnancy: Pregnant women will sometimes experience psychic attacks. These attacks can involve nightmares, sleep terrors, and awake-paralysis episodes, accompanied by feelings of dread and frightening presleep visions. Poltergeists activity may also be involved. These types of attacks can relate to prenatal hereditary attachments to unborn children. There are many similarities with these attacks and the hereditary Neg attacks that are commonly experienced by children around the age of three or four. Pregnancy attacks happen to only a small percentage of women and seem more common during first pregnancies.

Ill-Health Attacks: Ill health can attract attention from Negs and result in attacks. Injury and illness cause a lowering of natural energy defenses. Some Negs feed off sickness and death. It is common for seriously ill or dying people to reach a point where they begin seeing people and beings that others cannot see. These experiences show a weakening in the veil between the physical and subtle dimensions for such people. The environment around sick people is the main concern with respect to repelling negative influences. A clean, well-lit, cheerful atmosphere with lots of fresh flowers does wonders for the health of patients, as any nurse will tell you. Such an atmosphere is also great for repelling opportunistic Negs.

Side Effects of Neg Invasion

Once a major Neg attack has occurred, victims are often left with enduring weaknesses, specifically holes in their natural shielding. Because of this, similar attacks are possible in the future. Subtle changes occur in the mind and energy body of victims after the first successful attacks. People with histories of psychic attacks and Neg influences often realize that something about themselves has been altered. Subsequent attacks have similarities with earlier attacks, because the same weaknesses are exploited again and again.

People have remarked to me that it almost seems as if earlier Neg attackers left behind notes listing weaknesses and giving directions to other Negs. This is logical, as attacking Negs will always use whatever is available. Negs have strong psychic abilities and are very good at what they do. When they first see a person, they instantly see and know that person's weaknesses.

Real-Life Examples Involving Running Water

To illustrate the nature of these types of problems, and how the running-water countermeasure (introduced in Chapter 1) works, following are some experiences of mine. These also give a little background on how I got involved in this field and how I discovered some of my anti-Neg countermeasures. I will be referring to these experiences again further into the book.

CASE HISTORY 1: MICHAEL'S DINNER PARTY
This event happened around 1995. It triggered important realizations concerning the effects of running water on Negs. Here I recognize the

hand of my higher self instructing me through personal experience, for which there is no substitute.

I arrived at Michael's home in the outer suburbs around sundown. Michael and his wife are spiritual teachers. Two other guests had already arrived—a nice couple from India who worked in the hotel industry. We chatted about spirituality, metaphysics, books, and recipes, swapping stories and ideas.

After dinner, we continued our discussions. Another couple, Maggie and Tom, joined us later for drinks. Maggie was also a New Age teacher. I greeted her and Tom warmly, but I felt automatically repelled by this woman. Towards me, she was quite opinionated and disagreeable, even though she did not know me. She had a strong personality and manner, and I could barely finish a sentence without her cutting me off or disagreeing with me. She quickly steered the conversation over to her life and interests and ignored me. So I just sat and listened. Tom, an overtired shift worker, soon fell asleep on the sofa.

About twenty minutes later, I began feeling symptoms of a Neg attack. It started with a change in the atmosphere, cold shivers up my spine, anxiety, chest pressure, and a painful nerve cramp in my upper right back. This cramp soon spread down into my lower back, with sciatic pain down my right leg. I fought to relax and hide my distress. No one else in the room was affected. I did not fully realize what was happening at the time. Some of the symptoms I knew were Neg related, but I was unsure of myself. The implications were disturbing.

I tried to ignore what was happening, but the pain was becoming agonizing. Afraid I was about to collapse and embarrass myself, I excused myself and hobbled out of the house. In agony, with spinal cramps and sciatic pain searing up through my leg, I stumbled up the garden path towards my car, which was parked on the curb in front of the house. I went through the garden gate, and the cramps and pain vanished instantly. A few more steps, and I sagged against my car in wet-eyed relief.

Feeling fine again, I went for a short walk under streetlights of the tree-lined avenue to think about what had just happened. While it had all the hallmarks of a powerful Neg attack, with Maggie being the most likely source, I started to doubt myself again. Maybe I was just being paranoid. I did have some spinal injuries. Maybe I was just dehydrated or had somehow pinched a nerve over dinner.

I returned to my car and considered leaving. I touched my toes a few times, twisted, turned, and stretched. I had no pain or cramps whatsoever. I felt a little bruised from the earlier symptoms, but I was fine. I had not socialized for a long time, and this evening had been a real treat, so I decided to rejoin the party. I took one step back through the garden gate and collapsed to my knees in agony. Struggling to my feet, I hobbled back through the gate to my car. Once again, the pain stopped instantly as I passed through the gate. It was as if something unseen was attacking me—something in the shadows near the gate.

I eyed the gate suspiciously and decided to experiment. Gingerly moving towards the gate, I stood immediately in front of it and tried to feel what was happening, reaching out with my psychic senses. I felt absolutely nothing. I stepped through the gate, and there was instant, violent pain shooting up my leg and into my spine. I gasped and stepped back, almost falling over. The pain stopped instantly. I repeated this experiment a dozen times with the same result. I could not see it, but *something* was definitely lurking there. It had a precise border. I moved closer and slid my right foot forward an inch at a time until it almost reached the gate. At an exact point, sciatic-nerve pain hit my big toe and rushed up the outside of my leg. This was painful, but absolutely fascinating. I was now in full mad-scientist mode. I got out my notebook and started making sketches and recording my observations.

There was a nasty Neg on the other side of the gate. I could not sense it or see it, but it was definitely there. There was an invisible barrier across the front of the gate. I was on one side, and the pain Neg was on the other. It attacked me instantly whenever I crossed the line. There was an indentation several inches wide in the asphalt of the footpath that ran across the front of the property. This indentation looked to involve the watermain pipe for the street. It must have been dug up and patched at some time. This appeared to be a line the Neg could not pass. But why?

I walked to the far left side of the front yard, to where the water main crossed the driveway into Michael's yard. The same thing happened when I crossed there—instant pain. I continued walking to the front yard of the next house and repeated the experiment. Again the unseen thing attacked me. I moved a little further, past that neighbor's water meter, where the water pipe flowed into the house. I could hear this water meter ticking, indicating water was flowing through it. I repeated the experiment there and crossed over the water-main pipe—nothing happened, no pain. I went into that neighbor's front yard and walked slowly across the grass back towards Michael's home, till I crossed the smaller water-supply pipe that ran under the grass and into that house. An instant pain attack resulted every time I crossed that pipe.

I repeated this experiment in the neighbor's yard on the other side of Michael's house, with exactly the same results. I repeated the entire experiment again from start to finish with exactly the same results. I could accurately tell the positions of the underground water pipes that had water moving through them from the pain attacks.

The attacking Neg was trapped in a very specific area. This area was outlined by the water-main pipe that ran under the footpath across the front of these three houses and the water-supply pipes that ran into the houses on each side of Michael's house.

There was a water pipe extending from the footpath into Michael's home. But Michael was not running any sprinklers this night. The Neg appeared able to cross the domestic supply pipe that ran into Michael's home, but this had no water running through it. Both Michael's neighbors were running sprinklers at this time, so water was running through both those domestic supply pipes. The running water appeared to be why the Neg was limited to such a precise area.

With nothing further to be done, I returned to my car and drove home. I had no further problems with pain or cramps, although I felt a little bruised for a few days.

I tried to explain what had happened to Michael a few days later, but he did not understand and was insulted. So we broke contact.

Figure 3: Sketch showing layout of Michael's home and water pipes

This experience is a clear example of direct psychic attack by a free-roaming Neg. Even though the biological source of the attack seemed clear, the way the attack transpired showed the involvement of an aggressive Neg. It also shows how running water forms an effective barrier to Negs.

This incident was a real eureka moment. It caused me to realize the nature of running-water barriers. I had used running water many times in the past to stop attacking Negs from people, but I had not realized how effective this barrier was. I have thoroughly road tested running-water countermeasures since, sometimes in extreme situations. I have experimented extensively on myself and many other people, including children and infants, during direct Neg attacks. This running-water countermeasure has produced consistent results.

It has become clear to me over the years that Negs use people and animals to hitchhike across running water. In the above experience, either Maggie or Tom (he fell asleep) could have been the biological source of the attack. They crossed the running water on their way into Michael's home. The Neg did not appear to be resident in the house prior to the attack. I had visited Michael's house several times before, usually in the evening, and nothing bad had ever happened. So it was most likely that the Neg that attacked me was carried into the house by Maggie and Tom.

The above experience was a turning point for my work on psychic self-defense. I think it had been arranged by my higher self to demonstrate how running water profoundly affects Negs. It was at this point that my ongoing battle with Negs turned a corner, and I started to make real progress.

CASE HISTORY 2: FRED AND JESSE

This incident happened in 1991. It shows a powerful Neg attack on a man and a child. The man, Fred, was a tough, materialistic guy who did not then believe in spirits or anything supernatural.

It was mid-afternoon, and I needed bread and milk. Fred had dropped in for coffee, and my three-year-old son, Jesse, was taking a nap. I asked Fred to babysit while I went to the supermarket. I was only gone fifteen minutes, but all hell broke loose while I was away.

As I walked back to my front door, I was greeted with screams from Jesse and Fred, calling for help. I found them on their knees in the living room. Fred was white and shaking like a leaf and unable to walk, holding a crying Jesse. I could barely make out what Fred was saying. "Get me out of here! Something's got me!"

I grabbed Jesse and tossed him into the sandpit out in the backyard. Then I half-carried Fred out through the back door. He was shaking badly and could not walk alone. He gasped and straightened up the instant we passed over the threshold, saying, "It's gone. It's gone." Confused and shocked, he hunkered on the lawn and told me what happened.

A minute after I had left, little Jesse had started screaming. Fred found Jesse cowering in bed, pointing at shadows in the far corner of the room. Fred's hair stood on end as the shadows moved. He went to pick up Jesse, but an unseen force knocked him back against the wall. Everything went out of focus for him at this point. Fred had trouble getting to his feet as massive, bone-wracking shivers coursed through him. Not being one to give in, Fred shook his head and charged. He grabbed Jesse and staggered out of the room. He got halfway across the living room before he was driven to his knees by unseen forces. He was unable to walk or crawl any farther, and that's where I found them.

When Fred was settled, thinking the attack was over, we went back inside. Fred swore and fell to his knees the instant he stepped over the threshold. (Sound familiar?) Again, I half-carried him back outside, and again he straightened up after crossing the threshold. While I was not directly affected and could not sense anything, all my alarms were going off. This was a major Neg attack.

I experimented with Fred as best I could, crossing and recrossing the threshold with him, each time with exactly the same result. This was so disturbing that after we did this a few times, he refused to reenter the house.

As I could come and go as I pleased, I got Fred a cold beer to settle his nerves. He was badly shaken. We sat on the patio, trying to work out what had happened. While I had my suspicions, I could not explain them to Fred in any way that would make sense to him. He left to go home shortly after this point. We thought it was all over.

However, Fred returned ashen faced a few hours later. The attack had started again soon after he left the house; waves of shivering and goose bumps had hit him as he drove. He had strong compulsions to swerve into oncoming traffic. After a near miss with a truck, he pulled into a supermarket. He soon found himself shopping in what he described as a surreal, dreamlike mall. Fred filled a trolley with things he did not want and could not afford, then tried to pay for them with a bag of grass.

Suddenly realizing what he was doing, Fred made a hasty exit, leaving the unwanted shopping behind. Returning to his car, Fred drove home, fighting suicidal urges all the way. Things were so bad that he got a lift back to my home, hoping I could help.

I helped him as best I could with all I knew at that time. Mentally, he held his own against an incredibly nasty Neg. While the stronger symptoms of direct Neg attack eased after a few weeks, Fred's luck changed and his life went to pieces. He lost his job, his wife threw him out, and eventually he moved to another state to start a new life. Over the next three years, he experienced almost nightly Neg attacks. He did the best he could to overcome this. Mentally strong, he barely survived.

The symptoms eased after a few years, but only as Fred matured and changed his lifestyle. Looking back on all that happened, as bad as it was, in the long term, the suffering Fred experienced changed his life for the better. He now lives a more moderate, healthy, spiritual lifestyle. Fred was lucky to survive this level of Neg attack.

The experience with Fred was not entirely out of the blue. We had been having problems in our home for some time, and my family had just lived through several months of Neg attacks. Up until the time of Fred's attack, he had seemed immune to everything and sensed nothing during his regular visits. Our household Neg problems did not change after Fred's experience, so it seems he did not take our resident Negs away with him. However, he certainly picked up something nasty that day.

It was years later, and only after the experience I had at Michael's dinner party, that I realized what it was that broke the attacks on Fred at my back door: a domestic water pipe went across the back of the house and passed directly under the threshold of the back door. A garden hose was filling the swimming pool at the time and laying on the back step against the threshold. So water was passing through both these as Fred stepped over the threshold. The water running through the pipe and hose is what broke the attack on Fred each time he went through the back door, just as water running through water-main pipes had for me at Michael's front gate. I also realized that the Neg had been trapped inside my house until I turned off the garden hose a few minutes before Fred left that day. This may explain why the attacking Neg was able to follow Fred when he left.

···◆···

Now we have a solid grounding on the situation and a basic understanding of Neg behavior and types. Let's take a look at how people are exposed to these things and what symptoms are involved with different types of Neg-related problems.

CHAPTER THREE

Exposure and Symptoms

Core Affirmation: "I am loved and I am worthy. I am safe and I am free. I am powerfully protected. I am master of my body and ruler of my mind."

The signs and symptoms of supernatural activity are many and varied. The numerous complexities include the environment; the sensitivity, strengths, and weaknesses of persons involved; and the strength, experience, and nature of the Neg(s) involved. This chapter reviews some of the most common issues relating to supernatural activity and Neg attacks.

An interface must exist between Negs and the living biological human beings they invade and exploit, or this exploitation could not happen. The homunculus and the autonomous nervous system are the most likely areas involved. The homunculus is an area of the human brain that is directly related to the sense of touch. This area is also called the Little Man, because a cross-section looks vaguely like a little man with big hands and lips.

It is a common practice for some types of brain surgery to expose the brain while the patient is still awake. If surgeons touch or stimulate areas of the homunculus, patients feel various pressures and sensations in their physical bodies. The homunculus and its connections through the nervous systems of the human body have been mapped by medical science, resulting in diagrams like the one shown in Figure 4. The distortions in this body image result from concentrations of nerves. In the homunculus, areas connected with many nerves are larger, and areas with lesser concentrations of nerves are smaller.

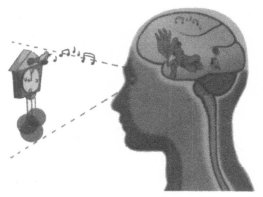

Figure 4: Homunculus (a.k.a., the Little Man)

A recent experience demonstrates the relationship between the homunculus, the physical body, the energy body, and Negs: I awoke at 4:30 a.m., just before sunrise, feeling painful pricking feelings in the middle of my right palm. I was partially paralyzed. At first this sensation felt like a physical nail was being used to pick a hole in my hand. After a few minutes, the invisible nail was forced slowly through my hand. This was excruciatingly painful, but fascinating at the same time. The feeling was so precise that I could feel the shape and texture of the nail as it was forced through my hand. It felt to be about six inches in length, with a square profile and rough, metallic texture. I countered this psychic-attack symptom with every countermeasure I know. The whole experience lasted several minutes. For days afterwards, my hand felt bruised where the invisible nail had gone through it.

I speculate that this type of interference, which is not uncommon, is caused by Negs directly stimulating the physical body through the energy body, the homunculus, and the autonomous nervous system.

I experienced that painful nail while editing the new edition of this book. This experience refreshed my memory of the time I was possessed many years ago and some of the things that happened to me then. Such experiences feel like warnings. They are painful, sinister, and threatening, but they are also great teachers.

One thing I know with absolute surety concerning this incident: if the Neg involved could have done more to harm me at the time, it would have done so immediately. Negs do not pass up opportunities.

So, logically, this experience was allowed by my higher self for a reason. It may have been just to refresh my memory. If that was the intention, it worked.

Every time I am attacked or interfered with by Negs, I learn something new. Over time, this new information adds up. The book you are holding grew from this process. (I would not recommend this as a learning method. It is hard on the body. When I look back, I am amazed that I have survived it all.)

The Skin and the Aura: a 3D Model

My decades of experience lead me to speculate that the outer edge of the human energy field, the aura sheath, is directly related to the skin of the human body. In my working Neg profile, this concept helps explain how Negs interfere with the human mind, the energy body, and, through these, the physical body.

The how and why of the involvement of Negs with the human mind and its energy field are difficult to conceptualize. The mind and energy field are, by and large, not 3D structures. But we have to work with a 3D model in order to apply this to the physical body and make it understandable.

According to this 3D model, most, if not all, attacks on the human energy body first flow up from below the feet and then over the surface skin of the human energy field. The feet connect with the field of energy that covers the surface of the planet, to which Negs are also attached. A penetration of the outer edge of the human energy field will have a direct effect upon the skin and flesh of the area of the physical body with which that part of the field is related. If the field is badly breached, pain will be felt and welts can appear on the skin.

If a Neg energy attachment is inserted through the skin, the skin and flesh will react. Red marks, swellings, infections, and eruptions can occur. These can include blisters, soft or hard lumps, or granulomas, on or under the skin. Various types of skin blemishes, like moles and nevi, can also appear. Birthmarks are possibly linked to energy attachments passing through the skin, though not all birthmarks are necessarily Neg related.

More on skin blemishes and lumps, and how to heal and remove some types, later in this book.

Associations and Energy Effects

The energies produced by people, places, buildings, atmospheres, and groups of people, can have significant effects on people. Some places energize us or make us feel happy or relaxed, and others drain us of vitality. Probably the most well-known study on these effects is feng shui. Feng shui practitioners adjust the décor, colors, layouts, shapes, and furnishings of buildings and places to improve positive energy flow. Our environment affects us in many subtle ways. Relating to psychic self-defense, a lot can be done to make homes beautiful, happy, and comfortable places in which to live. In this way, homes can be made to be repulsive to Negs.

The people with whom we associate also affect our energies. The closer the association, the stronger the effect. Some people's energies affect us in positive and healthy ways, and some people's energies are downright unhealthy for us. It is fairly easy to identify what is good and bad company to keep by observing people's morals, ethics, and behavior. It is more difficult to identify people with whom we are energetically in harmony or those who are disharmonious. Doing so is a matter for instinct, common sense, and personal experience.

For example, if you have an addictive-type nature and spend a lot of time associating with people who are actively feeding addictions, your chances of developing addiction problems are increased. So if you have addiction weaknesses, it is wise to spend time with people who have nonaddictive personalities and lifestyles. If you have an unhealthy lifestyle and diet, it is wise to spend time with people who have healthier lifestyles. These things really do rub off on you. Think of this as a frequency issue. If two tuning forks, producing two different sound frequencies, are brought close together, they will affect each other. This effect will change the ambient sound frequency being produced. This approach can make a big difference in the long-term quality of your life. This principle also applies to Neg influences.

People's pets will often reflect their owners' personalities and health. It is not uncommon for pets to develop health problems similar to those of their owners. For example, a woman I know is an overweight, type-2 diabetic with an eating disorder and heart problems. She has a cat with these exact same problems. Pets and their owners sharing similar health problems is not an uncommon situation.

In my experience, Negs can spread from person to person through close association. The computer analogy I gave earlier demonstrates the way this spread works. We all have our programs and baggage, and some of us have resident viruses and malware (Negs). If we spend a lot of close time with another person, chances are that some of these programs and viruses will spread into that other person, or visa versa. We can infect others with our programs and viruses, and in turn, become infected ourselves.

Overshadowing and Channeling

Channeling is a phenomenon whereby spirit beings communicate through living humans. This can be a good thing, albeit a risky thing, to do, as wise and helpful spirits do exist. Channeling can be described as a kind of temporary overshadowing, or possession, depending on how strongly the spirit is present within a person. Channeling usually occurs with the full permission of the channel—the biological host. Overshadowing and possession are very similar to channeling, but with no deliberate permission being given.

Channeling can involve anything from a light inspirational influence to consensual overshadowing to heavier forms of spirit control, where the personality of the biological host is absent, and no memory of what transpired during sessions is recalled afterwards. Again, there are marked similarities between channeling and Neg-related overshadowing and possession. So it is likely that similar mechanisms are involved with both.

Familiar sayings reflect the overshadowing experience in society, such as, "I'm not myself today," "I don't know what got into me," "He's got the devil in him," "She's in high spirits," "I don't know what came over me," and "I don't know what possessed me."

In negative versions of overshadowing and possession, the persons involved do not have full control over their thoughts, feelings, words and actions. These conditions can cause anything from minor changes in behavior to full personality replacement. Episodes can last from a few moments to many days or longer. This is often called a mood (e.g., "She's been in a bad mood all week"). Overshadowing episodes can happen unnoticed, depending on the usual personality and behavior of the person involved. Blackouts can also occur where there is full personality replacement, leaving the victim with no memory of what happened for a time.

Normal mood swings aside, the diagnosis of various mental disorders can be applied to explain some of these conditions, particularly the more severe forms of overshadowing and possession. Medications used to treat such conditions change the way the brain functions. These changes can chemically interfere with Neg controls and are, therefore, helpful in this sense for persons suffering with Neg-related disorders. Medications can also help to restore healthy sleep and eating patterns, which will also interfere with Neg controls by boosting natural defenses.

Overshadowing is one of the main devices used by Negs during episodes of psychic influence and attack. It is also often related to addictions and unhealthy and antisocial behavioral compulsions. Overshadowing affects not only the intended target, but also those people around him or her. It is used by Negs to affect situations in negative ways, to destabilize people, and to damage relationships. This influence unbalances and weakens people by causing arguments, spreading discontent, and generating violence, substance abuse, and toxic atmospheres. These things tend to isolate the target and reduce his or her support from friends and loved ones, all of which increases Neg vulnerability.

The most common signs of overshadowing are sudden mood swings, including marked changes in personality and behavior and loss of temper and self-control. These changes can happen quickly, and persons experiencing them can go from congenial to aggressive in seconds. The change can be quite noticeable. Body posture, gait, and facial aspects can change. Eyes can darken and even change color in severe cases. Often, it will appear as if a shadow has fallen over a person's face. This is where the term *overshadowing* comes from.

Over the years, I have worked with many people who were suffering from the whole range of Neg abuse. I am often told by Neg-abuse victims that other people are generally nasty to them. This sounds like paranoia, but in many cases these victims are right. I have seen people like this walk into a room and have felt the atmosphere change from positive to negative almost instantly.

An example came my way in 2004, while I was giving a residential workshop. I had invited a victim of serious Neg abuse to visit me there, so I could give her healing. She arrived just as I was finishing a class. She slipped in quietly and sat down politely near the door. I felt the atmosphere change from being positive and loving to negative and disturbed almost immediately. I watched carefully. The forty people in the room shifted about uneasily, and many glanced at the woman in unfriendly ways. I brought up their reactions during the next session; given the nature of the class, doing so was appropriate. Approximately half the group acknowledged this change, and many admitted to unexplainable hostile feelings towards this quiet and shy young woman. Some of these people were experienced spiritual teachers with decades of experience, so this was deeply disturbing for them. This example shows how a powerful Neg can influence many people simultaneously.

Victims of this level of Neg abuse feel isolated and disempowered for good reason, because everyone seems to be against them. Earlier, I spoke on how Negs use glamor. The Neg possessing this young woman at my workshop was projecting a field of intentional glamor around her. Everyone was repelled by her, even though she was actually quite sweet and beautiful. I am used to glamor, so the one around her did not affect me. But I felt it. (More on this later.)

Protection against Negs is always a personal responsibility. Very few spiritual teachers can offer any practical help if anything goes seriously wrong for a student. This is no slight on teachers, who are generally well meaning and would help if they could. But I have had so many people come to me for help after trying to learn channeling and similar things that I feel I have a duty to warn people about the dangers.

Channeling is a modern term for mediumship. This term is loosely used to describe a variety of psychic and mediumistic abilities, including psychic communication, trance speech, clairvoyance, clairaudience, transfiguration, and spirit writing (automatic writing). The type of channeling I am most concerned about here is when persons allow themselves to be overshadowed by spirits.

There is a disturbing modern trend towards simplifying spiritual protection. To do spiritual protection right, extensive spoken prayers, affirmations, visualizations, invocations, and evocations are needed. The way the old-school spiritualists activate spiritual protection is much safer than the way groups often do it today. Many groups gloss over spiritual protection or omit it completely, thinking it old fashioned and time wasting. It is also popularly believed that focusing on spiritual protection can attract negative problems (i.e., what you resist, persists). So many people focus only on the positives and completely ignore negative possibilities. While positive thinking is laudable, it is unwise to omit sensible precautions.

In my opinion, the practice of openly inviting unknown spirit beings to enter and control one's body and mind is both unwise and unsafe, to put it mildly. Permission is a profound spiritual issue. It is wise to be extremely careful what you invite into your self and into your life. Often, it is very difficult to rescind permission once it is given. Unfortunately, many people will risk anything just so long as some kind of phenomenon actually happens. Many times I have seen people get into strife through this phenomena-seeking approach. Whether it is worth the risk or not becomes a moot point once Neg problems are triggered. However, in all cases, no matter how frightening and painful such an experience might be, the end result is priceless firsthand experience and significant spiritual growth.

It is not necessary to work with spirits for psychic and spiritual development. It's far preferable to get in touch with your own higher self than it is to seek association with unknown spirits. One should not look outside oneself for spiritual knowledge, advice, and abilities. Everything is within. Psychic abilities are side effects of spiritual development and best not sought for their own sake.

If a good spirit wishes to work with a person, that person will not need to do anything to initiate it. A good spirit will approach a person gently and with respect. A good test is to ask the spirit to withdraw for a full month. If the spirit understands and withdraws graciously, its intentions are most likely good. If, on the other hand, the spirit refuses or returns after only a few days and gives excuses, it is most likely not a good spirit. Low spirits and Negs are impatient and will usually give *mission-bestowing messages*. These messages can sometimes appear to be profound, but are also often vague, silly, and illogical. If any of these things happen, it is wise to reject the spirit. If the spirit will not leave, then its identity is revealed as a deceiving or mischievous spirit.

Often, the appearance of an insincere, silly, or disrespectful spirit is an important test. It is right to reject such a spirit. A more sincere and evolved replacement can appear or can be requested. The appearance of the first spirit is a test of your own sincerity and gullibility. The gullibility factor is a profound spiritual test. This circumstance is often the prelude to a more serious, helpful spirit appearing. There may be more tests following the first one. After each test is passed, a more evolved spirit can appear. All that is needed here is a little common sense to discern good from bad.

Neg-related problems that can arise through group practices and psychic work are often not easily fixed. This is partly due to permission issues involved in openly inviting spirits to enter and take control. As I said, permission, once given, can be difficult to revoke. No matter what anyone might say to the contrary, removing a problem Neg, like a computer virus, can be extremely difficult.

Those who pick up problem spirits are usually told to surround themselves in white light and to send the problem spirit to the light. But if the spirit does not go along with this, what does one do to get rid of it? In addition, it's particularly difficult to do anything self-defensive when one is experiencing the disturbing symptoms of Neg invasion. More on this later.

Indications of a Neg Presence

When I am investigating a building for Neg problems, I stop in every room, hallway, and open area. I close my eyes and reach out with my emotional and psychic senses for Neg disturbances. Sometimes there will be tangible cold areas in the house. If I find anything—and most people can do this if they try—it causes a prickling, tingling, or cold shivers to run up my back. A strong Neg presence causes my mid to upper right back to cramp painfully. This type of nerve pain is a common response to Neg presences, as noted by many healers and sensitives I have known. I may also hear sounds, voices, or have visions relating to the disturbance. Such visions can be frightening in houses where murder or suicide has occurred. Powerful echoes from the past that cause such disturbing visions can linger for decades or longer.

Troublesome Negs tend to generate cold atmospheres in areas where they hang out in a building. These areas have a cold, creepy, tingly feeling to them that will make sensitives anxious. These areas are usually the darkest, quietest ones available. Negs retreat to these places during daylight hours. I have solved many household Neg problems simply by increasing the light and ventilation in dark or suspicious areas. This can be accomplished by opening curtains, doors, and windows, or by installing new light fittings, using stronger bulbs, and fitting mirrors or skylights.

If you relax and *sense* and *feel* as you walk through a Neg-troubled house, you will feel an uneasy, depressing atmosphere in the background. This atmosphere will have a creepy edge to it, making it similar to the uneasy atmospheres found at night in cemeteries, morgues, and funeral parlors.

Sensitives can have difficulties breathing, in strongly Neg-affected atmospheres. (The risk of direct Neg attack in such areas is always higher for sensitives.) Sensing cold patches in a room or feeling goose bumps and hair-prickling sensations on the body are all common indicators of a Neg presence.

Imagination and expectations must be taken into account when investigating potentially disturbed houses. If spooky Neg problems have been discussed, people will be on edge, and this fear can create bad atmospheres where there are none. If this happens, people can easily scare themselves and everyone else around them. If you are investigating such a house, it is better to play things down and not pass on everything you might sense. For example, I once scanned a disturbed house for a couple that claimed to be experienced with spirit matters. They had picked up many of the things I saw already. (There had been two suicides in this house, many years past.) I saw the echoes of both these events. A man had hanged himself, and a woman had cut her wrists in the bathtub. The imagery I saw was horrific. I passed on these details in a matter-of-fact way. The information so disturbing to the couple that they had trouble sleeping and moved house soon after. Having what they already knew validated was just too much for them.

Again, it is wise to keep such things to yourself or to play things down, so as not to increase tensions in an already-disturbed house. Ideally, information should be given on a *need-to-know* basis.

Negs are sensitive to light, particularly sunlight. Uneasy negative atmospheres will always get worse after sunset and improve after sunrise. Negs are always more active at night.

Strange noises, such as knocks and taps on walls, ceilings, furniture, and fittings, are common symptoms of paranormal activity. All buildings make noises as timbers and joints expand and contract through moisture and temperature fluctuations. These types of noises are identifiable. But moisture and temperature fluctuations do not explain the knocks and taps on walls, furniture, and fittings so often associated with supernatural activity. Many spirit noises come from empty space. The word *poltergeist* means "noisy ghost," which is apt. Poltergeists cause unexplainable noises and move physical objects, often in plain view. They can also interfere with or damage electrical and electronic devices and cause fires.

Spirit noises and poltergeist activity are always more intense during Neg attacks. Objects will sometimes go missing or be moved for no apparent reason. In areas of strong poltergeist activity, objects can even be hurled at people. I have been present while sledgehammer-strength blows have occurred, damaging solid objects like glass, doors, walls, bricks, tiles, and furniture. I have also seen heavy furniture sliding from one side of a room to the other. I have stood in kitchens where a dozen or more cupboard doors were opening and slamming shut simultaneously. As I said earlier, you may have read about this kind of thing, but you really have to see it to believe it.

Disembodied voices, another symptom of paranormal activity, are also common during psychic attacks. These are more frequent at night, especially during presleep and awakening. Common noises include the traditional dragging of chains, heavy footfalls, and the wailing and moaning of tormented souls—the familiar sounds of the dead in a haunted house. These noises are best classed as audio hallucinations or astral sounds, relating to astral sight and hearing, as discussed earlier.

Strange odors are also common during paranormal activity. Anything from perfume to cigar smoke to lipstick and body odor or feces can be smelled. Even very mild manifestations can produce noticeable odors. Many ghosts and spirits emit particular smells, almost like signature odors. Psychic smelling (the ability to detect nonphysical smells) is the most common of all psychic abilities. Most people have some level of this ability. The most common smell noted during strong Neg manifestations is something like a mixture of rotting meat, feces, and cat urine. The stronger the smell, the stronger the potential for serious Neg problems. Negs are generally attracted to bad smells and repelled by nice smells.

Astral lights and tiny pings and flashes and sparks of lights are common signs of paranormal activity. Pings are tiny pinpoints of light that appear and vanish in a split second. They are often brightly colored. Good spirits and ghosts of recently deceased persons will often cause colorful pings. Dark pings indicate the presence of Negs and are not a good sign. Even worse are clusters of dark pings that look like swarms of flies. This is a sign that a strong Neg presence is building up and trying to manifest. Areas with these dark clusters should be immediately evacuated until the manifestation ceases and appropriate countermeasures, like fumigation and incense, are used to improve the atmosphere.

The term *astral lights* refers to all types of light phenomena. These light phenomena are well known to occultists and parapsychologists as indicators of supernatural activity. Sightings of silver sparks and blobs of light, or groups of blobs, inside or outside affected houses at night indicate a high potential for manifestations and serious Neg problems. Blobs of astral light stay visible longer than pings, often for several seconds or so. Some blobs can be a yard across, but astral lights this size are rare and usually singular. The average size of an astral light blob is that of a tennis ball. Thick, ropey columns of pale, smoky light are also possible. Strong astral lights can be captured on video or photographic film. Many unexplainable pictures of astral lights have been captured. Books dealing with supernatural phenomena often contain examples.

The most common astral-light phenomenon relating to psychic attacks and Neg problems are tennis-ball-sized blobs. The most commonly sighted are silver or white. The most negative types are smoky black. Pay attention if smoky-black light blobs are sighted, as these are a major indicator of a Neg attack in progress. They move rapidly and are usually sighted for only a split second. Typically, they will suddenly come through a wall and fly across the room, disappearing through the far wall in a split second. A light but audible crack will usually be heard as they pass through a wall or windowpane. This phenomenon can indicate a human psychic attacker focusing on a victim at the time, although Negs are often involved.

More rarely, milky silver blobs up to the size of a human head can be seen. Such blobs will often clearly carry the shape and facial features of the human attacker. These blobs are like astral-projected partial apparitions of the attacker. This type of sighting is usually made during presleep in a dark or semidark room, or by people just awakening from sleep. Such things are most often sighted with peripheral vision—out of the corner of your eye.

Apparitions—ghostly shapes and figures—are common spirit manifestations. These are usually seen during presleep or with peripheral vision, as momentary glimpses of shadowy movements. One common type of apparition resembles full-sized, transparent images of people, as though the spirit were made of mist. Stronger apparitions can look like persons covered with glowing white sheets, showing blurred features—the classic ghost.

Disembodied hands, faces, and other body parts are also fairly common. Some apparitions can manifest strongly enough to physically touch people. Their touch always feels cold and clammy, as this is what spirit ectoplasm feels like. For example, persons may feel cold, clammy hands touching them during presleep. Or they wake up to feel a disembodied hand holding one of their hands. Any variety of real-feeling, disembodied hands and body parts are possible. This type of manifestation can sometimes have sexual connotations.

Symptoms of Neg Interference

Neg problems typically start with some kind of nocturnal interference, like obsessive looping thoughts, nightmares, sleep paralysis, astral sight and hearing experiences, cold shivers, touches from invisible hands, cramps, and jabbing-pin pains in the feet. Incidences of poltergeist activity, astral lights and pings, strange noises, unpleasant atmospheres, and seeing shadowy movements in peripheral vision will increase. The more of these indicators there are, the more serious are potential problems.

Care must be taken not to focus on phenomena too closely, as doing so can connect you to it and make matters worse. Imagination can also cause problems by increasing tension and worry, which can cause a fearful state of mind that increases exposure to Neg interference. Note the phenomena, but try to keep it out of your mind.

The following types of phenomena can occur in any combination and severity.

THE CLASSIC INCUBUS NIGHTMARE

The generic definition of the most common type of Neg attack is the incubus nightmare. An incubus is historically classed as an evil spirit, or demon, that visits sleeping persons. During an incubus nightmare, victims awaken to feel heavy weights pressing down on their chests, as if a heavy person were lying on top of them and making breathing difficult. This sensation usually includes some measure of awake paralysis. It can also involve astral sight and hearing phenomena. Victims feel incredibly weak, as if their vitality were being drained away, which can be what is occurring. There can be sexual connotations, but usually not. An atmosphere of dread is usually sensed. A typical incubus nightmare lasts only a few minutes, but is a terrifying experience.

LOCALIZED ATMOSPHERES AND PHENOMENA

Some people can be haunted. Victims of Neg abuse will sometimes be followed by disturbed atmospheres, which will grow in intensity in whatever place the victims stay. Supernatural phenomena will also tend to happen around Neg-abuse victims. For example, if a person suffering Neg abuse visits a house with a calm spiritual atmosphere, it will not be long before astral lights, knocks and taps on walls, peculiar smells, and fearful atmospheres begin to manifest.

PSYCHIC ANIMALS

Have you ever seen a dog viciously attack thin air for no reason, or a cat arch its back and hiss at empty space? I have seen this many times. Some, but not all, pets are psychically sensitive. Sensitive pets can react strangely, either defensively or aggressively, towards people who carry strong Neg attachments. Psychic pets can help identify and warn people about exposure to potential Neg problems.

If sensitive pets are forced to live in Neg-contaminated areas, these animals will act strangely, often becoming depressed or anxious. They may go mad or run away from home if the situation disturbing them continues. If they cannot get away, they may develop serious behavioral problems and need to be removed from the home.

Psychically sensitive people attract and are attracted to psychically sensitive pets. Such pets will grow in awareness and sensitivity through living with sensitive owners, and vice versa. Psychically sensitive pets can be encouraged through positive reinforcement to react to and warn their owners about Neg manifestations.

The aggression and noise of attacking pets makes an excellent countermeasure. This draws attention to and distracts Negs, making life difficult for them. Early warning allows other countermeasures—air freshener, incense, and music, for example—to be applied sooner. Negs are always at their weakest when they first arrive.

Some Negs are capable of shielding their presence from sensitive people. But the sensitive animals' ability to detect the presence of Negs appears to overcome this shielding.

NATURE'S WARNING BELLS

The human energy body has a sensitive outer field that extends in all directions beyond the outer edge of the aura sheath. The depth of this field varies, depending on the degree of sensitivity, and can reach from several feet to filling an entire house or more. This field reacts to the presence of spirit beings of any type, including astral projectors.

Cold shivers, goose bumps, hair-prickling sensations, tingling up the back, and feelings of anxiety—the feeling that someone has "walked over your grave"—are nature's warning bells. These reactions are similar to those that people experience when bees or other buzzing insects fly nearby and surprise them. Our minds can overcome these warning reactions through familiarity. If you worked as a beekeeper, you would get used to bees and tune these feelings out. Likewise, when persons are frequently exposed to spirits, they eventually get used to spirit energies and tune them out.

It is wise to listen to warning sensations and follow the instinctive urge to move away, or to double check what is causing them, just in case it is something negative that should be avoided.

These warning-bell sensations often do not indicate what type of spirit is present. The same sensations can be caused by good spirits, ghosts, astral projectors, nature spirits, and Negs. Further intuitive sensing and experience are needed to ascertain exactly what is being sensed. Sensations that start to become overly strong indicate that a spirit may be attempting to enter and overshadow someone or to manifest in some way. This is a good time to leave the area, to seek running water, and to apply other countermeasures as needed. This is always best done sooner rather than later.

Symptoms of Direct Neg Attack

Direct Neg attacks are heralded by nature's warning bells. These warning signals intensify and other sensations quickly follow.

Often, a noticeable patch of tingling and cramping nerve pain will be felt in the spine, usually in the mid- to upper-back area or under a shoulder blade. Tingling or pain may be felt in previously damaged areas of the spine. For example, the direct Neg attack on myself I described earlier, at Michael's dinner party, began with cramping nerve pain near the shoulder blade. This was soon followed by sciatic pain in my right leg, relating to an existing lower-back injury—a herniated disk.

In its strongest form, a direct Neg attack comes on very quickly. It can seem like a massive panic attack coming out of nowhere. It can cause one's whole body to feel pressure, causing breathing difficulties, palpitations, chest pressure, cold chills, and blurred vision. Partial physical paralysis can occur, and massive debilitating shivering that can make it difficult to stand or walk—as happened to my friend, Fred. This type of assault indicates that the Neg involved is trying to batter down natural defenses with brute force. Some Negs will expend all their strength to quickly breach human defenses. This is a time to take urgent action—take a shower, leave the house, cross running water, electrically ground.

Pricking and jabbing pain sensations will often be felt in the feet and toes and sometimes the ankles. These sensations may be why demons are historically depicted as small, horned devils carrying sharp tridents, and why hell was thought to be underground. If people suddenly feel sharp pricks and jabs in their feet while walking, it would seem as if unseen underground beings were jabbing at their feet with something sharp. These sensations can happen if you walk over an area of extreme Neg contamination.

Other common symptoms include loss of body heat; disturbing visions when eyes are closed; unpleasant or unsavory, out-of-character thoughts and compulsive urges with no discernable triggers; goose bumps and adrenaline rushes with no discernible causes; muscular cramps; sharp pains; nausea; vertigo; head pressure and headache; localized areas of buzzing (as if a fly were buzzing next to one's skin); localized patches of tingling or tickling; hot or cold patches; bad smells; throbbing sensations in the flesh; and feelings of being touched by invisible hands.

STRANGE NOISES AND VOICES

Astral noises and voices are usually only heard during presleep or while waking up. During Neg attacks, these sounds are best thought of as scare tactics. They can be unnerving, but they cause no direct harm. It is best to ignore them as much as possible. Focusing on them and reacting emotionally, becoming fearful, will weaken you and cause you to connect with and feed Negs and empower their activities. I think this is the main reason why Negs try so hard to scare people.

Audio phenomena will be more intense and frequent during psychic and Neg attacks. The types of astral noises vary enormously, as does their volume. Some noises can be startlingly loud. It is common to hear furniture being dragged about, spirit knocks and taps on walls and fixtures, growling, muttering voices, and strange voices talking among themselves. Sometimes, you may hear voices addressing you directly or discussing you by name with another presence, usually in critical and intimidating ways. Again, these are scare tactics, and the voices will do no harm, no matter what you heard. Ignore them as best you can.

Lighting incense, using essential oils, turning on overhead lights, playing music, and employing other countermeasures will reduce this type of phenomena considerably. (Placing a dark tee shirt over the eyes makes it easier to sleep with the lights lit.) Making commands, verbally or silently—such as, "I choose not to listen to this. I choose to relax and sleep"—will also help a lot. Repeat these commands as necessary.

The Core Affirmation will also help in these situations: "I am loved and I am worthy. I am safe and I am free. I am powerfully protected. I am master of my body and ruler of my mind." Repeat this affirmation continually, especially while falling asleep. Doing so will fill your mind with positive thoughts and petition your higher self for help. It will also help to block telepathic connections with Neg presences.

CIRCULAR THOUGHTS AND CORE IMAGES

Endlessly looping repetitive and worrying thoughts can be caused by Neg interference. Experiencing such thoughts is understandable if genuine problems are bothering you, but when the subject matter is trivial, silly, imaginary, old, or disturbing, it's likely to be Neg induced. If you awaken to these types of thoughts, you may be picking up telepathic Neg interference designed to weaken and disturb you. This can involve subconscious Neg programming that is being broadcast into your mind at this time. These thoughts can deprive you of sleep and further weaken your natural defenses. The subject matter of these thoughts can also be related to the creation of core images in your mind (which we'll discuss soon). Keep note of the subject matter of worrying thoughts, and save this information for core-image work later.

Listening to music, talking books, or natural sounds, like rain and surf is an excellent countermeasure for this type of disturbance. Record the core affirmation and play it on repeat. Drown out unpleasant sounds with something pleasant.

VISIONS AND NIGHTMARES

Disturbed sleep, bad dreams, and touches by unseen hands are common during Neg attacks. Spontaneous visions and lucid dreams are also common. Like other phenomenon detected with astral sight and hearing, these things are usually seen during presleep or waking. Sometimes you may see visions of accidents, often involving friends and loved ones, or monstrous faces. You may see your significant other in the arms of another person. You may see your beloved pet injured and dying. These are *false illusions* designed to scare and weaken you.

If you wake up from bad dreams and continue to see or obsess about these things, you are most likely witnessing the implantation of core images into your mind. Core images are created and used by Negs as a part of the typical attachments and controls they create within the mind and the energy body.

It is a mistake to think that these types of visions and dreams are real or prophetic. Doing so can lead to enormous worry and torment. Keep in mind that these things are Neg related—devices that can be used against you by Negs. Negs are intelligent and cunning. They will usually throw in some genuine prophetic scenes from the near future, something real, to trick people into accepting that which is false. It is wise to discount all dreams and visions you experience during suspected Neg interference. False dreams of positive events, such as gaining sudden wealth and winning lotteries, are also common. These dreams can also be destabilizing, if believed.

Do not accept disturbing images, ideas, and illusions. In your mind, firmly command, "I choose not to see this. I choose not to think about that. I choose to see beautiful landscapes. I choose to have happy dreams. I choose to sleep." This is a powerful countermeasure. Repeat as necessary.

GROUP INTERFERENCE AND STRIFE

Negs will go to great lengths to spread disharmony and strife. In groups and families, people will be used and set against each other. This can be a general attack on a group, or it can be used to disrupt the support network of the person being targeted. This is especially true if the target is managing to withstand other aspects of Neg interference. Friends, family, and work associates will begin consistently causing upsets and problems.

For the target of Neg attack, anything positive is worked against by Negs. For example, if the target is successfully dieting, he/she can expect numerous invitations to lunch and dinner. Negs can be extremely petty. If the target has problems with timekeeping, but is improving on these issues, he/she can expect lots of delays on the way to work and appointments. Watches will stop, alarm clocks will malfunction, batteries will go flat, tires will mysteriously deflate, and public transport will be untimely or break down. Murphy's Law will apply—anything that can go wrong will go wrong, at the worst possible time.

Sexual Issues

Sexual contact is a prime time for the transfer of Neg attachments. During sex, a strong energy bond temporarily forms. This bond can allow Neg influences to spread unnoticed from one person to the other. If such a transfer is suspected after an intimate encounter, it is wise to apply cleansing countermeasures as soon as possible. Neg attachments are weakest when they are new. Taking a mega salt bath and a long, energy-cleansing shower as soon as possible is wise, as these help to remove any new Neg attachments that may have been acquired.

SEDUCTION AND SEXUAL ASSAULT

Erotic dreams are normal, healthy experiences, and most people will get them occasionally. However, sex will often form a part of Neg attacks. Neg sexual interference is usually combined with sleep paralysis and direct genital chakra stimulation, making it difficult to break away from.

Neg-induced seduction appears to be accomplished by telepathic broadcast plus direct stimulation of the genital chakra. When stimulated in this way, people can awaken highly aroused, sometimes remembering erotic dreams, sometimes not. Unlike normal erotic dreams, strong genital stimulation will continue until orgasm is experienced. The genital-energy stimulation makes this type of interference unnaturally powerful.

During a Neg-induced seduction, several things are happening: erotic thoughts and imagery are telepathically broadcast into the mind, the genital energy center is stimulated, the energy body's natural defenses are weakening. Permission—surrender to the sexual urge— is sought. Sexual energy (vital life-force energy) is also drained during the act.

Submitting to Neg seduction and allowing its completion constitutes giving permission for further encounters of this type. Repeated sexual encounters can develop into a long-term relationship. I have known people to become addicted to unseen lovers. They simply cannot resist. If these encounters are allowed to continue, in time, Negs can begin approaching victims during waking hours, which can lead to Neg attachments and progressive possession.

Neg sexual interference can be particularly disturbing when it opposes one's natural sexual orientation. Traumatic, unnatural Neg-induced sexual experiences are a devious way Negs use to elicit permission, while also draining energy and forming powerful, natural core images. The trauma, worry, and guilt involved can also be psychologically devastating. These things create the perfect conditions for Neg interference and attachment to progress.

While uncommon, it is possible for a body part to become overshadowed or possessed. Such body parts can include a hand, an arm, genitals, an eye—anything. This phenomenon is often called *the sinister-hand syndrome*. The body part affected will at times act independently. People with this disorder will often bind the offending limb to their bodies to prevent its independent movement. When the genitals are affected in this way, physical touch sensations, movement, and corresponding arousal are experienced.

Internal organs like the bowels and bladder can also become similarly Neg controlled. An eye with this problem will eventually become useless. These are awful problems and difficult to deal with. These types of problems are generally diagnosed as tactile schizophrenia. In my experience, though, most people with these problems are quite sane. The only problem they have is a possessed body part.

I temporarily experienced something similar to the above condition, losing control of one body part at a time, during my own experience with progressive possession (a description of which is coming up later). In my case, this malady passed, but I experienced enough to know that body-part possession is not always a delusional mental disorder.

EROTIC FANTASIES
Natural hormonal enthusiasm aside, for many people, sexual fantasy is their greatest weakness. Neg-induced sexual fantasies are a powerful control device. If sexual fantasies and urges arise frequently and for no apparent reason, they are probably Neg related. For example, if a sexual fantasy arises in the middle of a soccer match, one should be suspicious of its source. If the urge to act sexually on such a spontaneous fantasy is obsessively strong, this is probably a Neg-related compulsion. If spontaneous fantasies are frequent and powerful, Negs are most likely involved. While such fantasies and urges may sound amusing, they can also ruin lives.

Neg attachments often form during childhood. When children begin masturbating, this is a prime time for the development of Neg associations and attachments. When young persons begin masturbating, they scan their memories for the most powerful erotic imagery possible. At this point, Negs can carry out psychological conditioning by telepathically transmitting and artificially empowering particular erotic scenarios. Negs will powerfully stimulate the genital chakra when Neg-chosen fantasies are used. Negs will numb the genital chakra when transmitted fantasies are not used. Through simple reward and punishment—positive and negative reinforcement—Neg-chosen sexual preferences and fantasies are implanted. This process can produce a range of sexual problems, including gender issues.

Mental-Instability Issues

Neg attacks are such weird, unnatural, and frightening things that they always cause some degree of mental instability, especially if heavy phenomena are occurring. If you do not have enough strength of character to cope with this kind of thing, Neg attacks can make you seriously doubt yourself. In the modern world, most people do not really believe in anything supernatural. Little empirical study has been done in this area. The availability of experience-based advice and practical support is minimal. Neg attacks are not common knowledge and are seldom discussed. This lack of information alienates victims and fills them with guilt and self-doubt. People experiencing the symptoms of Neg attacks often start to think they are going mad. Visits to medical practitioners will usually support this assumption.

When Neg interference causes you to believe you are becoming mentally unstable, it's time to slow down, take some time out, and have a good think about what is happening. Keep a journal of events and how they all started. It helps to examine the situation clearly and to come up with a sensible plan of action.

Seeking professional advice can help. The right supplements or drugs can help with sleep, eating, anxiety, and depression problems. A psychologist can help to clarify things and give commonsense advice. Alternative spiritual counseling is also available, if you widen your search criteria.

Bad Luck and Ill Health

One of the first questions I ask a person with Neg problems is, "How is your luck holding?" The answer tells me a lot about the situation. The presence of a Neg in or around a person grossly interferes with how that person interacts with life and other people. Bad luck is also an aspect of negative glamor.

Bad luck and ill health are common side effects of Neg interference—particularly overshadowing and possession—because the presence of Negs within people changes people's natural energy signature, which changes how they interact with other people and with life in general. One's natural set of attractions and repulsions (those unseen forces that guide us through life) are distorted by the presence of Negs. They can also be confounded in specific ways by intentional types of Neg glamor.

It is common for people under Neg interference to experience long strings of misfortunes. They lose their jobs, have cars stolen, have their houses broken into, make bad investments, break things, lose things, get mugged, have relationship problems, have accidents and illnesses. Life will not go smoothly when one has Neg-related problems. Some cultures describe such people as being cursed, jinxed, or afflicted with the evil eye.

It is wise not to overreact to unpleasant life events and thereby give Negs more ammunition that can be used against you. Look upon unfortunate events, such as losing a job or a relationship partner, as openings for change. These events might hurt at the time, but if you can do nothing about them, being optimistic and trying to work with them really helps.

Neg interference can affect everyone around you. For example, while you are driving it may appear that everyone on the road is trying to kill you or that they have suicidal tendencies. Being aware you are under Neg attack can help enormously.

At peak times like this, I have resorted to ridiculously slow speeds, driving across town at a walking pace. Yet even then pedestrians launch themselves suicidally at my wheels, and other drivers try to ram me at every turn. Walking can be even more dangerous, as it can seem like everyone is trying to run you over.

Understanding what can happen—and why—helps you weather this type of problem, as does thinking, planning, slowing down and being extra cautious. Extreme episodes of bad luck do not last very long, from a few hours or a day or two. While it's best to always think positive, it's also wise to take extra precautions at such times, or to just stay at home until the interdimensional weather clears.

People can be severely exposed to Negs without anything happening to them. Whether anything happens or not depends on individual susceptibility and other factors. Some people have strong natural defenses and can withstand just about anything without so much as a goose bump, while others need only momentary exposure to be badly affected. Lifestyle and health, beliefs, strength of mind, family history, and the company one keeps are all important factors. In addition, common sense, moderation, and tolerance help one to generally avoid Neg-related problems. A good sense of humor also helps enormously.

Innocence and Immunity to Negs

Innocence and being a good, spiritual person offers little protection against Negs. Youth, innocence, purity, and potential for good actually appear to be strong Neg attractors. Negs provide natural resistance in life. If people plan to be good and spiritual, they generally have to work at it. The concepts of "like attracts like" and "you attract what you focus on" are only partly true when it comes to Negs. Opposites also attract. Many other factors, including spiritual potential, are involved in one's propensity for Neg problems.

Think on this: if a person wishes to achieve significant spiritual development and to help the world become a better place, he/she many need to be severely tested in order for this wish to manifest. So in this sense, resistance and interference from Negatives are actually providing opportunities and lessons for real spiritual growth. We would never choose things to be this way, but this is what is. Every cloud carries a silver lining. Understanding and working with this principle is a serious help in weathering Neg problems.

Susceptibility

Psychic and emotional sensitivity, as introduced earlier, are the most important factors in determining how susceptible one is to Neg problems. Sensitive people are far more susceptible to psychic influences than nonsensitive people. Psychic insensitivity does not, though, offer total Neg immunity. It lessens one's chances of developing Neg problems, because Negs are less interested in nonsensitives, but it can also mask the symptoms. Sensitives will keenly feel the symptoms of psychic interference and Neg attacks, whereas insensitive persons will not.

The ability to feel Neg-related symptoms can be related to levels of hypnotic suggestibility. Some people are easily hypnotized, and others are not. Hypnotically suggestible persons respond quickly to hypnotist's methods. Nonsensitive people require a lot more work to improve suggestibility, but eventually everyone responds to hypnotism.

Circumstantial Exposure

A healthy lifestyle and care in the company one keeps are important factors in living a Neg-free existence. Most people have at least some standards of moral and ethical conduct that influence their choices of friends and associates, lifestyle and activities. It is wise to consider not only the moral integrity and personality of others, but also that of the company they keep and their families. This can be a difficult ideal to achieve; while everyone can pick their friends, we cannot pick our family and family friends.

If one associates with people who have ongoing Neg problems, the chances of picking up or becoming involved in Neg-related problems increase. While it's often difficult to tell if Negs are attached to people, risks are increased if one associates with persons of moral turpitude or with those who come from unwholesome environments. The more time spent in toxic areas and with toxic people, the greater the risks. There are, of course, exceptions to this ideal; some highly spiritual people—religious missionaries, for example—are born into or live in rough or toxic conditions.

Risky Practices

A common source of Neg trouble is occult dabbling. The occult attracts many inquisitive people chasing thrills and entertainment. You can buy all kinds of gadgets and instructional books to show how to contact spirits, cast spells, and the like. But these things carry risks. It is wise not to play with forces you don't understand and have no background to support.

Things like ghosts, witches, evil spirits, and demonic possessions are widely disbelieved in today. But the fantasy and sentiments and trappings relating to these things are engaged in by many. People often pretend to believe in this kind of thing because it is freaky and fun. Halloween deserves a special mention, because on that holiday, people pretend to believe in and play with the trappings of witchcraft and death because doing so is a freaky and fun tradition. For most people, things are best kept as playfully scary holiday fun. Having this intention of keeping things fun is very important. With the right state of mind, the trappings of Halloween stay as intended—as nothing but harmless fun. This distinction should be made very clear to children.

Probably half the Neg-related problems I have been presented with over the years grew from some type of occult dabbling. Many children play with Ouija boards, often making their own, and play games with spirits. Blanket permission is usually repeatedly given to any available spirits. Some children will even deliberately evoke demons, using real demonic names, rituals, and spells they find in books, the Internet, or TV. No matter what age their speakers are or how these spells and rituals are worded, they can involve the uttering of names and words of power and serious occult evocations and invocations. Ignorance is no excuse. By and large, no spiritual protection or precautions are taken whatsoever.

Just imagine the energies at work around several children playing witches or spirit communication by candlelight. They write demonic contracts and dare each other into signing their names in blood and then burning the papers—like they have seen done on TV. And later, while they are trying to sleep, all the associations, thoughts, imagery, and fears are at work, not to mention the occult actions that they have performed. This psychological state creates wide-open opportunities for any Negs that might be present.

Occult dabbling is a difficult subject to discuss with children. Many children will do the exact opposite of what adults and parents advise, just to see what happens. So this situation must be handled skillfully. Children will get away with occult dabbling 99 percent of the time—and then something bad happens. As the saying goes, "It's a lot of fun until someone loses an eye." In the case of Negs, a child's life can go down the sewer in this way. And as most people do not believe in the supernatural, you cannot just visit a doctor and have this kind of thing easily fixed. More than one person has said to me that they do not care what comes through, as long as something weird and fun happens.

Freaky is fascinating, but having a Halloween attitude about the occult and the spirit world can be dangerous. Most people are under the impression that if bad spirits come through, they can just tell the spirits to go away. And bad spirits are, of course, not actually real, so what's the problem? But occult dabbling with this attitude can cause lifelong Neg problems. What does one do if real bad spirits arrive and do not want to leave? Getting rid of bad spirits is no easy task. A golden rule is never to dabble with occult practices and spirit communication, and never to stay in a house where such things are being done. It is also best to avoid people who do such dabbling on a regular basis.

BLACK RITES

Probably the most intensely Neg-affected people I have encountered have been involved with black magic, or Satanism. This comes with its own unique set of problems. In some cases, victims have taken part in dark rituals and have taken vows that are binding. Being bound in this way can be likened to catching a serious spiritual virus or signing a mortgage.

Most people I have met with these types of serious Neg problems have made foolish, youthful mistakes and are genuinely contrite. They made some bad mistakes and are trying to sidestep the consequences. Many will hear horrible voices and suffer regular Neg abuse. They will often move town frequently, trying to leave Neg problems and phenomena behind, but the problems always catch up.

Permission is the key issue here. Powerful, ritually given vows have been given and then broken. These were often signed in blood and burned as offerings. Permission was *specifically* given to Negs to punish vow breakers, regardless of whether or not the persons understood the vows they made at the time or not. These vows can be likened to the classic selling your soul to the devil. There are serious consequences to breaking vows and contracts. To young people seeking thrills, making ritual vows might sound like fun, but it is actually like playing Russian roulette with live bullets.

While much can be done to help people in this situation, it is never easy. These things usually cannot be cured, because of the level of permission given, but they can be eased. For starters, serious physical and spiritual lifestyle changes must be made. Such people must maintain wholesome spiritual lives of moderation and self-discipline. Making such changes are not easy for some people. So, in many cases, people just put up with or try to sidestep their Neg problems.

Neg-related problems are more likely and usually more severe if people follow hedonistic and unspiritual lives. Regular drug and alcohol abuse, plus other unwholesome activities, progressively weaken natural defenses and generate a lot of negative energy, the same way poor diet and lifestyle progressively damage the health and eventually have serious medical consequences.

Neg-related problems can be a wake-up call for people to make lifestyle changes. They can also be part of spiritual testing and awakening. If ignored, Neg problems will progressively worsen. We are all creatures of habit, and lifestyle changes are difficult. But change is always doable with the right motivation.

Haunted Places and Ghosts

Places and things—including buildings, objects, people, and even areas of land—can become contaminated by Negs. There are many reasons. Currents of subtle energies, both positive and negative, flow through and over our planet. Areas where strong flows of negative energy exist, cross, or collect can create Neg hot spots. If you walk over a hot spot, you will feel sharp, jabbing pains in the soles of your feet, as if you were treading on tacks, and other Neg-related symptoms.

The spiritual echoes caused by violent and evil acts can also generate Neg hot spots. Sometimes these hot spots will endure for many decades after the events that generated them are forgotten. When human sensitives, particularly children, are present, spiritual echoes are amplified, and Negs are provided with the energy they need to become more active. This is why children are often associated with paranormal manifestations and haunted houses.

Some of the worst haunted places are old jails, mental hospitals, and asylums. These are all places where people have suffered and died. Sensitives will feel uneasy atmospheres in such places, especially at night. I would not deliberately choose to enter such a place, especially at night. Such places are best avoided.

Ancient burial grounds are often magically protected, and harm and curses are directed at anyone who desecrates them. Some curses are lethal and can last for thousands of years.

People often cling to their physical bodies after death and consequentially become temporarily earthbound. This is why ghosts tend to accumulate in cemeteries. Negs are attracted to cemeteries partly because of the energies expended there by grief and other strong emotions, partly due to the energies produced by many decomposing bodies, and partly because of the sheer concentration of ghosts. All of this generates an attractive atmosphere for Negs.

Negs that were attached to living people fall away at some point after the death of their hosts. These Negs will sometimes stay with the host's physical body for a time and can become trapped in cemeteries. In town and city cemeteries, running water adds to this equation. Water main pipes and power lines surrounding some cemeteries form barriers that trap earthbound spirits and Negs.

Day visitors to cemeteries are generally quite safe. Night visitors are more at risk because ghosts and Negs are more active after dark. There is some truth to the legends that vampires, ghosts, and other spirits cannot cross running water and are damaged by sunlight. All earthbound spirits, including ghosts, are driven into caves and buildings or below ground to avoid sunlight during daytime.

Negs and ghosts found in cemeteries will often actively try to overshadow and hitchhike rides with visitors, so they can leave the area. Spending time in haunted buildings and cemeteries at night is one of the easiest ways to pick up Neg hitchhikers. Alcohol and drug consumption will increase these risks. Picking up hitchhiking Negs from such places can also cause Neg-related problems to develop later.

Negative Energy Links

Neg-contaminated and cursed objects can cause problems for susceptible people. Such things can provide subtle energy links between their new owners and Negs associated with their previous owners. These links can attract Negs to places where such objects currently reside, giving Negs opportunities and footholds into new areas. Psychic attacks, Neg influences, and hauntings can result from having contaminated objects in one's possession.

The principles involved with such links are similar to the principles of psychometry (the psychic sensing of the energies of objects). Objects can also be magically charged to contain curses or bad intentions and be used as Neg-attack devices. For this reason, it is unwise to accept gifts from occult practitioners if there are any bad feelings or disputes between you and them. The gifts should be politely returned, unopened. This way the gift has not been formally received, so there is no permission involved to activate any magical devices that might be involved.

SECONDHAND ITEMS

Secondhand furniture and clothing, ornaments—anything—can contain residual impressions of previous owners. Sensitives will often feel the vibrations of previous owners when they touch secondhand items. In its most basic form, this type of sensitivity will cause an intuitive response.

It's always best to trust one's instincts when considering secondhand objects. They either feel okay or they don't.

Most secondhand items can be safely used after they've been cleaned and left standing on the bare ground for a day or two to become electrically grounded. Clothing can be washed and aired. If anything about an object causes bad feelings, or if Neg-related problems start after acquiring an object, further cleansing will be needed. Fumigations with incense and wiping with herbal tinctures and essential oils will solve most such problems. If these measures fail, the problem items should be discarded.

PERSONAL ARTIFACTS
Personal artifacts such as hair, nail clippings, blood, and body fluids contain very powerful energy links. These links can be thought of as spiritual DNA. Through them, Negs can locate a person anywhere. Occultists can also use these things to locate and magically interfere with people. For these reasons, care should always be taken to dispose of these things carefully. It's also wise to think twice before giving a lock of hair to anyone. I would suggest never doing this. Use a substitute if necessary. Get a lock of hair from a suitable doll or off the floor of a hair salon, and give this instead of your real hair.

Voodoo dolls and other such items used for magical practices need to contain a part of the person they represent, such as fingernail clippings, hair, body fluids, or blood. A photograph can also be used, but pictures are not as powerful as body artifacts. This type of practice is common to all traditions and forms of magic. While deliberate magical attacks are rare, they are always dangerous. If body artifacts or personal items, especially blood or body fluids, are acquired, magical attacks can be lethal. In some countries where magic and voodoo are widely practiced, entire family lines are wiped out in this way. On the surface, the destruction involves a string of unfortunate accidents and illnesses, but those who understand these things know what caused the family to be destroyed—black magic.

Any psychic attack will be stronger if the attacker has possession of personal artifacts or items, even if attackers have no significant knowledge of magical practices and no deliberate intent to harm anyone. For example, a jilted lover brooding or crying over a letter or photograph of a former lover can be enough to cause a strong psychic attack on that person. Any Negs attached to the jilted lover can also use this link to take action.

When two people marry or become regular lovers, a strong energy body connection forms between them, providing strong links whereby psychic influences and attacks can occur. Traditionally, it is said that it takes four years for such a link to dissolve for a man, and seven years for a woman. My observations show this timing to be fairly accurate. I do not know why this time is shorter for a man than a woman.

Books and information on magic are freely available. Some people will go to any lengths to get revenge. And some people will deliberately try to gather personal artifacts, like hair, blood, and nail samples, in order to try out their latest spells and rituals.

In this chapter we have explored a variety of issues relating to Neg exposure and contamination. Next, I'll introduce body-awareness energy work and explore ways of utilizing the energy body to repel Neg interference and to heal and repair Neg attachments.

CHAPTER FOUR

Utilizing the Energy Body

*Core Affirmation: "I am loved and I am worthy. I am
safe and I am free. I am powerfully protected. I am
master of my body and ruler of my mind."*

Negs seek to interfere with and attach themselves to people in a variety of ways. This chapter shows how your mind and sense of touch (body-awareness energy-work actions) can be used to stimulate your own energy body. Body-awareness energy work affects the substance of the human energy body like a magnetic wave. This effect can be used to stimulate the chakras and to raise energy. It can also be used to disrupt Neg interference and remove attachments.

Imagine that you have before you a plate of iron filings and a strong magnet. You draw a symbol in the filings to represent a Neg attachment device. When you pass the magnet back and forth over the filings, it disturbs and reorganizes the filings, effectively erasing the symbol. This is roughly what happens when you use body-awareness energy-work actions on areas of Neg interference and attachments.

Some of the most common symptoms of Neg energy-body interference are cramping, pricking and jabbing pains, and localized tingling, throbbing, and buzzing sensations. These can happen anywhere in the body, but are especially common in the feet. Just as in acupuncture, the insertion of a few small needles can dramatically change how the physical body functions, so can these Neg-induced sensations change how the energy body functions.

Body-Awareness Energy Work

Your center of awareness is normally focused between your eyes, but it does not have to stay there. It can be moved and focused on any part of your body. When your attention is focused in a specific part of your body, that part becomes energetically stimulated. When this focus of body awareness is given motion—meaning, when you focus on a specific part of your body and then move that focus back and forth through that body part—the underlying energy structures of that area become stimulated.

While the theory involved takes some explaining, body-awareness energy work is very simple to learn and to do. Everyone can do it successfully. Most people will start moving and feeling their own energy after just a few minutes practice with the following exercise.

Sit quietly and relax for a moment, with your eyes opened or closed. Rest your left hand on your desk or lap, with the palm up. With the fingertips of your right hand, stroke the palm of your left hand from fingertips to wrist, back and forth repeatedly. Take about a half to one second each way. While doing this, focus on and memorize the feel of the touch this action produces in your left hand. Continue stroking for about half a minute or so, until you can reproduce the feel and movement of this action in your left hand from memory of the *feel* of the touch alone.

Figure 5: Hand brushing hand

Stop physically stroking. Continue moving this *feeling* through the whole of your left hand, fingertips to wrist, repeatedly. You will begin to feel some peculiar sensations there—a fuzzy magnetic sensation, pressure, heaviness, tingling, buzzing, or tickling, cool or warm. Any sensation, no matter how vague, indicates that you are successfully stimulating your energy body in this area. Sensations will become stronger and more distinct with a little practice.

For the following exercises, rub the body part to be worked on until a residual sensation is caused, as we did with the hand. Focus on this sensation and move the *feel* back and forth, as we did with the hand.

- Continue moving the feel through your left hand for a few minutes.

- Repeat this exercise with your right hand.

- Repeat this exercise with your left foot.

- Repeat this exercise with your right foot.

- Try this on other parts of your body.

The key to making this exercise work is to focus on the residual sensation you caused, and then to move your sense of *touch* and *feel* through the hand or foot or body part you are working on. Spend some time practicing the above, until you are feeling *something* moving in response to your body-awareness actions. Then move on to the next exercise. You cannot overdo these exercises.

DUAL BODY-AWARENESS ACTIONS

To perform dual body-awareness actions means to work on body parts in pairs. For example, simultaneously brushing both feet, both legs, both hands, or both arms. Working on pair of body parts is easy to do and has many uses.

Clap your hands a few times, then make fists a few times, and then stop and relax. Hold out both your hands comfortably before you, arms slightly bent, palms down. Close your eyes and focus on feeling the residual sensations you just caused in your hands. Feel the air with the skin of your hands. Feel for the air temperature, and feel for the slightest movement of air. Relax and take your time over this. Continue for a few minutes.

Next, hold your hands comfortably out before you again, palms up. Focus on your hands. Move your body awareness through both hands simultaneously, fingertips to wrists, back and forth, repeatedly. Feel this action moving through the whole of your hands. Back and forth, about one or two seconds each way. Continue this action for a few minutes.

Next, remove your shoes and socks. Shuffle and rub your feet on the floor a little, and then focus on the residual sensations you have just caused. Next, rest your feet on your heels or a cushion, and feel with the skin of your feet and toes. Feel for the air temperature and for the slightest air movement around them. Continue feeling these sensations for a few minutes.

Next, as we did with your hands, move your body awareness from toes to heels, back and forth through both feet simultaneously, repeatedly. Feel this action moving through the whole of your feet. Back and forth, about one or two seconds each way. Continue this action for a minute or so.

Practice moving your body awareness through pairs of body parts by moving it up and down through both your arms and then both your legs.

ENERGY-WORK SENSATIONS

As said, when you focus your awareness on a part of your body, that body part becomes energetically charged. The physical nerves in that area charge up, and blood flow increases in preparation for physical movement. When you move your focus away, the nerves discharge. When you move your body awareness back and forth through a body part, the nerves charge and discharge repeatedly. This nerve activity is what causes the physical sensations produced by body-awareness actions.

When currents and waves of subtle energy move through your physical body, these also cause your physical nerves to become charged. So energy movement and activity in your physical body can cause physical sensations, even though you may not be performing body-awareness actions at that time.

A variety of sensations are possible, including warmth, coolness, heaviness, tightness, bone-deep tickling, tingling, prickling, and buzzing sensations. The intensity can range from soft, fuzzy magnetic feelings of movement to uncomfortably strong tingling vibrations. All these sensations are considered normal for energy work. These variations depend upon natural energy sensitivity, as well as effects caused by the condition of the physical nerves and by subtle energy blockages. Some people are very sensitive to energy movement, and others are less sensitive. But everyone will feel something if they persevere.

Typically, sensations are strongest during the first few months of practice, and then the sensations will reduce. This reduction is a good sign. Strong sensations are caused by the nerves of your physical body reacting to stronger-than-usual energy passing through them. Reduced sensations are caused by the physical nerves adjusting to stronger energy flows and handling them better.

Body-awareness energy work is safe to do, but it can cause a wide variety of activations in the energy body, including the major chakras and even spiritual awakening. Just working on hands and feet as we did above can cause major chakras to activate. An active chakra will produce throbbing, pulsing, and/or tingling sensations. Please consult my book *Energy Work* and my website, Astral Dynamics *(www.astraldynamics.com)*, if you have any concerns or wish to know more.

The Golden Rule of Energy Work: If you experience overly strong or uncomfortable sensations from energy work, stop what you are doing and take a break. When you feel completely normal again, continue with the energy work. This rule solves most energy-work issues. The stopping, resting, and then restarting a process allows the energy body to adjust itself and develop naturally.

BODY-AWARENESS HANDS

The focal points of body awareness are called your *body-awareness hands*. For example, when you are brushing both your feet, the parts that do the brushing are your body-awareness hands. These "hands" are not limited to the range and motion of your real arms and hands. They extend to any size, length, or angle and can move inside and outside the body.

SHAPED BODY-AWARENESS ACTIONS

Imagination and analogy are used to *shape* the effects of body-awareness actions to suit your intention and purpose. Most shaped body-awareness actions are also suitable for dual actions. Following are a variety of useful actions.

Brushing: Move your point of awareness back and forth along the surface of your skin, as if brushing that area with a wide paintbrush. Vary the size, depth, and intensity of this body-awareness brushing action to suit the task at hand.

Sponging: Imagine and feel that your body awareness is holding a large sponge and that it is sponging water (energy) through the area being worked upon. This sponging is primarily a whole-of-a-limb action. If sponging through a leg, for example, feel as if that whole leg were being sponged on the inside, as if you were moving a large invisible sponge through the whole of the leg to make the water (the energy) move up and down through its length.

Wrapping: Imagine and feel you are wrapping a wide bandage around your arm, starting from fingertips and winding the overlapping bandage up the arm and then down again. Vary the width of the bandage to suit the need. This wrapping action can be used on any body part—a finger, a hand, a leg, an arm, the head.

Moving Energy Balls: Imagine and feel a softball-sized white or electric-violet energy ball forming over your fingertips. (The color electric violet has a high vibrational rate, and using it raises the vibrational level of whatever it touches. More about this color later in the chapter.) Move this energy ball up and down through your arm. This movement is similar to the sponging action. (Some people find this analogy easier to grasp than the sponge.) Vary the speed and intensity of this action to suit your intention and purpose. Stronger and faster actions will have greater effect. Slower and heavier actions will have more penetration.

BODY-AWARENESS ANTI-NEG COUNTERMEASURES

You now have the fundamental body-awareness techniques required for disrupting Neg interference in your body and treating attachments. You can vary the actions in scope, intensity, depth, and speed to counter any type of energy-body interference. A good rule of thumb for a brushing or sponging action is about one or two seconds per sweep for the length of a limb. Experiment and vary the speed and intensity to find what works best in any situation.

Most Neg energy-body interference will be felt while you are resting and in presleep. Negs seem to prefer dark and quiet conditions and persons that are relaxed or sleeping. Body-awareness actions can be used to disrupt Neg interference that occurs at this time. For example, if you feel jabbing or pricking pains in your feet, as if someone were jabbing them with a thumbtack, brush the soles of your feet rapidly with your body awareness. If anything unusual or uncomfortable is felt happening to any other part of your body, brush, sponge, or bounce those areas with body-awareness actions. Continue the actions until the unwanted sensations cease. Apply shaped enhancements and other countermeasures as necessary. It's okay to experiment to find what works best. You will not break anything.

Please note that body-awareness actions themselves can cause widespread buzzing and tingling sensations. So do not be alarmed if you buzz and tingle a bit after doing them.

Imagination and Energy Work

Visualization and *imagination* are one and the same thing. There is no actual difference in the meaning of these words and the mind's-eye ability they describe. Many people teach or assume that visualization is different from imagination, because they do not understand this simple fact. However, although most people believe they have problems with *visualization* the way it is commonly taught, everyone can *imagine* and fantasize perfectly.

With imagination and fantasy, you usually do not actually see what you imagine in a visual way in your mind's eye, but the perception is just as clear as it would be with visual sight.

Anyone can easily imagine highly detailed scenes full of actions and sounds and colors and scents and textures. This is perfect visualization, and anyone can do it right now. (Seeing something visually in your mind's eye, like watching a little TV behind closed eyes, is an ability related to clairvoyance.)

Shaping body-awareness actions with imagination produces different effects. This can be used to create a variety of anti-Neg tools and countermeasures.

ELECTRIC-VIOLET COLOR

The color of cleansing actions is important, as different colors will have different effects. Electric violet is the most effective color, I have found, for countering negative energies of any kind. This color has a high vibrational rate, and using it raises the vibrational level of whatever it touches. Negative energies have low vibrations, so they can be changed or destroyed when they are flooded with higher vibrational colors.

Electric violet can be difficult to hold clearly with imagination. Doing so takes practice. You may find it easier to hold purple, magenta, pink or white, rather than electric violet. All of these colors have high vibrations, so they will work. Use what you can manage until you have more practice and can hold electric violet in your imagination. Always start with trying to hold electric violet. When this color fades or you lose touch with it, shift to an easier-to-hold color.

Tools

Imagination can be used to create energy tools with built-in intentions; swords cut, pincers pinch, spades digs, and hoses spray, for example. Create tools and combine them with colors and elements as need and logic require. For example, swords and blade tools are useful for cutting away energy-body-attachment cords connected to Negs. Pincers are good for digging into the energy body and ripping out attachment roots. An incinerator is used for disposing of lumps of negative energy. Swords need to be used enthusiastically for best effect. Create electric drills, grinders, chisels, needles, hammers—anything you need.

Body-awareness actions and tools can be used both inside and outside of the body. For example, if your feet experience pricking and jabbing while you are trying to sleep, start by using a body-awareness brushing action. If the interference continues, imagine and feel a large blade near your feet. Slice the area below your feet, as if the blade were almost touching the skin, rapidly and repeatedly. Then move the blade to slice the sides and backs of your feet, covering all areas. If more action is needed, use a blowtorch and electric-violet fire to burn the whole area.

An imagined blowtorch is a valuable tool for countering Neg problems and for general negative-energy-space cleansing. Create this blowtorch with your imagination, and feel yourself controlling and moving it with your body awareness hands. When you move the blowtorch, feel

Figure 6: A blowtorch

it moving as if you were physically moving it. However, this movement does not involve actually using your physical body. These feelings and movements are all body-awareness and imagination actions.

The blowtorch can be whatever size you need to suit the task at hand. It can be tiny to work on a finger or an eye, larger to work on a limb, even larger to work on the whole body, or massive to treat an entire room or house. Similarly, the flame can be wide and gushing, or small, hot, and focused.

The blowtorch is for cleansing and burning away negative energies of any kind. For example, you can burn your whole body, or parts of it, with electric-violet fire to reduce negative energy and burn away attachments. Just imagine and feel the blowtorch gushing fire and apply this fire to the problem area. Work through your body, burning away negative energy and attachments. This fire can be used both outside and inside the body, for treating skin, bone, organs, muscles, or any other body part.

The blowtorch can also be used to cleanse entire rooms or houses. To do this, imagine and feel a large blowtorch gushing fire. Move this blowtorch with your imagination, and imagine its electric-violet flame burning and cleansing everything. For treating an entire house and its grounds, imagine a blowtorch with a three-foot-wide nozzle. Thinking big can save time and use personal-energy resources more efficiently. For example, you can put a lot of energy and enthusiasm into a five-minute task requiring concentration, whereas doing the same for thirty minutes can be exhausting.

The Elements

The elements are a metaphysical concept relating to the process of creation. There are five main elements: fire, earth, air, water, and akasha (aether). The elements flow down from higher dimensions in varying combinations to form physical matter. The names of the four physical elements are based on the principles of magical analogy. For example, physical fire is not pure fire element. Fire has similarities that only approximate the fire element. Fire contains a lot of fire element, which combines with other elements to produce physical fire.

Elements can be added to a cleansing action to change its effects. Elements can also be enhanced with the addition of color. The fire element is a good all-rounder when countering negative energies, as its intention is to burn away. The water element can be used as an alternative, as this element has a cooling and diluting effect. The air element is best imagined as a light blue smoke. It is uplifting, cheering, and dispersing, which are good qualities for elevating atmospheres of depression and gloom. The earth element is very grounding and is good for calming, centering, and solidifying.

Commands of Intention

Commands and affirmations can be used to express intention and further empower energy tools and actions. Using commands engages the higher self to assist in the work being done. Use logic, and keep the command simple and descriptive. For example, when you use the blowtorch to cleanse a room, make the statements "I burn away negative energy" and "Electric-violet fire cleanses." Repeat as necessary. Saying these commands aloud is more effective than making silent commands.

The Power of Repetition

With ongoing Neg problems, it's good practice to spend a little time each day treating your body and home with electric-violet fire, even on the good days. Repeated use progressively strengthens all countermeasures. The more they are used, the stronger they become. This work also has progressive positive effects on your body and its natural shielding and on your environment.

More Energy Work

The body-awareness energy work given in this book is excerpt from the full system. See my book *Energy Work: The Secret of Healing and Spiritual Development* (2007) for more detailed information.

...◆...

We have explored the most important issues relating to the human energy body and how Neg attachments work. Next up we look at the human mind and how Negs utilize trauma memories. We also look at ways to remove core images and the Neg attachments they can carry.

CHAPTER FIVE

Core Images

Core Affirmation: "I am loved and I am worthy. I am safe and I am free. I am powerfully protected. I am master of my body and ruler of my mind."

This chapter explores some underlying Neg-attachment-related issues. I begin with a series of statements concerning consciousness, body and mind, and memory, and how these things can be compromised. These statements will hopefully paint a clearer picture of the non-3D side of the Neg-human equation.

Negs have telepathic and empathic abilities, because they can obviously influence people's minds, emotions, and urges. Some Negs can also hear your thoughts. Negs can also affect the physical body, causing a variety of physiological reactions.

All spirits, including Negs, are nonphysical conscious beings. Spirits can stimulate psychic receptivity in sensitive people by stimulating their energy-body chakras. The various forms of channeling and mediumship demonstrate how spirits communicate with or through people by activating those people's psychic abilities.

We know where the physical brain is, but locating the mind and its memories is not so easy. The most logical explanation for this difficulty is that the mind exists as a subtle energy field that permeates the entire physical body and its aura field. A mind-body interface must exist to allow human beings to function. This interface must have conscious and unconscious aspects to handle the complex workings of conscious and unconscious aspects of mind and body.

The human brain floats in silent darkness. It has no nerves or direct sensory input. Its perception of the physical universe comes solely through bioelectrical signals gathered and sent to it by its five senses—sight, hearing, touch, taste, and smell. This sensory-data stream gives a person a fundamental sense of self as a living being.

The physical aspects of the mind-body interface are handled by the brain and its nervous system. The brain can be likened to a transceiver between the mind and the body. Beneath these structures are the unconscious mind and the autonomous nervous system. These handle all the automatic functions, like regulating blood pressure, digestion, growth and cell repair, immune system, memory, and reflexes.

The mind, not the physical brain, contains the memories. This statement is supported by a surgical operation called a hemispherectomy, in which half of the brain is removed. If this operation is performed before the end of puberty, patients can recover from it with only a slight limp. The operation causes no memory loss, regardless of which hemisphere is removed. Again, the mind and its memories appear to exist in nonphysical form, in a field of subtle energy that permeates the physical body.

The subtle energy body itself contains a reflection of the entire physical body, including the autonomous nervous system, and the body's innate intelligence, responsible for the functioning of every cell and organ in the human body, and the homunculus (also called the Little Man), which is directly connected to the sense of touch. The subtle energy aspects of the physical body and brain are interfaced with the nonphysical mind. This means that every part and aspect of a human being extends into a nonphysical, subtle energy state. It is this nonphysical area that Neg interference and influence most likely occurs. This is common ground. A Neg-induced pain may appear to be physical, but its cause is nonphysical.

Psychic sensitivity increases during relaxation and sleep, as does hypnotic suggestibility. A deeply relaxed state is called a trance state. Heightened psychic sensitivity makes times of relaxation and sleep the prime times for Neg-to-human interference—for Negs to insert hypnotic suggestions and core images, to cause physical sensations, and to form connections within the human mind and body. Certain types of substance abuse can also create these conditions.

Core Images: Doorways for Negs

Physical and psychological traumas—bad life experiences—form powerful influential memories. These memories can be called core images, or core hurts. They can be conscious and recallable or unconscious and unrecallable. They can involve real-life, natural memories; *false,* implanted memories; or both. Core images are enduring psychic disturbances generated by traumatic experiences. They exist as discrete knots of mental and emotional energy, containing painful memories and unresolved conflicts and issues. They are powerful and influential, regardless of whether they are real or false.

The human mind has natural shields against intrusive psychic influences. Core images generate and accumulate negative energies, which cause holes in natural shielding. Negs make use of these holes to gain access to the human mind and energy body. Core images can also be said to cast shadows that allow Negs to penetrate and hide within human minds.

There are different types of core-image structures and various ways they can be created. All core images share similar properties. Most natural trauma memories eventually fade into the background as they are processed and healed, or at least forgotten. But if Negs latch onto them (like bacteria entering a wound), these memories can fester and transform into something different. Let's consider some types of core images.

NATURAL CORE IMAGES

Natural core images result from real-life traumas, bad experiences, and disturbing or unresolved conflicts. The more traumatic and painful the incidents, the more powerful the natural core images can be. After serious trauma, people will have nightmares, flashbacks, and various psychological disorders as they attempt to process the core images. Post-traumatic stress disorder (PTSD) is a well-known condition that demonstrates the psychological aftermath of serious trauma.

The effects of any bad experience are relative to one's perspective. For an adult, traumatic experiences may stem from such events as war, losing loved ones, car accidents, broken romances, and betrayal. For children, traumatic experiences may involve losing a much-loved pet or toy, being scared by an animal or a horror movie, being punished for something they did not do, or receiving bad potty training. Sensitivity plays a part in how severely an upsetting event will affect someone.

Everyone collects natural core images during childhood. These usually stem from trivial matters, and they quickly fade from conscious memory. As adults, we begin accumulating new types of core images. The human mind and society have ways of processing and releasing the emotions relating to trauma memories. We can cry, grieve, sleep, keep busy, and talk things out with friends and counselors. Eventually, we process or forget painful experiences and put them behind us. The memories still exist, but once processed, they lose energy and urgency and fade into the background.

When Negs first approach people, they will use whatever existing core images are available to gain access to people's minds. They will choose the strongest natural core images available. These core images represent the weakest areas of natural psychic shielding. A foothold here gives Negs tenuous connections, until they have time to infiltrate further and affix more securely. Some people do not have much for Negs to work with in this respect, whereas others have plenty. The more natural core images one has, the more susceptible one is to Negs.

FALSE CORE IMAGES

False core images are telepathically implanted within the subconscious mind. These false memories are inserted during sleep, through telepathic dream manipulation. Bad dreams, nightmares, and night terrors are often caused by this process.

Multiple false core images form networks of shadows within the mind, like a spreading infection. The larger a network of core images becomes, the more access and influence is gained by Negs.

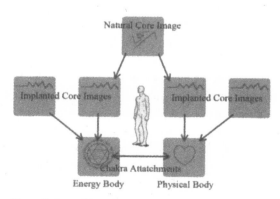

Figure 7: A core-image network

Discovering Core Images

I discovered core images by accident. I had long suspected that trauma memories were involved with Neg attachments. I had identified a number of my own real-life memories that I suspected might be involved in the Neg influences I experienced.

I became suspicious after a powerful series of disturbing dreams, each of which shared a similar theme. These dreams did not appear to relate to my real life. Each woke me, leaving me stressed and sweating, heart pounding. Once awake, I would obsess over the dreams for half the night. They were so disturbing that I had frequent flashbacks and anxiety attacks during the daytime. I am not an anxious, worrisome person, so this made me take notice. Examining the dreams during meditations also caused anxiety.

The setting for these dreams was the rail depot of a company I worked for in my youth. I did have a traumatic real-life experience there, but that experience had nothing to do with the imagery of the dreams I was having at this time.

The first dream scenario involved me making a foolish mistake, getting covered with acid, and dying horribly. The next dream scenario involved a similar foolish mistake, but this time many innocent people were covered in acid and died horribly. These were ridiculous mistakes that I would never have made in real life.

Suspicious, I used deep meditation to see what I could discover. I relived the dreams in this way and again experienced the anxiety. I chose the first dream and examined it more closely. I relived it again and again and studied how it was affecting me. Then I had flash of inspiration and used my body-awareness hands on it. I imagined and *felt* myself taking hold of the scene I was experiencing. I pushed it away from me, until it became an indistinct, pale rectangle about postcard size, which I could perceive in my mind's-eye. I then tried to turn it over, to see if anything was behind it. I felt a lot of resistance, and it would not turn over. This surprised me, because normally my body-awareness hands can do anything with ease.

I wrestled with the rectangle, but it was like trying to turn over a concrete slab with a toothpick. Gritting my mental teeth, I applied more and more pressure until I felt something move. Giving it everything I had, I felt a distinct shift inside me, and then I felt a ripping sensation as I forced it all the way over. In my mind's eye, I had a vision of a large, smoking tree stump with a jumble of gnarled roots half out of the ground. The exposed roots were torn and smoking, but some were still intact. I saw dark lines of force, like ropes, extending from this tree structure and curving back into myself.

Continuing the experiment, I imagined my body-awareness hands holding a sword and a blowtorch. In my mind's eye, I hacked at the roots with the sword and then burned them with the blowtorch. I continued this for twenty minutes or so. I then relaxed and cleared my mind before reliving the depot accident again in my mind's eye. This time, the dream scenario caused less anxiety. When I repeated the shrinking and turning process, the rectangle moved easily and had nothing beneath it.

After this, I called up the next dream image. I had similar difficulty turning it over and found a similar rootlike structure beneath it. I destroyed this tree structure in the same way as the first. After this, reliving these scenarios caused no anxiety.

Spurred on by this discovery, in the months to come, I dragged up every bad memory I could recall, including early childhood memories. I repeated the process on each memory. Some potential core images turned easily and had nothing attached. Others were difficult to turn and carried a variety of peculiar structures underneath. Some had trees and roots. Some had complex jumbles of plumbing pipes. Some had wires and electronic circuit boards. Some had abstract symbols and unidentifiable structures—probably my own subconscious mind visually interpreting the negative energy structures I was perceiving and dismantling.

Occasionally, I encountered a Neg while doing this work. For example, while turning over a core image, I could feel something move under my body-awareness hands. As I turned the image all the way over, an astral snake appeared between my body-awareness hands, thrashing violently. It was not happy, especially when I started hacking and burning it. Astral snakes are a common Neg type. They look like black snakes with thick, spiny fringes along their backs; they are one to two feet long and as thick as a man's wrist. When they are attacked, such as when I hacked and burned the one I found, they thrash and wriggle free and then disappear. (This work is less fear inducing when done in the daytime; doing it outside in the sunshine is best).

I have been hooked on core-image work ever since I discovered it. It is the most effective way I have found for dealing with Neg attachments and for processing trauma memories in general. I have been teaching this work at my live workshops since 2003, and it is quite common for people to discover astral snakes during core-image work sessions. Astral snakes will also sometimes be felt during energy work. If you feel one, use a blowtorch with electric-violet fire and a sword on them, and they will soon vacate.

Energy-Body Attachment Points

Core images generate 3D attachment points within the structure of the human energy body. Neg attachments generate negative energy, and so attachment points affect the cells and tissues and organs of the physical body at these points.

As discussed earlier, the most noticeable physical manifestations of energy-body attachments are skin blemishes. The end result of my first successful core-image removal session was that a granuloma in the back of my neck erupted and healed. I have also observed skin-blemish changes happen to people I have taught these methods to over the years. Such changes do not always happen, but occasionally they will. Often, while working on a core image, the physical aspect of it will react and produce sensations such as stinging, burning, vibrating, and throbbing.

Different types of Negs cause different patterns of energy-body attachment. The principles of how energy-body attachments can affect the physical body are similar to those of acupuncture, where needles are inserted into the physical body to affect the flow of subtle energy, which in turn affects how the physical body functions.

The most effective approach to core images is a combination of body-awareness energy work, core-image removal, the marking of skin blemishes, affirmations, and grounding. The help of a wise and loving psychologist can also be a huge asset when processing the traumas involved with natural core images.

Core-Image-Related Problems

There is more to core images than bad dreams and weird imagery. The energies that spring from core images can be the underlying causes of many real-life problems, including addictions, psychological disorders, and social problems.

The types of mental and dream imagery associated with core images vary considerably. All types involve powerful scenarios. These scenarios can include disturbing sexual fantasies, rape, murder, accidents, violence, arguments, fights, disasters, loved ones in distress, and other painful scenarios. Any imagery that is disturbing or has powerful effects is suspect and should be investigated.

Working on Natural Core Images

We now move into the subject of how to treat core images.

First, start a journal and record your progress. This record is important for future reference, as core-image work can become complex. Your journal will eventually contain lists of events and people (living and deceased) that, in the past, have caused you upset. This list can help identify people who may be affecting you in negative ways.

IDENTIFYING CORE IMAGES

To identify natural core images, spend some time recalling real-life traumatic events of the past and compile a list and approximate timeline. It is your choice whether you start from the present and work back, or whether you go back to your earliest memories and work forward to the present. List every traumatic or disturbing event you can remember into a rough timeline. Rate the degree to which each event affected you at the time, on a scale of one to ten. Also note how the memory of each event affects you now when you relive it.

Carry out core-image treatment on each event on your list. This is a distilling process. Most events will have no negative energy. The only way to discover which events are important is to test them through core-image treatment. Keep notes after each session.

A core image can be generated by anything that is disturbing to you. What can become a core image depends on how you were affected at the time an event took place.

A good real-life core-image example happened when I was about six years old. I had walked the couple of miles to school with some friends on a gorgeous spring day. On the way, we spotted a baby bird near the path. I picked it up and put it back into its nest. Happy with my good deed for the day, we continued on to school. After lunch, a girl in my class came up to me and abused me loudly. She had been told that on the way to school, I found a bird's nest, tipped out the babies, and stomped them to death. One of my friends had clearly lied to her about what really happened, though they all later denied doing so. My classmate told me what she thought of me in no uncertain terms. The whole class booed me. My denial and the truth were ignored. She felt she knew the truth with a capital T. I felt terribly wronged.

Almost half a century later, the memory of this event still wakes me up at night and pops into my mind occasionally. I can still feel the emotions I had way back then, as I am writing this. I was frustrated, embarrassed, and very hurt that someone had lied about me.

I have done core-image work on this natural core image many times. Occasionally, I will find low-level abstract imagery and energy attached to it. This is something I obviously need to let go of and forget. I have forgiven everyone and tried to let go of it many times, but it keeps regenerating. This core image is a work in progress. I suspect that something else is linked to it. I will discover its secrets one day.

Again, it is *the effect on you* that an event has that defines its importance as a core image.

FINDING CORE IMAGES IN DREAMS AND OBSESSIVE THOUGHTS

Once you start working on them, core images will begin to appear in your dreams, so it is advisable to practice dream recall and to keep a dream journal. Just having a descriptive title, the date, and a few basic details is enough to trigger the memories of dreams.

Dream-Recall Method: Keep a notebook and pen by your bed. Upon waking, keep your eyes closed, sit up with your feet on the floor, and relax, or do this in the washroom. If you have dream memories, jot down some key words about them immediately before the memories disappear. Dream memories are fickle and easily lost.

Hold your mind as if you were trying to remember something you have forgotten, like you would do if you misplaced your car keys and were trying to locate them. Use fantasy scenarios to help trigger associations with the dreams—for example, a variety of things you might have been doing in your dreams. Keep searching like this, and if all goes well, then fragments of dreams will begin to surface. When a fragment surfaces, focus on it and relive it, and pull back the rest of the memory. If this does not work, just record the dream fragments in your journal.

Dream fragments can lead to the recovery of more significant dream memories. The brain learns quickly, and if you practice this dream-recall method regularly, your dream memory will steadily improve.

Also watch for spontaneous dream fragments arising as you go about your day and make note of them. Associations with dream memories can be sparked by mundane events: something you hear on the radio or TV, that you see or read, or that people say.

Apply the core-image treatment method to all suspicious dream imagery. Recurring dream imagery should always be regarded as suspicious.

Obsessive Thoughts: Core images can also cause obsessive thoughts and urges. Record obsessive thoughts and imagery and test them with the core-image treatment method described next.

CORE-IMAGE TREATMENT METHOD

Core images are non-3D mind phenomena—meaning you cannot point to a core image in the physical universe. When you take hold of a core image with your body-awareness hands, you are locating and taking hold of a portion of your non-3D mind space.

It is the action of focusing your conscious mind, intentions, and body awareness on core images that affects them. This focus is the essence of the core-image treatment method. If you cannot turn over a core image, you will still affect it. Repeated sessions will weaken it until it turns over and reveals its contents or it dissolves.

The technique for treating core imagery is simple. Do it while relaxing with your eyes closed. It's slightly more effective when done in altered states, but this is not mandatory. With a little practice, anyone can do this method well.

1. Close your eyes, relax, and settle yourself well. Focus on feeling yourself breathing, feeling your stomach rising and falling, for a minute or so, and then begin.

2. Call up the mental imagery in question and relive it. Replay this memory with your imagination. Immerse yourself in it, and try to recreate all the emotions that came with the original event.

3. When you are ready, freeze and shrink the scene. Reach up with your body-awareness hands and grab the edges of the scene from each side of your head. Then imagine and feel yourself pushing this image out and compressing the

scene down to postcard size. Hold the feeling of this image in your body-awareness hands, as if you were holding a real postcard at arms length before you. Now you have a chunk of mind space that contains the essence of the memory. (Holding the visual details of the image when you shrink it is not important. An indistinct blurred image is the goal. Do not think about how you will shrink the image. It's easier to just do it. Reach out, grab it, push it out in front of you, as if you were holding a postcard out at arm's length before you.)

4. Turn the image over by pushing with one body-awareness hand and pulling with the other, as you would in real life. Turn this postcard shape over with your body-awareness hands. If the image turns over easily, and you sense nothing, then there is no significant energy attached to it. Turn and rotate it several times in all directions just to be sure. (It's a good idea to quickly treat every image with electric-violet fire, just in case. This only takes a few seconds.)

5. If the postcard shape is difficult to turn over, it is a core image. Considerable effort may then be required to turn it over. Concentrate and exert as much mental force as necessary. Do not allow your physical body to tense. These are all imaginary and body-awareness actions. If the image will not turn, hack at it with an imaginary sword and then burn it thoroughly with your blowtorch. Take note of this resistance, and return to this core image during your next session of core-image work.

If an object, place, or person appears beneath a turned core image, note this for future reference. This appearance may be a clue relating to the nature or source of the core image in question. Also record any background details, such as the setting, the weather, clothing, colors, and events. If the people that appear are not already on your suspects list, add them to it and reexamine your relationship with them.

Repeated sessions may be necessary to remove stubborn core images. The core-image treatment process appears to catch Negs unaware. This

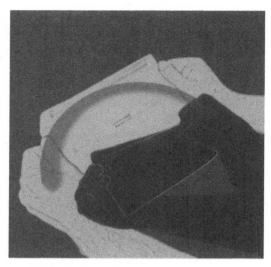

Figure 8: Turning over the core image

technique is new, and they have no idea what is happening or how to avoid it. Negs are generally poor at adapting to change.

LOOKING BENEATH CORE IMAGES

Sometimes, when a significant core image is turned, it will produce visual mental imagery. This means you may have a spontaneous vision as clear as if you had suddenly turned on a TV inside your mind's eye. You might, for example, see twisted rootlike structures, circuit boards, electrical wiring, insane plumbing, or other strange symbols and structures. You may see false events of a very disturbing nature, as if you were watching a dream playing in your mind's eye.

More rarely, you might see snakes, insects, scary faces, someone you love in danger or injured—anything. Some of the things you might see can be very unsettling, even traumatic, so be prepared. Always remember that you are in full control. This is all happening in your mind's eye. You can stop it any time you want.

Whatever appears, attack it with your sword and blowtorch, and dismantle and dissolve it. Repeat the Core Affirmation. Make commands to engage your higher self, such as, "This imagery dissolves. I choose to dissolve this imagery."

Regardless of what strange things you might see or feel, they signify Neg attachments, holes, and wounds in your mind's-eye space and energy body. These things need to be removed from your space. You can stop the process any time and return to finish it another time. Again, some people find it less fear inducing to carry out core-image treatment outdoors, in the daytime or in full sunlight.

Core-Image Maintenance

After you have treated a core image and whatever was under it, in the next session repeat the process using the same imagery. This is a test. First use the original imagery scenario and treat it with core-image work. Then remember and use the image of whatever you found beneath it. Shrink and turn it, then chop it up and burn it.

From time to time, return to core images you have successfully treated and retreat them. Doing so will help to stop them reforming.

Occasionally, you will discover a network of false core images hiding beneath a single core image. For example, you may treat a natural core image and discover a false core image beneath this. You turn that false one over and find yet another beneath it. Then you find another beneath that one, and so on. If this happens, dismantle and burn each as you find it. Make notes after the session and return to work on any newly discovered core images during future sessions. Continue this process until all the core images are empty and turn easily.

When significant core images are destroyed, the negative influences associated with them will vanish, or at least be significantly reduced. This loss can cause temporary feelings of emptiness and depression—a dark night of the soul. This sense of emptiness will heal as you grow to fill that emptiness. There will also be a corresponding reduction of Neg-related influences and activity in your life.

Negs will sometimes attempt to reconnect or to form new core images after they have been ousted. So countermeasures and further core-image work may be required. Recheck significant core images from time to time. Keep a record on any disturbing dreams and obsessive thought episodes, and treat these with core-image work as they arise.

When you start working on core images, your higher self will immediately start working with the process. It will begin giving you information through dreams and intuitive feelings. In this way, you will progressively become more effective at the core-image discovery and removal process.

Core-image work is a powerful life tool. Use it wisely and often. The more you use this core-image-treatment method, the more powerful it will become.

Now we have examined the relationship between core images and energy body attachments, let's investigate how these things affect the human skin and flesh. We will also explore some other ways of removing Neg attachments.

CHAPTER SIX

Energy-Body Attachments

Core Affirmation: "I am loved and I am worthy. I am safe and I am free. I am powerfully protected. I am master of my body and ruler of my mind."

Before we delve into energy-body attachments, the following information and reminders will help clarify this topic.

By and large, the most troublesome Negs are bound to the surface of the earth and can be described as earthbound. They appear to exist in or are attached to the thin layer of perpetually dissipating energy that is created by constant lightning strikes on our planet.

Every cell of the human physical body contains and produces electrical activity, so the body can be said to be full of bioelectrical energy. This electrical activity generates electromagnetic (EM) fields that can be scientifically measured and used for medical diagnosis. This biological EM activity is connected with our planet's stronger EM fields. This EM activity is an aspect of the human subtle energy body and its chakras.

Negs also have an EM component to their makeup. The EM component that both humans and Negs have is, logically, one of the primary ways that Negs invade and interact with humans.

Human subtle energy fields and Neg subtle energy fields are comprised of both 3D and beyond-3D aspects. In order to describe these, only a 3D model can be used, as it is impossible for a human being to conceive of anything that is beyond 3D.

Human biological EM fields, along with subtle energy fields, extend out in all directions and into the planet below the feet. For this reason, earthbound Negs first invade the part of the human energy body that extends down from the feet into the planet. It can be said that Negs reach up through this belowground structure and through the feet to invade the surface skin of the human energy field, in order to penetrate it and form energy-body attachments.

The physical sensations in the feet that Neg invasions cause are often light and unnoticeable. If people do notice these sensations, they usually will not see the relationship between these and other more obvious Neg-related sensations. However, given how running-water countermeasures work, it is clear that the feet play an important part in Neg invasions. I have tested this factor exhaustively, and the role of the feet in Neg human interactions is consistent.

As we discuss Neg energy-body attachments, please keep in mind that when I speak of the human energy body, its surface skin and its chakras, having energy attachments, that the feet are always involved goes without saying.

···◆···

Energy-body attachments are how Negs are able to affect human beings. These attachments are complex devices. They comprise both mental (core images) and energy-body aspects. The energy-body aspect of an attachment can be likened to a small core of negative energy within the human energy body. These areas of attachment can be located in any part of the body, internal or external. They are often found directly or indirectly attached to a chakra.

Neg attachment points seem to affect the physical body in ways similar to the ways acupuncture needles do. These needles alter the flow of subtle energies within the human energy body by connecting, disconnecting, or redirecting subtle energy currents. These changes affect the physiology of the physical body. They also alter how the energy body, mind, and emotions function. Thus, energy-body attachments give Negs varying levels of access and control.

I speculate that some malignant tumors and other diseases may be caused by the physical body's response to Neg attachments, particularly where Negs attach to internal organs and tissue. More research is needed, but I feel there is a connection.

Skin Blemishes and Neg Attachments

There is a direct relationship between Neg energy attachments and certain types of skin blemishes and disorders. The skin is the largest organ of the human body, and the surface of the skin is connected directly to the surface of the aura energy field (the energy egg) that surrounds human beings. Every part and pore of the skin is related to a specific area of the outer aura energy sheath. Where negative energy devices attach to or pass through the outer energy sheath, the skin and flesh are affected. To use a normal, 3D description: when negative energy attaches to or passes through skin and flesh, the cells that maintain these areas become disturbed. This disturbance can produce a variety of immune-system responses, which cause lumps, granulomas, and skin blemishes to appear in the skin and flesh.

During the witch hunts of the Inquisition, suspected witches were first given thorough physical examinations. Witch examiners searched for physical evidence to prove suspects were witches. The examiners

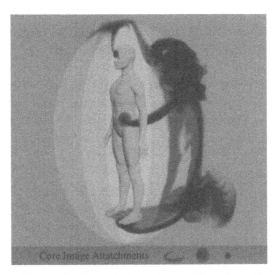

Figure 9: The aura sheath, an attachment line, the skin, and a core image

looked for gristly tumors (granulomas) that would not bleed or hurt when pierced with a needle. Such marks were said to be the devil's mark *(Stigmata Diabolis)*, the devil's seal *(Sigillum Diabolis)*, or witch's marks. This last type of mark was a later addition to the criteria for identifying witches. It included protruding tumors at which demons were said to suckle. The discovery of such tumors was considered definitive proof of being a witch, and justified torture and a sentence of death, regardless of any other evidence. If no physical evidence (no tumors or gristly lumps) was found, then suspects were not tortured or burned. They were often released and compensated, and accusers charged with false accusation.

The popular opinion of what happened during the witch hunts and why is quite a bit different from the actual records. The witch hunts obviously became widespread, horrific mercenary madness. But in my opinion, at the beginning of the witch hunts, some people knew what they were doing.

Ancient theories of certain types of skin growths being indicative of demonic possession and witchcraft seems consistent across various cultures, religions, and traditions. I speculate that knowledge of the relationship between Negs and granulomas (gristly lumps that, when pierced with needles, cause no pain and do not bleed) came from the experiences of demonologists of long ago. It is difficult not to notice this connection if one works with demonic-possession cases.

This type of lump appears as a swelling at the instant demonic possession happens, hardening and growing into a gristly lump over a few days. It will burst at the instant the victim is released from the possessing demon. The Vatican still performs demonic exorcism today, and I also speculate that today's Vatican may know a lot more about the connection between possession and granulomas than it admits. (I have been unsuccessful with obtaining comment on this matter from senior Vatican demonologists. I have sent messages and letters, including letters written in Italian. I know my messages were received, but so far there has been no response.)

A granuloma phenomenon was involved with my own possession and release, and with the demonic possession and release of many others I have observed and helped over the years. The connection between possession and granulomas is a consistent but little-understood phenomenon. I have only scratched the surface with my work on the mechanics of demonic possession. However, my experiments indicate that a wide variety of common lumps, skin blemishes, and other skin and flesh anomalies, including gristly granuloma lumps, moles, nevi, and even rough, hard, or inflamed patches of skin, can be related to energy-body attachments.

Energy-body attachments are not necessarily always demonic, as a wide range of spirit entities can be involved. A single energy-body attachment may involve a single skin blemish or a network of interconnected skin blemishes.

Granulomas are gristly nodules that the immune system forms in response to particles it senses are foreign. The particles are surrounded by cells that form into a gristly lump. While these foreign particles can have a natural physical cause, they may also be caused by Neg attachments. The energy of a Neg attachment is different from the energy of a natural part of the human energy body. So a penetration of the human energy body by a Neg attachment line of force could cause the physical body to sense that area as containing foreign particles. The immune-system response is to surround this area with protective tissue, resulting in the appearance of a granuloma. This response can be likened to how an oyster coats a grain of sand with layers of protective secretions, which eventually build up to form a pearl.

The best way to discover the significance of any skin blemishes is to test them by applying the skin-blemish treatment method (described later in the chapter) and observing reactions. This treatment is also a diagnosis. If a skin anomaly containing a Neg attachment is treated, changes and side effects will demonstrate its significance.

Many lumps, blemishes, and skin conditions have natural physical causes, so please do not jump to conclusions without testing. Most common skin blemishes caused by energy attachments are insignificant. These can be likened to the barnacles on a ship's hull in that they are of no real significance or threat. They will often, though, still respond to the blue-ink treatment method. (As a side note, warts do not respond well to this treatment.)

Major Chakra Attachments

A serious Neg attachment can produce blemishes anywhere on the skin and have other physical attachment points inside primary chakras. The skin blemishes mark the points the Neg originally penetrated the outer aura sheath; from there, threads of force extend inside the physical body to attach to chakras. The skin blemishes are often the only visible signs, but Neg attachments always extend inside and attach to other internal areas of the energy body.

Base Chakra—situated between the anus and genitals. Attachments here are often related to sexuality, fear, guilt, materialism, and rigidity issues.

Navel Chakra—belly area. Attachments here are often related to physical appetites, sex drive, and intimacy issues.

Solar Plexus Chakra—solar plexus area. Attachments here often relate to personal power, assertiveness, and self-esteem issues.

Heart Chakra—heart area. Attachments here often relate to love, emotional, and self-control issues.

Throat Chakra—base of throat. Attachments here often relate to communication, control, and decisiveness issues.

Brow Chakra—middle of forehead. Attachments here often relate to intuition, perception, beliefs, and understanding issues.

Crown Chakra—whole top of head above hairline. Attachments here often relate to creativity, mental processes, cognition, and mental stability.

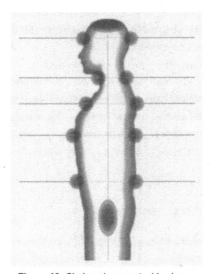

Figure 10: Chakra placement, side view

Skin blemishes relating to major chakra attachments can be located anywhere on the body. For example, a skin blemish relating to a heart-chakra attachment may be located on a hand or a shoulder. A blemish resulting from base-chakra attachment may exist on a leg. The site of a skin blemish relates to the area of the outer aura sheath where the sheath has been penetrated by a Neg attachment line of force. More than one skin blemish can relate to a single Neg attachment.

Acupuncture and reflexology charts give some idea of the potential significance of visible attachment points. Some chakra attachments, though, are invisible. In these cases, the psychology and behavior of persons, and the sensations they experience, can help to identify chakra involvement.

Treating and removing major chakra attachments requires addressing related skin blemishes, as discussed below, as well as core images and the psychological and behavioral issues involved. Combinations of other countermeasures will also be required, depending on Neg reactions to treatment methods.

Skin-Blemish Treatment Method

Following is the method for treating skin blemishes and the Neg energy-body attachments connected to them.

I discovered this treatment by accident in 1990. My then–three-year-old son, Jesse, had been born with a strawberry nevus birthmark, about three-quarters of an inch across, on his upper forehead. At that time, I was experimenting with ways to remove skin blemishes, but without success. This was just a crazy idea at the time. On a whim one day, I marked Jesse's birthmark with a large, thick cross, drawn with a blue ballpoint pen. He was very proud of his new decoration. A week later the ink had faded, gradually washing off in showers. Something extraordinary appeared in its place—a bleached-white cross on the birthmark. Closer examination showed the swelling and redness of the birthmark had faded under the ink, leaving a clear, white indented cross. This cross was a little crooked, following the outline of the original ink symbol exactly.

Since then, I have seen this treatment work on hundreds of people, including myself. Here is how to perform it. Note that the type of ink used is the most important factor; use *blue ballpoint* pen only. A large to medium ballpoint pen is best.

1. Clean and dry the skin area. Use skin cleanser or soap to remove skin oil. (Oil will make the skin difficult to mark and will block up the ballpoint pen.)

2. Draw a simple X in a circle over the blemish, so the arms of the X touch the circle. Alternatively, draw a circle with a spiral inside.

3. Leave the ink on the skin for as long as it takes to affect the blemish, and touch up or reapply the ink symbol as it fades or washes away.

With moles, granulomas, and other distinct blemishes, the symbol should be slightly larger than the blemish and centered over it. If treating indistinct areas, such as a raw area of skin or a group of tiny spots close together, the symbol does not have to be larger than the area being treated. Using several symbols can be more effective, as this uses more ink.

Open symbols (ones not enclosed by circles) do not work as well as those enclosed within circles. In some cases, when a symbol is not enclosed, only the skin directly under the ink will respond, as happened with my son. When enclosed within a circle, the entire area inside it becomes affected.

Figure 11: Treatment symbol—X and circle with mole

Figure 12: Treatment symbol—circle and spiral with mole

How Does It Work?

All Neg attachments involve delicate energy arrangements that are partly 3D and partly non-3D. When energy-attachment points (the physical skin blemishes) are painted with blue ballpoint ink, the Neg attachments experience interference. The blue ink alters the natural flow of energy on the surface of the skin, resulting in a variety of side effects. Most skin blemishes wither and fall away in time—sometimes in only a few days. The negative energy attachment is, in this way, disconnected.

There are two possible explanations for how the ink interferes with the attachment:

1. An ink symbol drawn on the skin causes subtle energies to flow along its lines. Enclosing the symbol within a circle creates a small vortex that accumulates subtle energy. This increased concentration of subtle energy interferes with energy-body attachments and or burns them away.

2. The reverse may apply. An ink symbol may block or shield subtle energies from skin blemishes, thereby starving Neg attachments.

Regardless of which of the above is correct in any given situation, the blue ink clearly interferes with the subtle energies of attachments and helps the human energy body to reject them. The physical body then rejects the biological aberrations (the skin blemishes or granulomas) and repairs itself according to its natural template.

In my early days of experimenting with this treatment, the possibility was raised that I may be causing its effect—unwittingly performing an unusual type of healing or hypnotic suggestion. One of my volunteers, a young woman, undertook to test this possibility. Without telling me, she began treating a large (almost an inch in diameter), black, flat mole on her stomach. She'd had this mole all her life. Four weeks later, I received an excited late-night phone call. She had just peeled the mole off while taking a shower. The spot bled a little after she'd peeled the mole off, but it did not hurt and healed quickly. The next day, she showed me the place where the mole had been. It was partly bleached white and partly scabbed where it had bled. The scabbed area turned white when it healed. The white area faded over the course of the year as she tanned, leaving no visible scar.

How Skin Blemishes Respond

Skin blemishes respond to the treatment method in a variety of ways. The types of blemishes that respond quickly may involve more delicate energies than others. The color and composition of the ink used may be responsible for some variations in effect.

Moles: A typical mole can begin responding within forty-eight hours. The change is barely noticeable at first, but the mole will slowly dry and change into a dry scab over a couple of weeks. The scab will eventually fall off or can be easily peeled off.

Once a mole begins to change and dry, its edges should be lightly scratched with fingernails while you are bathing. This scratching will show the mole's progress and indicate when it has changed into a scab or is ready for peeling away. When the edge begins to lift, the mole can usually be peeled off like a minor scab. It may bleed a little. Apply iodine as necessary. Ideally, wait a little longer so the mole can be peeled off with no bleeding.

After a mole has been removed, the area will usually heal to pure white. The skin will have no tan or pigmentation in that area. In most cases, removing the mole will leave no discernible scar tissue. However, it may take several months before the white blends in and tans properly. Be patient. Peeling a mole off too early can leave a slight scar.

None of the moles that I have removed by this method have ever grown back, even after many years. I recently examined the aftereffects of one of the first large moles I ever removed. Located on a woman's wrist, it was a large (over a quarter-inch across), dark, raised mole with the classic dark hair growing from its middle. The woman had had this mole for as long as she could remember. This mole was peeled off a bit early during the removal process and bled a little at the time. When nineteen years later I reexamined the area under strong light and magnifying glass, I could only see a barely discernable, lighter-tanned patch of skin where the mole had once been.

Not all skin blemishes will respond to the treatment in the same way. For example, two people may start treating similar-looking moles at the same time. One person will have a good response and remove a mole in a few days, while there will be no perceivable effect on the other person's mole. However, with extended treatment time, most, if not all, moles will eventually respond.

Granulomas: When granulomas begin to respond to treatment, they will often flare up, becoming painful and infected, sometimes erupting, before shrinking and dying. If they erupt or are lanced, there will often be an offensive, strong, cheeselike smell. Apply iodine and see a doctor if the infection does not quickly respond.

The granuloma may shrink and grow back several times during the removal process. Sometimes a new lump will appear next to one being treated as the original begins to die. At other times, a new lump will appear on the opposite side of the body. Applying iodine and then placing an ink symbol on top of the iodine can be effective. (Iodine seems to generally enhance the ink method. Let the iodine dry and wipe away any residue before applying the ink symbol.)

New attachments often begin as small watery blisters, which soon grow into small boils with hard, gristly centers. These boils change into hard, gristly granuloma lumps under the skin. If new lumps respond to treatment and start to fade, the old lumps they are related to often begin growing back. This regrowth can be frustrating, but each time a lump is removed, it grows back slightly smaller and weaker and is then more easily removed. If treatment is continued, it will eventually go away completely.

Adding Body-Awareness Actions and Core Images

Body-awareness actions can be combined with the use of ink symbols to enhance the skin-blemish treatment process. I removed a number of granulomas from my own body using a combination of ink symbols and body-awareness energy-work actions. These granulomas appeared to carry significant Neg attachments. While using powerful, rapid body-awareness actions on a small lump on my right hip, I felt a noticeable stinging sensation there. I then felt stinging lines connecting this lump with several other areas up and down my right side. Some areas had small moles or granulomas, and some had nothing. These skin blemishes were connected and highlighted a network of attachments. I marked them and continued working on them. Most of these skin blemishes fell away after several weeks of working on them.

While removing small granulomas from myself and treating them with body-awareness actions during meditation sessions, I often found spontaneous core imagery appearing in my mind's eye. Treating this core imagery as it appeared aided in the removal of the granulomas. Due to the peculiar way granulomas respond to ink-symbol treatments, they seem to indicate stronger types of Neg attachments than moles and other types of skin blemishes.

Ink or Symbol?

The symbol used does not seem that important. I have tried a variety of sacred and nonsacred symbols and found no discernable difference in their effects. I settled on using an X within a circle, with the arms of the X touching the outer circle. Spirals have the same effect.

It is the ink that is most important and not the design. Blue ballpoint-pen inks contain iron salts, which may be a contributing factor, as these iron salts change the skin's conductivity.

Other colors do have an effect. Black, violet, and other dark colors work reasonably well. Red and lighter colors, like green and yellow, are not very effective.

Stamp-pad ink, bottled ink, magic markers, and dye pens do not appear to work at all. Blue ballpoint-pen ink works the best, so I have stuck with this. There is, however, plenty of room for experimentation here.

Time Factor

The time factor involved with skin-blemish treatment is important. Approximately half of all treatable skin blemishes will respond in some way within two weeks. However, the time factor is an unpredictable variable. Some skin blemishes respond very quickly, often causing immediate side effects, and change noticeably within forty-eight hours. Other blemishes take several weeks or more before they begin responding.

As the time factor is so unpredictable, it's difficult to say exactly how long it will take a blemish to respond, but as a rule of thumb, most treatable blemishes begin changing noticeably within fourteen days. The shortest time for moles to die and be peeled off is forty-eight hours.

The most stubborn blemish I ever treated on my body took several months of regular attention before it responded. Once a mole or blemish begins to respond, it will usually die fairly quickly.

RESULT RATES

My early experiments with more than thirty men, women, and children (ages three to seventy) showed an approximately 50 percent success rate at totally removing blemishes in a reasonable length of time. Only three of my volunteers showed no response. Given the success in treating other similar types of skin blemishes, it's possible that if treatment had been continued, these volunteers would also have shown good results.

I have had some limited success with volunteers treating scar tissue with the skin-blemish treatment method. I do not have enough data to say more at this time. However, if this method works on scar tissue, then it would suggest that the skin-blemish treatment method is having a more general effect on the skin and that the removal of energy-body attachments may be coincidental to this effect. There is much room for experimentation here, too.

I have removed twenty or more skin blemishes from my own body, including moles, freckles, and lumps. Even if treatment is discontinued immediately when noticeable side effects are experienced, blemishes will often still die.

SIDE EFFECTS

Side effects caused by the skin-blemish treatment process are varied and unpredictable. About 25 percent of people will experience some noticeable side effects. The most common include mild nausea and diarrhea. These side effects can be compared to the symptoms of mild food poisoning. These relatively mild side effects will mostly be of short duration, often lasting only a few hours.

Stronger side effects can last longer and include all the above symptoms at more severe levels. In most cases, these symptoms will occur only at night, between sundown and sunrise.

Most of my early volunteers were not told about side effects. We did not know what to expect at that time, which rules out psychosomatic causes.

Strong side effects have occurred in less than 5 percent of people I have worked with over the years. In one case, a white male teenager was stricken with severe nausea, followed by vomiting and diarrhea, within thirty seconds of applying a blue-ink symbol to a dark mole on the side of his neck. After an hour, during which time he was in distress, I washed off the ink symbol. All symptoms disappeared within a few minutes. This reaction happened during the early evening. The young man did not wish to continue the experiment.

In another case, a dark-skinned Burmese adult male had two raised moles on the side of his forehead. He had carried these since birth. After the treatment was begun, there were no immediate side effects. But when I checked him two weeks later, I learned he had been stricken the first night with unexplainable nausea, vomiting and diarrhea, anxiety attacks, and nightmares. These symptoms continued every night for the week after his moles were first marked. At first, he was touching up the ink symbols with a pen, as instructed. He then suspected the ink symbols had something to do with his sickness and he removed the ink. The marked moles fell off in the process and never returned.

At a seven-day residential workshop I gave in 2005, I introduced the skin-blemish treatment method on the second day. A white adult male challenged this. He marked three prominent moles on his head, in front of the group. On the second-last day, he peeled off one mole in class and showed it to me. I then called the group around to watch as he peeled off the others. He said he had experienced mild nausea the first two nights after he first marked the moles. Because the nausea had been nothing serious, he had put it down to the change in water and food.

In general, stronger side effects seem more likely to occur with moles on the head and neck areas.

A common side effect of treating major Neg attachments is infection. These infections can be virulent and occur in the most unlikely places. If an infection, including boils, appears, apply iodine and seek medical help sooner than you normally would, as antibiotics may be required. (Iodine helps fight granuloma-type infections because it penetrates the skin.)

While working on Neg attachments years ago, at different times, my coccyx and then my right elbow became severely infected. There was no break in the skin at either area, and my doctor was mystified. The painfully infected coccyx burst and healed after I'd taken two courses of antibiotics and applied iodine regularly. It took a week in hospital on intravenous antibiotics to clear up the elbow infection. I was delirious for two days. At one stage, amputation was scheduled. Fortunately, this measure was not necessary, and the infection healed completely. Again, extra care is needed when working on energy-body attachments.

Side effects appear to be a positive sign, though, as they mean that the skin blemishes being treated are responding to treatment. If side effects are too uncomfortable, wash off the ink before sundown and reapply it the next morning, keeping the symbols on only in daylight hours.

It is wise to have any skin blemishes checked by a doctor, particularly if they noticeably change or get infected. They may need to be surgically removed, and the surgical procedure will often remove the energy-body attachment as well.

However, it is unwise to attempt to explain the ink-based skin-blemish treatment process to others, particularly doctors, as this will be considered crazy talk. If I had not experienced the skin-blemish treatment method myself, I would also consider it crazy.

Treating some types of skin blemishes also may cause some temporary changes in health. Existing medical conditions, like diabetes, should be monitored during treatment.

I have very little data on treating skin blemishes during pregnancy. I do not recommend this treatment during pregnancy, because if severe side effects occur, they could cause medical problems.

Precautions for Treating Children

Extra care should be used when treating children with ink symbols. While these methods are apparently harmless, children should always be monitored during treatment. I have seen strong side effects, including sudden very high fevers, occur several times in small children.

High fever can cause convulsions and even brain damage. If fever appears and analgesics fail to quickly reduce it, remove all ink symbols. Treat the fever as a normal illness, and immediately give the child a lukewarm shower or bath to reduce body temperature rapidly. If an ink symbol is causing a fever, the fever should quickly reduce once the symbol is removed. Seek medical attention immediately if you have any concerns for your child's health.

If a child experiences a fever or other side effects, I suggest applying the treatment only during daylight hours and washing off the ink before sundown. If fever still occurs, discontinue the treatment.

General Considerations for the Skin-Blemish Treatment Method

The effects of ink symbols on skin cancers, or on potential skin cancers, are unknown. I am not advising the use of ink symbols as a treatment for skin cancers. If any doubt exists whether a mole might be cancerous, see a doctor and have it checked. None of my volunteers experienced any dangerous changes in the moles they treated. If benign moles and skin blemishes are removed, though, they obviously cannot then become cancerous in the future.

Skin-blemish removal obviously has strong cosmetic applications. Disfiguring skin blemishes, such as moles and lumps, can be removed just to improve appearance. There is no reason not to do this.

It can be socially difficult to use ink symbols. Embarrassing questions are sure to be asked if they are visible. If you are applying the ink to a noticeable area, say on the hand or face, covering the symbols with an adhesive spot bandage or makeup, applying the ink symbols only at night, or wearing more expansive clothing to conceal the ink symbols will help you avoid awkward questions.

If people do see the ink symbols and ask about them, just say you were doodling. People may roll their eyes and think this strange, but this answer is often enough to satisfy people's curiosity. Alternatively, you can offer no explanation and watch people go crazy with curiosity. As noted earlier, it is not a good idea to attempt to explain this treatment to people.

Alternative Method for Removing Moles and Warts

Edgar Cayce gave a method for removing moles and warts in his readings (573.1 and 1179.4). This method is given in the book: *The Edgar Cayce Handbook for Health through Drugless Therapy* (See bibliography).

The method involves mixing a few drops of raw caster oil with a pinch of bicarbonate of soda (baking soda) into a gummy paste. This paste is applied to moles and warts and covered with a spot bandage or bound on each night.

Cayce also recommended massaging raw caster oil into the general area of flat moles daily until they fall away.

I speculate that this method involves similar principles to the blue ballpoint pen method. The Cayce method is a useful alternative for mole and wart removal.

···◆···

Now that we have gained some context for Neg-related problems, the following chapter contains the main arsenal of anti-Neg countermeasures. These countermeasures include direct methods, as well as ways to defuse situations before they become problems. No single countermeasure provides a total solution to Neg problems. Combinations are needed for the best outcomes.

CHAPTER SEVEN

Anti-Neg Countermeasures

*Core Affirmation: "I am loved and I am worthy. I am
safe and I am free. I am powerfully protected. I am
master of my body and ruler of my mind."*

This chapter contains (1) advice on defusing Neg problems, (2) countermeasures that interfere with, weaken, and ground Negs and negative energies, and (3) ways to make an environment repellent to Negs. Used in the right combinations, these provide a formidable arsenal of protective measures.

The first task when dealing with Neg problems is to try to identify where they're coming from. They may have started after a certain event, after a visit by someone to your home, after a confrontation with someone, or after a visit to a particular place or building. Sometimes there are no identifiable sources or reasons. However, more can be done to defuse the situation if the source or cause can be determined.

Think back to when your Neg problems first started. Did you have any bad dreams or sleep disturbances? Did any disagreements, conflicts, business difficulties, family problems, or emotionally charged events occur within a few weeks prior to that time? Include situations with loved ones and family here. It is not uncommon for family members to accidentally or deliberately psychically attack each other. The person most likely to precipitate attacks will be the type that tends to brood about things and hold a grudge for a long time.

Defusing Attacks

If the source of an attack can be identified, make a serious attempt to defuse the situation. This may entail swallowing your pride and apologizing for your part in the problem, even if you believe you are in the right. You can, for example, say, "I'm sorry we argued. I care about you." A quick phone call can save a lot of grief.

If a situation cannot be defused, break all contact with the suspected source of attacks. Every contact and communication will increase and prolong the problem. If breaking contact is not possible, reduce contact to a bare minimum, so that bad feelings will not be rekindled. "Out of sight, out of mind" applies here. Try your best not to antagonize this person further. Do something nice for him or her. A surprise gift can do wonders.

Try not to feel angry with attackers, if they can be identified. Complete forgiveness is a powerful spiritual act. Forgiveness does not mean submission. And it helps if you look at the bigger picture. These things happen for a reason. This often involves the gaining of personal experience, learning, enforced growth, spiritual tests, and being moved and redirected by life.

Often, without realizing it, people cause their own Neg problems. They might, for example, be angry and unforgiving towards other people and be inadvertently psychically attacking them. These attacks can have a rebound effect. With this in mind, when attempting to find the source of attack, also include people against whom you hold bad feelings. Again, forgiveness and defusing real-life problems can be effective ways of stopping Neg-related problems.

If you are angry with someone, there will be energy-cord connections between you and that person. This cord can open you to negative influences and attacks. Just thinking or talking about this person can strengthen the connection and rekindle negative-energy problems. It is wise not to talk about or think of someone who might be attacking you. However, if you do and you get an immediate increase in Neg activity, then you may have identified a source of Neg attack. If this increase in Neg activity repeats on other occasions when you talk about this person, then this person is most likely the source of Neg attack.

If you cannot identify a specific source, start working through the most likely suspects. Wherever possible, make amends and resolve conflicts, or at least agree to differ. Again, these actions may be difficult, but they are effective ways to neutralize attacks. These actions can also help identify the source of problems, as other people's reactions will tell you a lot about how they are feeling towards you. Forgiving and making amends is also high spiritual work. Life is too short to do otherwise.

Attitude

Attitude makes a big difference. Fear broadcasts energies that attract and feed Negs and gives them something to work with. A courageous attitude broadcasts energies that repel and weaken Negs. This dynamic can be compared to how walking the streets of a modern city with a fearful attitude will tend to attract muggers, but walking with a fearless attitude will repel them.

It's difficult not to feel any fear while facing supernatural problems, but you don't have to let fear get the better of you. Being brave does not mean not feeling fear. It means controlling fear while continuing to function in a reasonably effective manner.

It is best to have a matter-of-fact attitude when dealing with Neg problems. And anger, while not a perfect solution, is preferable to fear. Anger should be considered a short-term solution only, to help you through a difficult situation until you have time to think. If you continue to use anger to cope, this emotion will eventually be used against you.

Challenging Negs

It's unwise to openly challenge or abuse Negs, verbally or mentally. Doing so could antagonize them and make matters worse. The idea behind most of the countermeasures in this book is to make life difficult for Negs so they will just leave. Make your home atmosphere as uncomfortable for Negs as possible, but do not openly antagonize or insult them.

It is also very unwise to let Negs know that you are aware of them and what they are. Negs generally try to hide their true existence. If Negs drop the pretense, the gloves can come off, and problems and phenomena can escalate. Please take this caution seriously.

Not Being There

One of the wisest actions anyone can take during Neg attacks or supernatural manifestations is to not be there. Move away from areas of disturbance as soon as possible. Negs travel slowly and have difficulties moving from point A to point B due to running water and electrical-grounding obstacles. Negs seem to move at a slow walking pace. Moving away from areas of disturbance can avoid many potential problems.

Many people suffering major Neg disturbances and attacks stay put where the phenomena are happening. Do not do this. Take action. Sleep in another room or on the couch in front of the TV, leaving a light on and the TV on low. Changing rooms, plus adding extra light and sound, will help reduce disturbances. Place a dark tee shirt over your eyes if you cannot sleep in the light.

If the problem follows you into the new room, take a long shower or find somewhere to walk over running water, such as by walking over a water main or garden hose gushing water. Also perform the imagination, running-water, and electric-violet-light cleansing exercise (described later in this chapter). If these measures do not alleviate the problem, go for a drive or a walk. You will pass over many water mains, and the driving or walking will help keep your mind occupied and grounded. Turning the music up while you drive will also help.

If none of these measures help, arrange to sleep at a friend's home or stay at a motel. I know people who have slept in motor vehicles or in backyard tents for days, thereby escaping serious Neg problems. A tent circled by coils of a garden hose with trickling water is a strong Neg defense. Even better, spread many coils of hose under the tent and sleep on top of them. Add some essential oil or incense, a bright light, and some spiritual music, and you have created a formidable defensive position.

Avoid hot spots—places where Neg manifestations frequently occur—like haunted buildings, basements, and cellars. Also, try to avoid people who are experiencing Neg problems, if being around them affects you adversely. Alternatively, encourage such people to take action and reduce their Neg problems. Giving them a copy of this book would help.

Permission Issues

Most Negs require some level of permission before they can significantly interfere with a person. Ancient knowledge of this permission requirement is hinted at in myths that say vampires need permission to enter homes. Once Negs obtain permission, even as a result of trickery, it can be difficult to revoke. Permission can be likened to real-world legal contracts.

The level of permission needed and what Negs are capable of doing after getting it varies considerably. In the experience in which I became possessed (coming up later), the Neg in question did not strike until the exact moment I gave it full permission. I gave mental permission (I thought the words), which demonstrates the Neg was aware of my thoughts. Therefore, caution with thoughts, as well as spoken words, is well advised.

After many years of pondering the hows and whys of permission issues, I have come to the conclusion that permission involves the higher self. Your higher self is a part of you, and it holds all the keys to your natural shields and defenses. No Neg is powerful enough to directly go against your higher self. So Negs resort to trickery, deceit, and other ways to gain permission, as happened to me.

I voluntarily gave permission in the hope of saving a five-year-old child. Granting this permission told my higher self that I wanted to experience this Neg. The higher self sees these things as potential learning experiences. I would never have deliberately chosen to have that experience. I barely survived. However, looking back with the wisdom of hindsight, I would not change a thing. That experience was clearly part of an initiation process that would lead me into the greater spiritual reality, which was something I greatly desired. The opportunity was arranged by my higher self, so I would have a chance to realize the nature of the greater reality and to evolve to a higher level of spiritual understanding.

Many Neg-abused people I have worked with over the years have also greatly desired and prayed for spiritual development. These were cases of "be careful what you ask for, as you might just get it." Again, the higher self does not see things as we do. A serious Neg-attack experience may be the most efficient way to give you what you desire.

Some people are prone to compulsions that can force them to obsess about giving permission. They worry they might accidentally give permission or be tricked into doing so, or that they might give permission in their dreams. They also worry they might weaken and deliberately say words that give permission. I have worked with Neg-influenced people where this fear has been a big issue. Some could not resist the compulsion to deliberately give blanket permission repeatedly. Their influential Negs did this, I am sure, in order to scare and weaken them. However, in all cases, this did not change anything.

The higher self may seem distant and obtuse, but it is actually incredibly wise and close. Permission cannot be truly given by obsessive-compulsive urges, because your higher self knows your true intentions. A duty of care is involved with natural shielding. The higher self rejects such things. Also keep in mind that people who can't resist the compulsion to give blanket permission already are struggling with Neg attachments. Permission has already been gained for those initial attachments, and further permission will not change the situation.

Agreements and Permission: If you come under Neg attack, the Neg will have obtained some level of permission from you already, or it would not be able to seriously affect you. That permission may be part of an agreement or contract that you made long ago or at a higher level of consciousness to which you are not privy. Remember, Neg problems are huge growth and learning experiences. In the bigger picture, they happen for specific reasons. We may not consciously agree or fully understand these reasons, but it helps to keep this bigger picture in mind and to work with what is.

Revoking Permission: Actively revoking permission can help to reduce or break a Neg attack. Revoking permission is a form of banishment. It is done with commands and affirmations, made aloud and/or silently, depending on the situation. Revoking permission petitions your higher self to take action to restore your natural shielding and to block, remove, or reduce the Neg intrusion or attachment.

Spoken words are far more powerful than silent thoughts, because the spoken word activates the throat chakra and projects words directly onto the astral level, making them more powerful. Your higher self is far more receptive and proactive on the astral level.

When you feel an attack or a negative influence or sensation, focus on it and firmly say, "I cancel and revoke all agreements, contracts, and permission, known and unknown, with this energy!" Repeat this several times and as necessary. Repetition adds power to commands and affirmations. Revoking a serious Neg problem is worth serious effort and attention. Also repeat this revocation silently while you are falling asleep, so this intention will continue in your dreams.

The Compassion Approach

Compassion is a powerful thing when it is genuine and based on a true realization about the nature of Negs and the greater reality. Compassion cannot be faked or pretended. There must be respect, an absence of fear, and genuine compassion and understanding for this countermeasure to be effective. Using compassion as a countermeasure involves showing love and understanding towards troublesome spirits and asking them nicely to leave and/or to go into the light. The most common approach involves praying for help while imagining the offending spirit moving into a tunnel of white light. Words can also be spoken to this effect. Calling upon angels and good spirits to take troubled spirits into the light can also help.

Showing compassion and sending spirits into the light is always worth a try, because it is a good test for discerning the nature of spiritual problems. This method works only when spirits are willing to be helped or moved on, or with genuinely lost and confused ex-human, earthbound spirits. It is usually ineffective when applied to serious Neg situations. If there is a lot of fear—and there usually is—I would suggest other countermeasures be applied first. With few exceptions, angels and advanced spirit beings will not usually interfere in serious Neg situations. Good spirits may have the best of intentions, but expecting them to forcibly drag Negs away, kicking and screaming against their will, is not realistic.

Projecting love, understanding, and compassion to Negs is generally ineffective. Negs do not understand higher human emotions. By and large, they have the emotional capacity of predatory insects. Negs consider higher emotions a weakness and will take advantage of them. While people are being loving and compassionate, they are not doing anything constructive to interfere with Neg activities. Negs are incredibly devious and notorious liars. They are also very secretive, hiding what they are and what they are doing. They seem to know that if humans realize the truth, it will not be long before we develop effective ways of dealing with them. They do have weaknesses. This book is a step in the right direction.

I have had the opportunity to connect with many Negs over the years. By and large, they are like insane children. The character Golum in *The Lord of the Rings* trilogy is a good depiction of a typical Neg—childlike, playful, petty, egotistical, devious, untruthful, vengeful, selfish, and generally capable of the most awful things.

Again, showing compassion towards Negs must be supported by true realization and understanding of the greater spiritual reality. This understanding removes most of the fear involved when dealing with Negs. If Negs are shown true compassion of this measure, backed by a real understanding of what they are, they become deeply disturbed and will, at least temporarily, withdraw. Compassion for Negs is a profound matter of faith. Until this faith is gained through hard personal experience, though, it is wise to be cautious and to use what works.

Mental Defenses and White Light

Strength of mind alone will not in itself protect one from serious Neg abuse. It's an invaluable asset, but not a perfect defense. The minds of intelligent nonhuman Negs are incredibly strong. They are mental beings with strong psychic, telepathic, and hypnotic abilities. Also consider that Negs never rest or sleep, but much of what they do occurs while people sleep. And even the strongest-minded person must sleep.

The term *white light* today has grown to become a matter of popular belief. I often hear people talking about this, saying things like, "I just called down the white light, and the problem went away" or "I surrounded myself with white light and was instantly safe." However, this white light is not a divine force that can be summoned, shaped, or directed. White light is a frequency of energy. Electric-violet light is a more effective frequency for cleansing negative energies.

I tried using white light exhaustively in my early days. I have been involved in many cases in which people have tried using white light and sending spirits to the light, and in every case, this technique has not been effective. These people contacted me because popular methods failed. Such people are often blamed by their peers and teachers for doing something wrong or of being somehow defective when this white-light approach fails. Again, the white-light technique is a matter of popular belief that is not based on *what works*. Common sense and combinations of anti-Neg countermeasures need to be applied to get good results.

Priests, Psychics, and Healers

It is worthwhile to seek advice and healing from some psychics and healers. You may have to try a number of these before you find one you are compatible with and that can help.

Some priests can also help. Again, you may have to shop around and try a few. It is not the brand of religion or the books or the rituals that work, but the personal experience, strength, and faith of the priest or healer doing the work.

The old saying "God helps those who help themselves" is very apt here. It's wise to do what you can to overcome Neg-related problems for yourself. This includes seeking outside help. The higher spiritual reason for seeking help relates to the reason why you have Neg problems in the first place. For example, the underlying reason behind serious Neg problems may be to enforce change. These changes may involve spiritual growth and big life-direction and lifestyle changes. Many people I have helped have become better people and more spiritually aware in the process of overcoming Neg-related problems.

If asked, representatives of many religions will help people who are not members of their faiths. Many priests will perform blessings on homes regardless of your faith. You just have to ask. Have a priest or lightworker bless you and your home, and, if the Neg problem eases, even if it only for a short time, something worked. Then it would be worth having that blessing repeated by the same person. Some countermeasures have a cumulative effect. If something works, keep applying it, and its effect may increase. If one person's blessing is ineffective, do not give up. It is worth trying others.

There are organizations that offer help for spiritual problems. This includes a healing center connected with the healer John of God in Brazil, and an international organization called The Modern Mystery School. I have sent many people there for help, and the feedback I have received is positive. Again, you may have to try a few places if you want outside help. Never give up.

Bodyworkers and Healers

All forms of bodywork and healing—including Reiki, Quantum Touch, massage, acupuncture, reflexology, osteopathy, chiropractic work, the laying on of hands, shaman drumming, and anything else that works on the physical body—can help release core images and Neg attachments from the body and mind.

It is common during energy-healing or bodywork sessions for people to have emotional releases when they are touched in a certain place. This place can be anywhere on the body. Healers and bodyworkers are familiar with this tendency and are often guided to do certain things to facilitate emotional releases. Such releases can involve the dissolution of core images and energy-body attachments. (Trauma memories have 3D physical placements in the flesh, as well as non-3D placements in the energy body and the mind.)

Religious Symbols and Paraphernalia

Religious symbols, pictures, ornaments, jewelry, or charms can be used as anti-Neg protective wards. Through the spiritual law of analogy, these items have intentional energies inherent to what they represent. Some Negs find religious paraphernalia offensive and will avoid areas containing such things. If items are reverently cared for, and what they represent is believed in with sincerity, their effectiveness is increased. It is wise, though, to use such things in combination with other countermeasures.

Working With Your Higher Self

Your higher self holds all the keys to your life, including natural shielding and the power to evict Neg attachments. Working with your higher self is more commonly known as *manifestation*.

Manifestation: Manifestation is the essence of prayer and of all magical systems—supernatural ways of making things happen. The fundamental idea is to communicate intentions (wishes) to your higher self through affirmations, commands, and other expressions of intention. Your intention must be stated as if it were already so, because the higher self does not understand the concepts of past or future. For example, to manifest a new job, you must communicate the idea that you already have it. Once this idea is received by your higher self, the job will magically appear in your life.

Manifestation is a powerful spiritual act, but it is also tricky, and making it work takes practice. Most people discount affirmations because they sound like wishful thinking and too good to be true. People will often try doing affirmations for a while and then give up. This is normal. Often, a year or so later, what was being affirmed will appear.

Manifestation requires faith. Faith can only be gained through personal experience. This is a catch-22 situation. Ideas can be intellectually accepted, but faith is gained only by doing and experiencing. For this reason, it is best to start manifesting small things. Start by manifesting dinner invitations and visits and phone calls from friends. As these start to happen, your faith will grow. As you gain confidence, move on to bigger things. Working with manifestation is an excellent way to grow closer to your higher self.

Manifestation is not just about manifesting objects. You can also manifest changes and healing. You can, for example, use the manifestation process to heal yourself or to develop psychic abilities. You can also use it to get rid of Neg problems, which is a form of healing. Manifestation is the essence of the Core Affirmation at the start of each chapter. This affirmation is charged with spiritual intention. Its every word and idea states that there are no Negs in your life.

The alternative to manifestation through positive thinking and statements is what is called *realism*. To be realistic is wonderful in the sense of accepting what is. However, accepting bad situations and not doing anything about them is also to be negative and fatalistic, which does not help matters. Positive thinking focuses on the good things and expects more good things, which empowers them. The more positive thinking and positive expectation you can put into overcoming negative problems, the better. Positive thinking works with and encourages your higher self.

Manifestation usually works best when it is used indirectly. For example, to give up smoking, focus on having clean lungs, a healthy heart, and good circulation, and not on not smoking. So to use manifestation to remove Negs, focus on being peaceful and relaxed, sleeping well, having happy dreams, and being happy, content, and balanced.

Vigilance: When you are manifesting something, you need to be vigilant. Once your intention is received by your higher self, guidance will appear in many forms. Know that help and advice are trying to get through to you. Your higher self will attempt to guide you to what you need to make your intention a reality. The higher self works mainly through life and will use everything and everyone around you. It is connected with everything else and causes the universe to conspire around you. It can do so because you are an integral part of the universe and are connected to everything. Help and information will arrive in many shapes and forms: through dreams, through coincidence and synchronicity, through other people, through TV and movies, through books and magazines, and even through the Internet. Recognizing the information can be like going on a treasure hunt, searching for and following clues provided by life. Being vigilant is a matter of allowing yourself to be led to the solutions you seek. I call this process *bee following*.

Being vigilant means you have to open up to life, to work with life and to allow it to work its miracles, to get you into the flow of life. Be on the alert for coincidences and synchronicities. These will guide you to information, people, and things you need. A coincidence may not appear to be related to what you are manifesting, but because it is a coincidence, you need to pay attention and to follow it, looking for clues.

Action: The acts of opening up to coincidences and synchronicities, following your heart, and taking action (following signs and omens) opens you up to life's guidance. You cannot be guided unless you are moving and taking action. So don't just sit there waiting for the cavalry to arrive. Be vigilant and take whatever positive action you can think of to help yourself and to help this manifestation process.

For example, you may be sitting at home affirming and praying for help, and nothing seems to be happening. Then the postman calls to deliver a parcel. You chat, and he tells you he had a lovely meal at a little pub on the other side of town. It would then be wise for you to go to that little pub for a meal. This act opens you up to further guidance. You might meet someone there who can help. You might also get food poisoning and end up in hospital in a bed next to a very wise person who will help you. Keep taking actions like this, and you will sooner or later be led to help. This method may seem convoluted and unrealistic, but it works. It has saved my life on many occasions.

Gratitude: Over the years, I have learned to work with the manifestation process. It requires you to clearly state what you want and to hold this intention. Then you need to be vigilant for signs and guidance. Then you need to take action. Finally, once the manifestation is accomplished, you need to express gratitude. Gratitude is an important part of the manifestation process. Gratitude acknowledges the source of the help—your higher self. You don't have to call it this. Use any name you like—spirit guide, God, Monad, Source, Deity of choice, or just say thank you to the great unknown force that has just helped you. Acknowledgment and gratitude makes the act of manifestation complete.

Intention + Affirmations + Vigilance + Action + Gratitude = Results

Affirmations and the manifestation process provide serious help for overcoming Neg-related problems. Manifesting is working with the ultimate power in the universe. Have a good think about this statement. You may not understand how, but you do have access to the ultimate power, if you allow it. The only thing standing in the way is you and your beliefs.

You need to get yourself out of the way and to allow your intention to happen. My best advice here is to not try to work it all out. Accept that some things are beyond our understanding.

Again, the biggest barrier to higher-self help is yourself and your beliefs. The more you realize this truth, the more powerful your affirmations will become, and the more powerfully and openly will your higher self work on your behalf.

Affirmations, Commands, and Prayers

Praying is much like dictating a letter, aloud or mentally. Pray to Source or to whatever deity or aspect of God you believe in most. If you do not know any formal prayers or do not feel comfortable using them out of a book, just talk with God as if you are writing a letter. You could simply say, "Dear God, please guide me and protect me from all evil." Then follow this request with more specific pleas for protection and help with whatever is currently troubling you. The clarity and heartfelt sincerity with which prayers are said empowers them.

Prayers are also beneficial when they are used to occupy the mind and clear it of Neg mental influences and compulsive thoughts. Prayer holds the mind centered and balanced during stressful times. It focuses the mind on a strong source of positive energy. For this purpose, memorize some prayers, spiritual songs, or poems that you like. They can be said or sung aloud or silently thought.

Affirmations and commands are the most powerful tools we have to cause real change. Creating and working with change is the essence of the manifestation process. We are focusing on revoking and repelling the negatives in life and on attracting the positives. Affirmations and commands work best when they are simply and clearly phrased with unambiguous words in the present, active tense. Use them as if what you are affirming already exists. The Core Affirmation at the start of each chapter is a good example.

Commands are directives, like affirmations, but phrased differently. They direct your higher self to take immediate action. During an out-of-body experience, for example, your higher self will react immediately to a directive. If, for example, you command, "Take me to the moon," you will feel a powerful force take hold of you and start moving you. If you keep your focus on your destination, you will arrive there in a short time. If you get distracted and look at a tree, your higher self will drop you there. Restate your directive, and you will start moving again. This stopping and starting can happen many times. Keep your intention focused, and you will get to your destination sooner. This principle also applies directly to the act of manifestation.

Commands and affirmations are similar in that for best results they need repetition. For example, in an out-of-body experience, if you make a command and then keep repeating it like a mantra, you will get results much faster than if you say it only once. In the same way, affirmations and commands in the real world need repetition to be effective. The more they are repeated, the more effective they become.

Affirmations, like the Core Affirmation, are powerful statements of intention. They petition your higher self to bring about change. Affirmations can be used to manifest anything from a new automobile to healing from disease, injury, or Neg attachments.

Commands can be used in many ways as anti-Neg countermeasures. For example, if you have obsessive thoughts and urges, you can firmly think or say, "I choose not to think about that. I choose to sleep." Or "I choose to think about sailing." (Think of something nice you would like to think about.) These types of commands also work when you see disturbing images in your mind's eye while trying to sleep: "I choose not to see this. I choose to see beautiful trees." Then imagine trees to help manifest them in your mind's eye.

Other ways of using affirmations and commands to remove negative atmospheres and manifestations are to affirm "My home is blessed and peaceful" or command "This disturbance is ended!" or "This energy leaves my home!" Make up a sentence that is logical and phrased in the present, active tense, as if what you are saying is already true. And when your intention manifests, say a simple thank you to complete the act of manifestation.

THE CORE AFFIRMATION

The Core Affirmation given at the start of each chapter is a powerful tool for manifestation, and for getting help from your higher self to remove or ease psychic and Neg abuse. It can be spoken aloud or thought silently, but the most powerful way is to speak it aloud and to feel the words as they are spoken.

The Core Affirmation can also be written or printed out in bold letters and taped to walls and furniture. Placing printed versions around you will help keep your mind focused on it. The written version has a detrimental effect on Negs because of what the words represent. The Core Affirmation can also be printed or written on paper and kept in a pocket as a talisman.

Mantras and Versicles for Shielding the Mind

A balanced mind is an asset during any type of Neg or psychic abuse. Control over one's thoughts helps counter the polluting thoughts and compulsions common to Neg attacks. Repeating prayers, mantras, versicles, and positive statements helps to occupy the mind and will reduce Neg influences. If you have religious beliefs, finding something aligned with your faith will help.

The Core Affirmation is perfect for this purpose. It expresses exactly what is needed to manifest a Neg-free life: "I am loved and I am worthy. I am safe and I am free. I am powerfully protected. I am master of my body and ruler of my mind."

An excellent protective versicle was given to me by my mother many years ago: "God and goodness alone governs and guides me. No other presence. No other power." I use it myself and have had a lot of positive feedback on it over the years. This versicle is another good affirmation to print out and tape to walls or keep in a pocket.

When anything is thought or repeated regularly, it grows in power. Thinking about it will eventually become habitual. Repeated thoughts sink into your mind and take root. This applies to obsessive negative thoughts, as well as positive and protective thoughts and affirmations. So be discerning with what you allow into your mind; this includes the books you read and the movies you watch, as well as the thoughts and fantasies you allow. With frequent use, positive thoughts will become powerful enough to crowd out negative and polluting thoughts. The positive energy attached to repeated positive statements, mantras, prayers, and versicles will also attract higher positive energies.

Taking control of your mind is the best approach for removing negative thoughts and imagery from the mind. To help in the battle to keep your mind positive, use commands as well as affirmations. Every time a negative thought or image or urge arises, think to yourself, "I choose not to think about that" or "I choose not to have that thought" or "I choose not to feel this urge." Follow this thought with the Core Affirmation, a short prayer, or some positive statements. Keep repeating the positives until the pressure eases. If you have serious Neg problems, keep this up during every waking moment if necessary. The negative thought patterns will eventually lose their hold and be replaced.

Take action. Regaining your peace of mind may take a lot of work over days, weeks, or even months, if Neg problems are severe, but it is achievable. The more time and energy expended, the faster the results will appear. Never give up. Try to get yourself out of the way. Do the affirmations, be vigilant, take whatever actions you can, and know that help is trying to get through to you.

Sound and Music

Some types of music and sound generate positive energies and atmospheres and, consequentially, repel Negatives. Like incense, music is a quick way to positively charge the atmosphere. Incense and music make a good combination.

Certain songs and music pieces—for example, *Swan Lake* by Tchaikovsky and "A Kiss from a Rose" by Seal—stimulate or are in harmony with the human energy body and its chakras. You will recognize the effects of this type of music when you hear it, as you will feel tingling energy-movement sensations throughout your body.

Music can also be used to fill the mind with positive thoughts and sounds, which is why many people find they can concentrate better while listening to music. Listening to music does not require attention, but it occupies the surface mind and deadens internal dialogue. It is for these reasons that most teenagers can study well with music blaring, but find it difficult to focus in silence.

During Neg attacks, it is always difficult to concentrate. The internal onslaught of negative thoughts, feelings, and urges can be greatly eased by listening to beautiful music.

Play music in your home. Use headphones when you leave the house. Wear headphones at night, use pillow speakers, or have soft music playing nearby. The music will help you sleep and help generate a positive atmosphere around you. Do what works for you. Music can be combined with prayers, affirmations, and commands.

The type of music used is important. Avoid heavy metal and most modern music. Use uplifting spiritual and feel-good music. This music must be something beautiful and uplifting that you like, or can at least tolerate. It is important that you like the music you listen to, or it will add to your stress. The music you need to make Negs feel uncomfortable may not be the music to which you habitually listen. Some experimentation may be required. You can also use spiritually uplifting or funny audio books and movie soundtracks. Play positive, uplifting music in the background of your home day and night, if necessary. Have music playing even while you are out of the house, as this will encourage a positive atmosphere.

Children's Music: Some of the most powerful anti-Neg sounds for clearing a house are children's nursery rhymes and songs. I think this kind of music works through a simple annoyance factor. Humans have the ability to tune out repetitive sounds and music. Negs do not seem to have this ability. If you find it too annoying, this type of music is best played while you are out of the home or in rooms where you will not hear it.

Negs will hide in the darkest, quietest area of a house, often the basement or cellar or a little-used room or closet. A CD player with a nursery-rhyme CD on repeat can drive Negs nuts and force them to move elsewhere. An old radio playing classical music will also help.

Soundtracks of children's cartoon movies are excellent for building positive energy in a home. Some of these music tracks are superb.

Percussion: Using percussion is an ancient method of driving away ghosts and evil spirits. Gongs, drums, cymbals, bells, wind chimes, and firecrackers have long been used for this purpose by Eastern cultures. Loud noises affect any type of Neg manifestation. Even clapping hands or loudly banging pots and pans will help. These sounds break up astral lights and negative atmospheres, weakening and disrupting Neg manifestations. They are especially effective while Negs are gathering energy and building up an atmosphere, which is their weakest time.

Loud Music: Loud music will also help break up manifestations. The type of music—modern, classical, heavy metal, rap—does not matter. It just has to be loud and lively. Playing loud music, along with turning on all the lights, spraying with air fresheners, and starting incense, is a good countermeasure to use when a Neg atmosphere first appears.

Wind Chimes: Wind chimes made of bamboo, wood, or metal are good passive countermeasures. I recommend at least one wind chime for each cold spot of supernatural activity in the home. Place one in or near each room of your house so it can catch occasional drafts of air and regularly tinkle. You can also sometimes place wind chimes outside near windows, depending on the wind strength.

Attention Shifting

When episodes of Neg phenomena begin, shift your attention away from them and do not allow yourself to react emotionally. Focusing on Neg phenomena induces emotional fear reactions that will feed the problem. Fear will increase the power of Neg activities and phenomena.

When Neg activity starts—such as with a fearful atmosphere, flashing lights, taps on walls, or bad smells—it is natural to reach out with your perceptions to identify the source. Doing so has the effect of psychically tuning you into and connecting you with the Neg that is causing the phenomena.

Keeping your mind off phenomena will help to reduce its severity. When Neg activity begins, focus on something else, or nothing in particular, and in a matter-of-fact way go about setting up your countermeasures, such as turning on the overhead lights, getting some incense going, playing some music, taking a quick shower, and reciting some affirmations and prayers.

Morphing Spiders into Unicorns

If you are having Neg- or psychic-attack problems, you might see disturbing images during presleep or any other time you relax with your eyes closed. These images may involve monsterish faces, scary pictures, or disturbing visuals of any type. They can make it very difficult to fall asleep. Sometimes these images are Neg related, and sometimes they are created by your own fears—or a combination of both.

People often scare themselves during presleep. When you are deeply relaxed, your mind's eye can swirl with vague, indistinct clouds. If you have been disturbed by Neg-related problems, you are primed and on the alert for trouble. Trying to sleep during such times can make you feel vulnerable. You may be reminiscing about what has happened and trying to find solutions. The swirling clouds behind your closed eyes start to take the shape of something almost recognizable. In a heartbeat, you pay attention, and suddenly the image of a monster appears. Startled and not knowing what to do, you stare into the clouds, hoping that nothing else will happen.

Your subconscious mind is now focusing on watching for monsters. This focus affects your mind's eye, and more monsters appear. The more disturbed and frightened you become, the more energy goes into this process. Pretty soon, your mind's eye is full of frightening images.

Part of the problem here is that your attention is on the swirling clouds of your mind's eye and being on the alert for scary imagery. The clouds start to form an indistinct shape, you gasp and hope it's not a scary face, and your subconscious mind turns it into a scary face. The face appears because you are half expecting it to. Negs may or may not be involved, but you are always a part of the process.

The first step to dealing with this type of disturbing mental imagery is being aware of what can happen and not allowing yourself to emotionally react. Next, make firm commands: "I choose not to see these things. I choose to see happy and beautiful things." Also use the Core Affirmation repeatedly.

You can creatively change your own mind's eye imagery in the same way you can contribute to creating scary imagery. You can take control of this situation and turn it around.

Focus on the swirling mind's eye clouds and imagine a beautiful unicorn taking shape. Imagine you can already see its outline, and it is getting clearer. A unicorn will appear in your mind's eye. If you are seeing scary imagery, reach out with your body-awareness hands and clean your mind's eye as if you were wiping a blackboard clean. Imagine and *feel* yourself doing this action. Next, make the command "I choose to see unicorns." Strongly imagine another unicorn appearing, and it will. If a scary face jumps in, strongly imagine this changing into a unicorn. Repeat the command "I choose not to see that. I choose to see unicorns," and the face will change to a unicorn. If more disturbing images appear, immediately change them into unicorns.

This method is an excellent way of taking control and shifting your attention away from the source of Neg problems, which will weaken any telepathic connections that are contributing to this situation. Again, it's important not to react emotionally to disturbing mental imagery. Take control of this process. Push the memory of what you might have seen firmly out of your mind. Focus on creating unicorns. You might end up with a lot of unicorns, but this beats the alternative. As you keep creating unicorns, you will at some point fall asleep. (Creating unicorns is a bit like counting sheep.) Because your focus is positive and your mind's eye is full of unicorns, you will most likely have a peaceful night's sleep. If you get woken up later, repeat the process.

Getting healthy amounts of sleep is crucial when you have Neg problems. Taking control of your mind's eye space during presleep is a big step forward. Negs will always try to deprive you of sleep, because this weakens you. Stopping this from happening gives your mental and psychic shields time to restore themselves.

Breaking Sleep Paralysis

As discussed earlier, sleep paralysis is a disturbing problem that can sometimes happen when Neg problems are being experienced. There are ways of reducing the likelihood of sleep paralysis and of breaking out of this state when it does happen.

Paralysis is more likely to occur in certain resting and sleeping positions. For most people, lying on the back is the most likely position in which sleep paralysis can happen, though the most susceptible positions vary from person to person. It's worthwhile to check to see if your resting position is a factor and to avoid positions most likely to promote sleep paralysis.

When sleep paralysis strikes a deeply relaxed, but still awake person, or one trying to fall asleep, it starts with a sudden falling sensation. You get only a split second of warning, and this instant is the best time to fight it off.

Rolling out of bed quickly will stop the paralysis before it can take hold. Do not return to bed for at least fifteen minutes, or sleep paralysis is likely to happen again. Overtiredness makes sleep paralysis far more likely, so catching up on your sleep reduces the chances of it happening. An empty stomach also tends to increase the chances of sleep paralysis. A bedtime snack helps.

To break out of sleep paralysis once it has happened, focus on breathing deeply, or on moving either a single big toe or an index finger. Try all three methods. I find that a big toe is the easiest body part to reanimate during a sleep-paralysis episode. Once it moves, even slightly, sleep paralysis ends instantly. This will normally work. If for some reason it does not, fill your mind with the Core Affirmation, protective prayers, versicles, unicorns, and positive thoughts, until you can move again.

Sleep paralysis will not in itself cause any harm. Your body is just asleep, and for a short while you are unable to reanimate it. This condition will pass in a few minutes. Stay positive, work on breathing deeply, and moving a big toe or index finger, and it will end soon. Again, once you've reanimated your body, get up for at least fifteen minutes. A snack will promote sound sleep and lessen the chances of sleep paralysis happening again.

For more detailed information on sleep paralysis, please see my book *Astral Dynamics*.

Creating Shields

Mental shields are thought creations, or thought-form barriers. They can be effective, although they are not a quick fix. Building mental shields takes time and effort to do well. Hastily erected shields formed under duress are ineffective. It is too late to build shields once a serious Neg attack begins. Direct Neg attacks are mentally destabilizing and make it difficult to focus on anything. Shields need to be built beforehand. Then you can activate them when you need them.

To build a shield, relax and imagine an egglike structure around you. Hold your arms wide; the width of your arms is the best width for an egg-shaped shield. Hold up your arms; the height your arms reach is the height of the shield above you, and it extends this same distance below your feet.

Imagine your egg-shaped shield is made of steel, concrete, unbreakable glass, or a composite of these, several inches or more thick. Look around yourself with your eyes closed, and imagine this shield shimmering and glistening around you. Spend some time reinforcing it.

To program your shield with qualities while you are imagining it, make commands like "This shield is impenetrable. My shield protects me from bad energies. My shield protects me from psychic attack. I am powerfully protected by my shield. My shield keeps me safe." The Core Affirmation can also be repeated and used for programming your shield.

Add some more qualities, if you like. You can be specific and program a shield to protect you from a particular person or people. You can also bless your shield, if you have religious beliefs, saying, for example "I bless this shield in the name of _____ ."

Use the big blowtorch described in chapter 4 to cleanse and reinforce this shield with electric-violet fire. Imagine a big blowtorch appearing above you, gushing electric-violet fire. Move this fire all over your shield, including the area under your feet. Imagine the fire sinking into your shield and imbuing it with electric-violet color. Imagine your shield glistening and growing thick with this color. Imagine the blowtorch appearing inside your shield. Use it to clean and reinforce the inside of your shield. Also use the blowtorch to treat your body with electric-violet fire and light, burning away attachments and negative energies. Spend some time reinforcing the shield.

Repeat the same words used to program your shield's qualities. Spend a few minutes each day repeating these intentions and reinforcing your shield. As you do, look around yourself with your eyes closed, and imagine the shield sparkling and shimmering with electric-violet energy. Your shield will grow in strength and solidity the more you reinforce it, and imagining and seeing it in your mind's eye will become progressively easier.

Once your shield is created, repeat the reinforcement procedure whenever you are exposed to Neg-related situations, to further activate it. Spend a few minutes per day reinforcing your shield. More layers of shielding can be created and used to hold different properties, including the elemental properties of fire, earth, air, and water.

Again, a shield is only as good as the time, energy, and intention put into its creation and maintenance. No shield is totally impervious. Other countermeasures and common sense are still necessary.

Running-Water and Electromagnetic Barriers

Negs have an electromagnetic (EM) component to their makeup when they manifest close to the physical dimension. They are bound to a thin field of energy that covers the surface of the earth. They are affected by electrical grounding, magnets, and electromagnetic fields, among other things. They cannot cross running water unaided and must avoid electrically grounded areas and structures. They have problems with certain types and strengths of EM fields.

Negs can also produce EM fields and can affect and damage electrical and electronic devices. I was involved in powerful Neg attack in 2001 that left the distinct shape of an adult-sized nonhuman head burned into a computer monitor. The murky-green discoloration from this image was so dense that the desktop graphics could not be seen through this shape. We had to degauss the monitor multiple times before it could be used again. This type of green discoloration is identical to that caused by running a strong magnet over a monitor's screen. Some electrical and electronic devices and wiring configurations may even produce types of EM fields that attract Negs.

Anything that produces an EM field will affect Negs. The full extent of these effects is currently unknown. What I do know has been enough to formulate some EM countermeasures. Field tests have confirmed their effectiveness, based on the principle of what works, works. Further experimentation will, in time, produce more countermeasures.

The Science Behind Running Water and EM Charges: Running water generates voltage and EM fields, as demonstrated by physics experiments and papers and YouTube *(www.Youtube.com)* science videos included in the "Further References" section at the end of this book. Following are descriptions of two scientific experiments that show links between physics and my theories on the nature of Negs. The second experiment can easily be done at home.

The first experiment shows how running water can produce an electrostatic charge. Two thin streams of water are poured close to each other from two metal cans, held several feet above, into two grounded metal cans on the floor. Wires connect the cans to two electrodes, which are held about an inch apart. A charge builds up between the streams as they are poured. When this charge peaks, the water is seen to flatten, and then a visible spark is seen jumping across the gap between the electrodes. The spark occurs at regular intervals, seconds apart. The charge involved is many thousands of volts, which shows an enormous potential difference.

The second experiment, which you can do at home, demonstrates how water interacts with EM fields. On a dry day and using dry hair, take a plastic comb and brush your hair or something furry repeatedly, until the comb is charged with enough static to make hair stand up. Now go to a sink and turn on a tap so you have a stream of water *as thin as you can make it* without it breaking up. Move the charged comb (or charged rod) close to the stream of running water. The stream of water will bend towards the comb. Move the charged comb up and down the thin stream of water and note how the water bends. (This experiment will not work in damp or humid conditions.)

The previous experiment demonstrates that a rod (or comb) containing a static electrical charge causes running water to move towards it. To be more specific, the EM charge is attracted to the running water, and the same charge is repelled at the other end of the water, which could be in the water-supply reservoir many miles away. The tap's water bends towards the charged comb because the water is free to move while the charged comb is not. If the EM field were free to move, having no weight, it would be drawn towards and into the running water, and then pushed instantly out of the other end, many miles away in the water-supply reservoir. The charge would be instantly spread over the entire surface area of the reservoir and strongly electrically grounded. If this charge includes a Neg, then that Neg is toast. The EM component of the Neg is drawn into running water via the charge attraction and instantly transported to the water-supply reservoir. The deep electrical grounding involved in this process appears to drain the Neg's EM component, effectively demanifesting the Neg.

When Negs are demanifested in this way, they are not destroyed, but are absorbed into the planet. Some types of Negs may be capable of returning at a later time.

Humidity greatly reduces the ability of EM static charges to accumulate in objects and to interact in the atmosphere. (As said, the charged-comb-and-running-water experiment given above does not work in damp or humid conditions.) For this reason, increasing the humidity in an area can reduce Neg phenomena. Humidity can be raised by using a humidifier or by spraying a mist of water. A small pump up garden mist spray is a useful anti-Neg tool for moistening the air (and for applying Neg-repellant scents).

The Feet and Negs: We stand and walk, and our feet are connected with the ground for a considerable amount of time each day. In a natural sense, we are supposed to be electrically grounded to our planet. The human energy body has subtle roots that extend into the ground. There is a natural exchange of energies and electrons between the human body and the planet when we are electrically grounded. Going barefoot on damp grass or soil helps restore a healthy balance of the natural EM forces within our bodies, as well as helping restore natural shielding. Because of this exchange of energies with the planet, the feet are obviously the most Neg-exposed area of the human body.

As said, Negs exist in the thin layer of energy that covers the surface of our planet. Parts of our biological EM and subtle energy fields extend like roots from our feet into the planet and through this energy layer. Because of this connection, Negs always invade the human energy body through the feet first. Even though sensations may be felt elsewhere, the feet are always where the invasion first takes place. It can be said that Negs latch onto these roots before they reach up to attack the outer energy sheath and penetrate the human energy body and its chakra system.

Remember the experience I related in chapter 2, where pain shot through my foot and up my leg each time I moved a toe across the underground water-main pipe? This experience shows that Negs gain access to the human energy body—and from there, the mind and the physical body—through the feet. The feet are the natural interface between human beings, the planet, and Negs. The importance of the feet in Neg-human relationships should not be overlooked.

How Negs Are Affected: Crossing running water has two powerful effects on Negs. If a Neg is forced into contact with running water, it is instantly demanifested. If a Neg stops before contact occurs, it is effectively blocked by a major barrier, like a person standing on the edge of a chasm.

All Negs are affected by running water and EM grounding. How badly they are affected depends on a number of variables, including how strongly and in what way Negs are attached to their living hosts. Negs appear to use humans and animals as shields against running water and grounding effects. They get around in our society by hitchhiking on living beings.

Hitchhiking Negs: The surface bioelectrical activity of human skin can be compared to the dissipating-lightning-caused EM field that covers the entire surface of the earth (discussed in chapter 1). I think Negs can easily move up over the surface of human skin and, in this way, hitchhike and avoid being affected by running water. The widespread electrically insulated ways of modern life, with insulated floors, shoes, clothing, and vehicles, makes it easier for Negs to avoid exposure to electrical grounding.

When Negs first attach to persons, they usually only have a light and tenuous hold. This hold may, though, still cause Neg-attack symptoms. This tenuous state will last for several hours or so, until Negs have time to reinforce their attachments while people sleep. In this hitchhiking level of attachment, Negs are shielded enough to be carried across running water and underground water pipes and insulated from electrical grounding.

However, experience tells me that the degree of shielding hitchhiking affords Negs is still relatively light, and they are still affected by heavy exposure to running water and electrical grounding. They can be demanifested by activities such as swimming, showering, standing over many coils of garden hose, standing or walking over water-main pipes and streams, or spending time on shores of rivers, lakes, and oceans.

Driving across running water in a motor vehicle has much less effect on Negs than crossing the water on foot. Motor vehicles are heavily insulated.

Hitchhiking Negs will be felt to detach when people are several yards from shorelines of lakes or oceans, or outside shower cubicles, and then reattach when people return and move away from the water. Negs on the shoreline will follow persons moving in the water, so paddling some distance parallel to the shoreline before getting out of the water will not keep Negs from reattaching. However, crossing a stream on foot, by either wading or using a low bridge, can remove hitchhiking Negs.

A free-roaming or hitchhiking Neg that is attacking a person either detaches and stops at the edge of a running-water danger area, or gets dragged into it and is demanifested. Negs will usually detach in this scenario. Negs will attempt to reattach when the person returns from across the running water. This principle also applies when people enter showers or other areas involving running water and electrical grounding.

Draining Neg Attachments: The length of time involved since exposure and how deeply Negs penetrate the energy body and natural defenses of humans are factors with attachments. Long-term exposure to deep electrical grounding is needed to reduce and/or to drain entrenched Negs from people. This grounding is best accomplished by sleeping on electrically grounded bedding. (More on this later.)

Building on the above, following are a variety of countermeasures utilizing running-water and electrical-grounding principles.

Running-Water Countermeasures

The practice of counteracting Negs by crossing running water is not new. Many people have heard legends saying that witches, vampires, ghosts and demons cannot cross running water. The ancient Celts and Druids knew the power of running water. For example, in years of old, by law, a Celtic doctor's house had to be built next to or over a stream of clean, flowing water. This mandate may seem ridiculous today, but if you take into account that running water is detrimental to Negs, it becomes logical. Sick and injured people have low natural defenses to Negs, so recuperating in a house close to running water would be beneficial to health.

BASIC WATER-CROSSING METHOD

The basic water-crossing method is to find any running water available and cross over it, get into it, or stand over it as soon as possible when Neg attack begins. (Negs are at their weakest when they first attach.) In cities and towns, underground water-main pipes line every street and flow into all buildings. Taking a walk or going for a drive will often do the trick, though walking is more effective for this purpose. Be sure to cross the road a couple of times to make sure you cross a water-main pipe. Crossing rivers and streams (including underground streams) will also work. Crossing or paddling at the edges of lakes and oceans will also help.

The symptoms and sensations of Neg attack will usually disappear the instant running water is crossed. However, the volume of running water required and the length of exposure needed are directly proportional to how strongly Negs are attached. So if you cross running water and still feel a Neg attached, seek greater volumes of running water or spend more time directly exposed to running water.

Be aware that if you paddle in an ocean or lake, an attacking Neg will usually detach several yards away from the shore. It will wait there and attempt to reattach when you get out of the water.

GARDEN-HOSE METHODS

Lay down a garden hose and turn it on so it gushes water over the ground. Step over the hose. Better yet, step through the gushing water, wetting your bare feet during the process, so your physical body is also electrically grounded. The attack will be broken. If the attack recommences when you cross back over the hose, some tactics are needed.

Tactics can be used to trick Negs into becoming exposed to running water, so they will be demanifested. For example, lay out many coils of empty garden hose—as many coils as you have available. Stand on them, and *then* turn on the water or have it turned on. Stay there until the Neg is drained away; at least five minutes.

If crossing a garden hose is used to successfully break a Neg attack, the hose can then be thrown into a loop over the Neg to trap it. The Neg will be directly opposite you and will follow you up and down the length of the hose if you move. Once the Neg is trapped, the hose can be pulled tighter to create a smaller loop. Keep the hose touching the ground, or the Neg will get away. Water can then be gushed through this smaller area to forcibly demanifest the Neg.

Another version of the garden-hose Neg trap is to stand inside loops of empty hose and then turn on the water and step out of the loop. Shrink the loops and then gush water through the area inside the loops to demanifest the Neg. (Demanifesting a Neg is like returning a fish to the ocean).

Repeat the above and use other countermeasures as necessary. Remember, the volume of water and duration of exposure are important.

All the above can be done in an apartment bathroom, but you will still need a length of garden hose. You can get hand-shower-hose attachments that will fit over a standard tap fitting. A garden hose attached to this fitting can then be used to carry out anti-Neg treatments in a bathroom. Remember, hoses should be empty before persons are placed into looped-hose areas or over many coils. Then turn on the tap and run the hose water into a drain, or spray it over the person's feet.

NEG-DRAINING WATER METHOD

An extension of the garden-hose methods above greatly increases the volume of water Negs are exposed to. Place many coils of garden hose (all you have) on the ground so they overlap. Stand on top of the coils—in wet bare feet is most effective. Then turn on the water. Close your eyes and relax. Imagine electric-violet or brilliant white light pouring into your head from above and filling your body like thick fluid from the head down. Take your time with this visualization. When you get to your ankles, imagine discolored fluid draining from your feet into the ground. Continue this visualization for several minutes or more, until the Neg pressure ceases. Spend some time repeating the Core Affirmation before you finish.

If you cannot be in your bare feet due to low temperature, add electrical grounding by holding onto a conductive metal spike or metal garden tool driven into the ground next to you while you stand over the coils of hose. You can also use a towel soaked in saltwater; hold one end in your hand and have the other electrically grounded—touching a metal tap, metal water pipe, or touching the ground.

Running water and grounding countermeasures are just as effective when done in high-rise apartments. While Negs are capable of moving over the surfaces of buildings, including internal walls and ceilings, combined running-water and grounding methods have the same effect inside a building as out.

SHOWER AND BATH METHODS

The running-water method can be done in a bath or shower, if a garden hose is unavailable. The most important ingredient is exposing the feet to lots of grounded running water. The visualization aspect is also important, as it expresses the intention involved and engages the higher self.

The shower method is usually more convenient, and you can use warm water. Showering is also better for long-term regular treatment of more serious levels of Neg attachment. It drenches the entire body, so it can reach Negs that may be attached to parts of the skin and energy body above the feet.

Stand under the shower and close your eyes, feeling the water running over your body. Imagine the water is brilliant electric-violet light (or brilliant white light), saturating your body. Next, imagine this color is filling your head as a thick liquid. As strongly as you can, imagine this liquid spreading down into your body and filling you from the head down. Then when you get to your ankles, imagine discolored fluid being forced out of your feet and draining away. Repeat this action numerous times, as often as necessary. Repeat the Core Affirmation several times before you finish.

If you have only a bathtub, first stand in the bath and run the water over your feet as the tub fills. Perform the visualization exercise as you do this. (While the tub is filling, the water is grounded through the tap, making this the most effective time to do the visualization.) Once the tub is filled with enough water to cover your body completely, lie down and cover yourself completely. Leave a tap trickling so the water is grounded, or use a wet towel to connect the water to the tap. Soak for a while, then briefly duck your head underwater. Then pull the plug and stand in the tub as it drains. You will be electrically grounded through the water running into the sewer pipe.

A quick alternative to the full bathtub method is to just stand with your feet under the water from the running taps, perform the visualization, and then repeat the Core Affirmation. This is not as powerful as complete submersion, but it is good for a quick fix, for maintenance and for generally reducing Neg energies.

Another alternative is to use a sink. Hold your hands under running water, perform the visualization, and repeat the Core Affirmation. Imagine electric-violet color filling you and discolored fluid draining from your hands down the sink.

BUCKET METHOD

This method is convenient and requires minimal setup and effort. You will need a bucket, a few handfuls of salt, and a way of electrically grounding the water in the bucket. Soak your feet in the electrically grounded bucket of warm, heavily salted water. Imagine that your body is filling with thick, electric-violet-colored fluid and that discolored energy is draining out of your feet into the bucket. You can soak your feet in the bucket for extended periods of time.

Electrical grounding can be accomplished by using a metal bucket and standing it on the bare, damp ground. You can also use automobile jumper cables or towels soaked in saltwater to connect the water to a nearby metal tap or water pipe.

INDOOR WATER FEATURES

Any source of running water will generate EM fields that will deter Negs. If the water is electrically grounded, this effect is enhanced. Grounding can be achieved with a length of copper wire. Insert one end into the water and solder or clip the other to a metal water pipe, a metal tap, any grounded fitting, or a metal spike driven into the ground.

Note: Some metal-looking taps are actually plastic with metallic coating. These are not good for electrical grounding. If this is the case, use the metal pipe under the sink.

Water features are small indoor fountains, like Japanese water sculptures, where small electric pumps drive the water. Any type of indoor fountain makes an excellent Neg countermeasure. They can be placed next to a bed to provide personal protection during sleep. They can also be placed near the front door to deter free-roaming Negs from entering a home or hitchhiking Negs from entering with visitors.

Aquariums also make good countermeasures, especially if the water is electrically grounded.

Many old churches have a spring-fed well next to their main entrance or a font of holy water just inside their front doors. These water features were originally designed, I think, to stop Negs from entering these churches.

MEGA SALT BATH

When salt and water are mixed, a chemical reaction generates an EM field. Salt has been used in healing for centuries. Some energy healers (such as Pranic healers) use saltwater to cleanse and dissolve negative energy. Salt baths are also widely used in various traditions. Usually only small amounts of salt are used. However, larger quantities of salt create a more powerful countermeasure and attachment-draining method. This section discusses how to prepare and use mega salt baths.

What You Will Need

- For the average bathtub, about 3 kg (6.6 lbs) of coarse crystal or rock salt, preferably sea salt. Use the larger type of salt crystals (1/8 inch or larger) that will not dissolve too rapidly, so wet salt can be clumped onto the body. If sea salt is not available, use whatever you have.

- Cloth flannels, tea towels, and bath towels.

- A diving snorkel or piece of hose (if you want to submerge your head)

- For ambiance, some candles, incense, music, and scented bath salts.

- An hour or so of your time. (A box of chocolates helps.)

The Procedure

Step 1: Drink a large glass or two of water or Gatorade. Have water on hand to sip during the bath. Eat a banana before the bath. These things will reduce dehydration caused by the salt.

Step 2: Draw a bath. You might be in it for a while, so leave room in the tub for more hot water to keep it at a comfortable temperature. Do not overfill the bath, so you can clump salt to your body more easily.

Step 3: If you have attachments in your back, lay an old towel on bottom of tub and pour half of the salt crystals over the towel. The towel will hold the salt crystals against your back.

Step 4: Wet and pour salt on the cloths and flannels, and wrap these around any body parts that will not be submerged and around problem areas.

Step 5: Get into the bath. Pour the remaining salt crystals over yourself from foot to chest. Use flannels and clothes to keep the salt crystals pressed against your body as they slowly dissolve.

Step 6: Use wet cloths to clump salt around your neck and head. Duck or submerge your head several times, or use a snorkel to stay submerged for a few minutes. Getting the salty water on your head helps reduce head attachments.

Step 7: Soak and relax. Imagine the water and your body are filled with electric-violet light.

Step 8: Afterwards, shower or rinse thoroughly, as salty skin increases dehydration.

Cautions

- If you have medical problems, such as liver, kidney, low blood pressure, high blood pressure, or heart problems, check with your doctor first before taking a mega salt bath. If in doubt, use the bucket method.

- Do *not* drink excessive alcohol before or during a mega salt bath, as doing so will greatly increase dehydration. Do *not* take a mega salt bath if you are hung over.

- Strong saltwater is very dehydrating. If you feel dizzy, get out of the bathtub, drink more water, and shower to remove the salt from your skin. Rehydrate before taking another salt bath.

- Heavy salt baths will affect pH (alkalinity) for women and, thus, can increase the risk of yeast infections. A vinegar- or garlic-water douche after the bath can help avoid this problem.

- Dehydration is a particularly important concern with small children. Consult a medical doctor before giving any child a mega salt bath.

- If you have septic fields, beware that large amounts of salt can cause problems, especially with clay soil. Salt can bind with the clay, and the porosity of septic fields can be lost. In this event, the septic field may need replacing. Use a siphon or bucket to carry used saltwater onto a road or other location to avoid damaging your septic system. Dumping saltwater into a city sewer is safe.

- If you get salt in your eyes, rinse them with tap water.

- The effectiveness of mega salt baths is increased if the water is electrically grounded. Soaking some clothes in saltwater and draping them over metal taps or water pipes so that they are also hanging into the bathwater will ground it.

Mega salt baths are effective for countering psychic and Neg attacks. A wide range of energy symptoms and energy releases can be experienced when taking a mega salt bath. There is a direct relationship between the amount of time spent bathing, the quantity of salt used, and the level of relief that can be experienced.

Shower Alternative: If a bathtub is not available, a shower cubicle can be utilized. Place the salt in a bucket and add enough water to cover it. Sit on a bath chair or on a wet towel on the shower floor. Direct the shower water onto the shower cubicle wall, so the salt is not washed away too quickly. Use cloths to clump wet salt over your feet, legs, arms, body, and head. Follow the same instructions and cautions for a mega salt bath, including how to avoid dehydration. Shower afterwards to remove the salt from your skin.

Bowls of Saltwater

A simple countermeasure is to place bowls or bottles of saltwater under your bed. To mix the saltwater, add a handful of salt to each pint (500ml) of water.

Bowls can be placed at the head and foot of the bed or at each corner. Place the bowls in position before sleep. Change the saltwater daily.

If using bottles, any type of bottle, glass or plastic will work; empty soda bottles will suffice.

Saltwater bowls or bottles can be made more effective by duct-taping strong magnets to them.

Dry Salt

Dry salt also has an effect on Negs and Neg attachments. There is no EM field involved, but it is possible that salt, being a crystal substance, may absorb subtle negative energies. Experience shows it has positive effects. Dry salt is convenient to use as a Neg deterrent and attachment treatment in bed. Salt can be placed into packets or plastic zip bags and placed in pockets or under pillows, or taped onto clothing. Magnets can also be added to salt packets.

Fire

Fire can be used as a countermeasure and barrier against Negs. Like running water, fire generates energies that interfere with Negs. I have used fire at times when running water was not available. Fire as a countermeasure has not been as widely tested as running-water countermeasures, but it does work.

Place a few sheets of newspaper on the ground. Set them alight and then step over the flames. As with the water method, Negs can be trapped inside a ring of fire and demanifested. Of course, when using the fire method, be careful not to set yourself or the surrounding area on fire. Keep a bucket of water, a hose, or fire extinguisher handy in case of mishap.

Being Grounded and Sleeping Earthed

As previously mentioned, the surface of the earth carries an energy field that is contributed to by the several thousand lightning strikes that occur each minute around the world. The earth's surface is conductive.

Electricity travels virtually instantaneously, and this results in a constantly dissipating field of energy that covers the entire surface of the earth. It is this field of energy to which Negs appear to be attached or to exist within.

When your bare skin touches the earth's surface—say if you stand on wet sand in bare feet—you become electrically grounded to the planet. Your skin also carries its own electrical charge, which can be measured. One test for this is called the *galvanic skin response*. This test measures electrical resistance in the skin. This measurement is known to vary according to emotional states, which alter the skin's salt content. The level of salt in the skin changes its electrical resistance

I speculate that Negs need to be attached to a safe energy field to avoid becoming grounded into the planet and demanifested. It is, therefore, possible that Negs may attach to the electrical field that covers the surface of human skin. This connection protects them from running water and electrical grounding. This idea throws some new light onto the mysterious behavior and motivations of Negs. It also supports some of the countermeasures given here and how they work.

As mentioned earlier, I say Negs are demanifested when they are electrically grounded into the planet, but it is not clear whether they are absorbed by the planet and, therefore, destroyed, or whether they simply move through the planet's massive electrical field and can return at a later time. Both may apply, and which result happens may depend on the type and level of Neg involved.

Spending time being grounded and sleeping electrically earthed are known to be beneficial to the health. If you spend some time barefoot and in contact with the earth, you will find that your respiration, blood pressure, and heart rate all lower. Camping out and sleeping on the beach or by a lake or ocean offers similar health benefits, in addition to the natural Neg protection of the running water and/or saltwater.

(A recent book by a cardiologist shows how being grounded to the planet has a scientific basis and many health benefits. See *Earthing: The Most Important Health Discovery Ever*, by Stephen Sinatra, Clinton Ober, and Martin Zucker.)

In earlier times, our predecessors were much more grounded beings. They spent the majority of their time in contact with the earth. They wore electrically conductive leather shoes or walked barefoot on bare ground.

They also slept in more grounded ways, like curled up on animal skins or natural fibers, lying on straw in caves or huts or positioned around fires. Not so long ago, humans probably spent 99 percent of their time electrically grounded to our planet. This is a natural state of being.

In our modern world, we spend the majority of our time insulated from our planet. We wear shoes with synthetic electrically insulated soles and walk largely on electrically insulated synthetic surfaces. We drive motor vehicles that insulate us and sleep on beds that are insulated from the planet. The most significant electrical-grounding contact we have with the earth comes from washing and bathing. By and large, today we probably spend less than 1 percent of our time grounded. This is an unnatural state of being.

Added to the above, we also have to consider how plumbing, electrical wiring, and the synthetic, static-electricity-generating materials we wear and walk upon affect us and Negs. We are also exposed to a huge range of EM fields via such things as electrical and electronic devices, computers, cell phones, Wi-Fi, and radio and TV broadcasts. All of these things have an effect on human health and Neg-human interactions.

SLEEPING EARTHED

Sleeping in contact with our planet may not always be convenient in our modern world, but the same effect can be achieved by electrically grounding your body during sleep. You spend a third of your life asleep, so sleeping grounded is something good you can do, with no effort, to help yourself.

Electrically conductive sheets and cloths are widely available. A shiny fabric called lamé, for example, has metal fibers woven into it. Bedsheets and materials especially made for electrical grounding during sleep are also available. Conductive sheets can be connected with alligator clips and copper wires to water pipes, gas pipes, or to other electrically grounded structures and outlets. Aluminum duct tape can also be used for this purpose.

Do-It-Yourself Setup: A simple setup can be achieved using anti-static computer wrist straps connected to automobile jumper cables. The cables can be joined and clipped to metal water pipes or any conductive structure to provide electrical grounding during sleep. For convenience electrical grounding, you can get special power-outlet plugs that have only the ground wire connected. You can also attach a cable to a metal spike driven a couple of feet into the ground. Consult an electrician if you need advice or have any doubts as to its safety.

Power Extension Cords: These can be used as barriers to Negs. When plugged in, power extension cords produce EM fields; they also contain insulated grounding wires. Electric blankets and other electrical devices have similar properties. These things are generally repellant to Negs, who will actively avoid them. Close physical contact with electrical wiring, though, is not beneficial to the health. So this countermeasure should be used with caution. However, placing power cords on the floor around beds puts a fairly safe distance between you and the wiring.

You can lay power cords around a room's perimeter or around a bed, or place coils of power cord under a bed. A small appliance, like an electric clock, can be plugged into a power cord so that power is flowing. When plugged into a wall outlet, but with no device attached, the insulated, electrically grounded wires in the cords are still useful against Negs. Some experimentation will help to determine what works best.

I have solved many serious Neg problems using power extension cords.

Steel and Grounding Structures

Negs are drained or demanifested when they come into contact with electrical grounding. Ungrounded, heavy steel objects and fixtures also have an effect on Negs, much as steel has an effect on a magnet. The heavier the metal object, the greater the effect—that is, a horseshoe will be more effective than a teaspoon.

Iron or steel objects can be placed near the entry of a home to deter Negs. A steel horseshoe placed on a door will help. If it is electrically grounded, a steel doorframe will have an effect similar to that of a running-water barrier. This doorframe will stop free-roaming Negs from entering the building. Heavy steel plates under doormats will also help. Steel chains can also be placed in rooms, under beds, and even under pillows to repel Negs.

Another idea is to sleep on steel-framed beds that are electrically grounded. Using conductive sheets or cloths held in contact with the steel bed frame makes it easy to sleep electrically grounded.

Fumigation, Scent, and Incense

Scent, smoke, incense, herbs, and other airborne substances and smells affect the atmosphere and energy of a place. These things are historically and experientially known to affect Negs in various ways. The application of scented smoke or mist is the quickest way to change the atmosphere of a room or building. This smoke or mist can be used to deter and repel Negs and create harmonious atmospheres. A happy ambiance in itself is generally repellant to Negs. Incense sinks into all surfaces and materials of a home. Frequent use has lasting effects.

There are numerous ways to apply scent, including burning, evaporating, and spraying methods. These methods include burning incense as sticks, blocks, and granules in censers; evaporating essential oils; setting out potpourris in bowls; and using spray cans or bottles. The fastest way to fumigate large areas is with charcoal censers or with spray cans or pump sprays containing scented water.

Incense: Incense is available in the form of sticks, blocks, and granules. Various types of incense holders and burners are available. A glass jar filled with sand works well for holding sticks, and blocks can be burned on a saucer. Have one incense burner for each main area of your home. To create an anti-Neg ambiance, the idea is to produce noticeable quantities of scented smoke throughout the home. Increase the quantity of smoke according to the severity of Neg disturbances. Use lots of incense as soon as a Neg disturbance is felt, before the disturbance gets worse. You then have a chance of breaking up the Neg atmosphere with incense alone. For the average-sized home, six to eight incense sticks is a good start for breaking up a Neg atmosphere. Use more incense if problems escalate.

Types of Incense and Oils: Many varieties and qualities of incenses and essential oils will help with Neg problems. My preferred incenses are white sage, dragon's blood, nag champa, sandalwood, lavender, and frankincense. Many types of incense and scents are suitable for anti-Neg purposes. Personal tastes also matter, as using something you do not like will not encourage a happy mood.

Charcoal Censer: Charcoal censers are used for burning incense granules. They can also be used to burn herbs, like garlic, chili, rosemary, and sage. Using a censor is the most efficient method for quickly fumigating a home or building, as they produce lots of incense smoke. If you have ongoing Neg problems, a censer is an essential tool. You can purchase packs of smokeless charcoal disks especially designed for use in censers. Charcoal disks are quick to light when they are held over a stovetop or flame with a pair of pliers. You can substitute barbeque briquettes, but these take longer to light and produce smoke.

To use a censer, first light a charcoal disk (or briquette) so it is glowing, and then cover the top of the disk with incense granules. Do not overload and smother it. The disk will soon begin producing copious quantities of smoke. Airflow is needed for the disk to stay lit, and so censors are designed to be swung on a chain or wafted from side to side. The more airflow there is, the more heat and smoke the censor produces. Add more granules as needed.

Using censers takes a little practice. The secret is to have the charcoal burning well and to not overload it. Start with just a few incense granules. Homemade censers can be made from steel food cans. Remove tops, clean the cans, punch multiple holes in sides, and make wire handles. Add some dry gravel or small rocks inside the can so there is air movement around the charcoal and the bottom of the can does not overheat. Charcoal is essential to make censers work.

Fumigation: With serious Neg atmospheres, do not be afraid of filling a building quite thickly with incense smoke, even if doing so means you have to temporarily vacate. Heavy fumigation has a strong effect on Neg manifestations. A fumigation procedure can be combined with music and light, verbal affirmations, prayers, positive statements, and banishments. Walk through the house, swinging the censer and repeating a suitable affirmation or mantra aloud. (For example, "This home is happy and full of love. This home is filled with love and grace.") Do not mention Negs. Focusing on positive thoughts and statements will help connect you to positive forces.

Strong incense smoke can cause coughing, headaches, and sting the eyes. Asthmatics may wish to wait outside until fumigation is completed or to breathe through a mask or wet towel. Remember, the thicker the smoke, the stronger the effect. Leave the house for a few minutes until the smoke clears, if it bothers you. Alternatively, use only essential-oil burners while you are home, and burn incense while you are out.

Numerous essential-oil burners are needed to create a sufficient amount of scent to fumigate a home. Humidifiers can be used for this purpose and to continue scent production during sleep. You can also add essential oils to a small saucepan and simmer them on a stovetop for a greater volume of scent.

Sprays and Air Fresheners: Commercially produced air fresheners can be used to treat Neg atmospheres quickly. Some experimentation is required to find what works best. Pick a scent you like. Anything that adds a pleasant scent to the atmosphere, including air-freshener spray cans, blocks, and liquids, will have an effect.

Spray bottles that will produce mist can also be used. Add water and essential oils, shake, and spray. Pump-up garden spray bottles with brass nozzles are the best for this purpose. These can be bought in most supermarkets for a few dollars. A whole home can be treated in a minute using one of these. Add scented essential oil and water, shake the mixture, and then pump up the pressure and spray with a fine-mist setting.

Spraying your home immediately after arguments or after disagreeable visitors have left is a good general countermeasure for maintaining positive home energies. You can also spray and air your bedsheets each morning.

Chili Peppers: Hot chili pepper is an effective Neg fumigant. When burned, it emits a vicious smoke. This smoke has a violent effect on the lungs and stings the eyes. Swim goggles and a damp towel held over the mouth and nose will help.

Black mustard seeds can be added to the mix or used as a substitute for chili peppers. A tiny pinch of ginger or mint added to the mix will increase its effect.

Fresh or dried chili peppers can be used. A censer or a small cast-iron fry pan can be used for burning chili flakes. Heat the pan and throw in chopped chili peppers. Copious amounts of smoke will soon be produced. The fry pan or censer can be carried around the home from room to room, or it can be placed on a suitable heat-proof plate and left to smoke. Close the doors and windows, and leave it to fumigate for ten minutes or so. Then enter the room, holding your breath, and air the room. Repeat as necessary. Burning chili peppers is a good way to cleanse the energies of a home. Take care not to set fire to anything.

Chili smoke can also be used to remove Neg hitchhikers. This countermeasure is best done outside the home, ideally in combination with running water. Have the person stand inside coils of garden hose, then turn on the water. Take the smoking fry pan or censer and walk around the person several times, holding the pan close to him/her and moving it low and high, so his/her whole body is touched (smudged) by the smoke. Smudging with white sage is also beneficial. Finally, move the person out of the coils of hose and gush lots of water through the coils to dispose of the Neg.

Sulfur: Elemental sulfur, also called brimstone, is a naturally occurring crystalline substance and the most effective material for Neg fumigation.

Elemental sulfur is produced through geological processes, including hot springs, volcanoes, and salt domes. Sulfur has been widely used for thousands of years as a medicine, bleach, fumigant, fertilizer, fungicide, and insecticide. It is still widely used today, including on organic farms, as a biologically friendly agent for dusting vegetables and fruit.

Sulfur burns with a blue flame and has the smell of burnt matches. Burning sulfur produces toxic gasses, including carbon disulfide, carbon oxysulfide, hydrogen sulfide, and sulfur dioxide. Because sulfur produces toxic fumes when burned, great care must be taken when using it as a home fumigant.

First, prepare the area to be fumigated. Remove all people and pets from the area, and turn off air pumps to aquariums. Place censers on safe, fireproof surfaces. Close all outside windows and doors. Burn charcoal briquettes until they are glowing, then place them into censers. Use a wet towel or a breathing apparatus to protect your nose and mouth. Alternatively, just hold your breath when you apply the sulfur to the charcoal.

Add a small mound of sulfur powder to the glowing coals in the censer. Do not overload them, or they will go out fairly quickly. Swing on the censer until the sulfur burns with a blue flame. Do *not* breathe the fumes. Then leave the area, shutting the door behind you. Return approximately twenty minutes later and, again holding your breath, extinguish any remaining burning sulfur. Open all windows and doors to air. Still holding your breath, leave the building and wait for the air to clear.

A whole house can be fumigated by using multiple censers or by repeating the procedure in all main areas. Fireproof ashtrays or tin cans with a few holes punched in them can also be used to hold smoldering barbecue charcoal pieces for sulfur burning.

Elemental sulfur powder is freely available from gardening-supply stores. Please check the label first to make sure the powder contains only elemental sulfur. (Some sulfur powders contain copper. This copper-containing sulfer can be used in a pinch when pure sulfur powder is not available). Sulfur sticks (like thick incense sticks) are also used in the wine industry, where they are used to fumigate oak barrels. If you can obtain them, these are more convenient to use than elemental sulfur powder.

Again, do not breathe sulfur fumes. When mixed with the moisture in your lungs, sulfur fumes create sulfuric acid, which is toxic.

A Quick-Fix with Matches: When struck and ignited, matches release sulfur. They can be used as a quick fix for treating negative atmospheres. Say, for example, a visitor has left behind a bad atmosphere, or there has been an argument in your home. Ignite several matches at a time. Do so again multiple times until the affected areas have been exposed to the smoke. This procedure does not produce dangerous levels of toxic fumes, even if you ignite a whole box of matches, but it is still wise not to breathe the smoke.

Matches have long been used as an air freshener, and sulfur smells strongly of burned matches when burned. However, after a home has been fumigated with sulfur and aired, it will have a very clean, fresh smell. Sulfur absorbs and destroys all bad odors, as well as negative energies. It will also kill insects, mites, bugs, silverfish, and mold.

Garlic: Legend has it that garlic repels evil spirits and vampires. The truth is, garlic contains a lot of organic sulfur, which makes it an excellent anti-Neg countermeasure. I have used garlic for many years with good results. Just placing a few bulbs of garlic around a room will not work. The sulfur-carrying odors must be released into the atmosphere to be effective. Fresh cloves of strong red garlic are best. The stronger the garlic, the stronger the sulfur and the anti-Neg effect.

To reduce a negative atmosphere, slice a few cloves of garlic into thin rounds. Spread these over small plates and position around rooms. Alternatively, place slices of garlic on pieces of foil or paper, and then place them on tables, counters, windowsills, and the tops of doorframes. You can also wrap slices of garlic in tissue and place them in pockets and under pillows.

A garlic crusher or press can also be used, and the resulting paste smeared on plates or cardboard.

The amount of garlic used to treat a room depends on the severity of the problem. The stronger the odor, the stronger the effect. Used garlic should not be used for cooking, but put in the trash.

If you have ongoing Neg problems, increase your daily consumption of garlic in food and as garlic oil in capsule form. Odorless garlic capsules do not work. When ingested, garlic permeates the body and acts as a built-in Neg deterrent. It is also a natural antibiotic and antifungal, and it has blood-thinning properties and many other health benefits.

Garlic can be applied directly to skin to deter or treat Neg attachments and to counter Neg interference during sleep. Apply garlic to the feet and hands by rubbing them with broken garlic cloves or the oil from broken garlic-oil capsules. Raw garlic is stronger than you might think. Take care to not get any garlic juice in the eyes or on sensitive or broken skin, to avoid stinging and burns.

The feet are the areas most vulnerable to Neg influences, especially during sleep. You can rub garlic juice into them, or slices of garlic can be wrapped in tissue and placed inside socks. If your mouth is affected by Negs, sucking a piece of garlic will help. If you have never chewed raw garlic, be careful, as it's hot.

Protective Herbs and Oils

Many herbs and essential oils can be used to help with Neg problems. Sprinkling protective herbs around the home is a simple countermeasure that helps with Neg problems. Herbal oils can be wiped on furniture and fixtures. Some can be mixed with water and used as sprays and rinses. Some can be used as incense and fumigants. While not as effective as sulfur or garlic, herbs and essential oils smell a whole lot nicer and are more socially agreeable.

Herbs, scents, and perfumes affect subtle energies and will change and positively charge the atmosphere or mood of a home. If applied to the physical body with soaps, shampoos, body rinses, herbal baths, perfumes, and creams, they change the energy vibrations of the skin, which affects the frequency of the energy-body aura field. When herbs are taken internally, they permeate the physical body and also change its energy. When carried on the body, the energy of the body is affected.

Sprinkles: Fresh or dried herbs can be sprinkled in corners of rooms and across or beside entry points to deter Negs from entering. Vacuum up the sprinkled herbs and replace them when their smell fades. Herbal teas and oils can also be used as sprinkles.

Herbal Teas and Rinses: Teas can be made from herbs in much the same way as normal tea, by soaking in boiling water. These herbal teas can be used in atomizing sprays and as rinses to wash entryways, doors, window frames, floors, and walls and thus counter bad atmospheres and Negs. Teas can also be used as body and hair rinses after bathing, as a personal deterrent.

Activating: Herbs and oils can be activated to enhance their natural properties. Verbalize statements of intention, affirmations, or prayers over them. State what you wish the substance to accomplish.

Following are some useful herbs and ways of using them:

Agrimony: Can be burned or sprinkled to repel Negs.

Anise: Can be placed under pillows to repel Neg dream interference.

Broom: Boil tops in water and use the water as a sprinkle or rinse to repel Negs.

Clove and Cinnamon: These raise vibrations and repel Negs.

Citrus and Bergamot: Good all-round Neg repellents, promoting positive atmospheres.

Camphor: Repels Negs and reduces negative atmospheres.

Eucalyptus: Oil can be mixed with water and evaporated in oil burners, used as sprays or sprinkles, or rubbed into the feet. Leaves can be burned as a fumigant. A good general Neg repellent.

Fenugreek and Dill: These herbs reduce negative atmospheres and repel Negs.

Lavender: Can be used fresh or dried, and as a sprinkle, rinse, perfume, or essential oil. A good general Neg repellent.

Mint and Ginger: These are energizing, activating herbs. They increase the efficiency of any herbs with which they are mixed. Use only a very small quantity.

Mugwort (Wild Sage): Traditionally used for smudging and fumigation. Mugwort moxa sticks are available from Chinese herbalists.

Pine: Fresh pine branches can be woven into wreaths and placed around home as general atmosphere improver and Neg repellent. Many other woods can be used for this purpose. Check what is available in your local area.

Rosemary and Marjoram: These absorb negative atmospheres, raise positive vibrations, and repel Negs. Can be used as sprinkles or as a rinse. Living rosemary bushes can be placed in pots near front doors and in bedrooms to deter Negs. They can also be grown outside near entries to a home.

Thyme and Lemon Thyme: These repel Negs and weaken attachments.

Tobacco Leaves: Untreated tobacco leaves can be used for smudging to repel Negs and remove attachments. Do not use cigarette or other commercially produced tobacco products.

Sage and White Sage: Sage is grown around the world. There are many different varieties. All are useful for smudging or as incense. White sage (from California, also called buffalo sage) has a wonderful sweet smell and is my personal favorite as an incense, smudge, and fumigant to counter negative atmospheres and repel Negs.

Cleanliness

Cleanliness is a consideration with regard to what attracts or repels Negs. Negs are less attracted to and have more difficulty operating in clean, well-aired buildings. When you are faced with Neg problems, the first thing on the to-do list is a good spring cleaning and decluttering of the home. If a home is run down, redecorating will help. These measures can solve many Neg-related problems before they become entrenched.

Maintaining good personal hygiene and wearing clean clothing are also important for the same reasons. Regular bathing clears away accumulated negative energy from the skin, along with dirt. The absence of these increases the quality of subtle energies surrounding the human body and helps reinforce natural defenses. Clean clothing and bedding, for these same reasons, also have positive affects. Tight clothing restricts natural energy flow, while loose clothing promotes a greater flow. Natural fibers are always preferable. It is also advisable that you do not wear street footwear within the home, to avoid spreading negative energies that you might have been picked up outside the home.

A shower and change of clothing helps counter negative influences and Neg attacks. This is the first thing to be done when you feel the effects of negative energies or Neg problems.

FOOTCARE
The feet are the main interface between Negs and humans. For this reason, extra care should be taken of your feet. Give yourself a pedicure. See a podiatrist. Get some reflexology. Rub essential oils or lotions into your feet after bathing. Change into fresh socks in the midafternoon. Use natural cotton or wool socks when possible. Wear comfortable shoes. Walk

barefoot on bare ground every day. Walking on damp grass or sand is very grounding and healthy.

Using good quality herbal soaps and shampoos with nice scents is a wise everyday precaution. These scent the skin, hair, and clothing, all of which enhance natural shielding.

Light as a Countermeasure

Darkness makes it easier for Negs to operate. Negs are weakened by well-lit conditions. Turning on the main overhead lights is a good basic countermeasure. If it's hard to sleep with the lights on, cover your eyes with a dark tee shirt.

A 100-watt overhead bulb, when lit, will reduce nocturnal Neg activity by around 50 percent.

Children should always be given a decent nightlight or have the overhead light on if they have problems sleeping. Children are more sensitive than adults and will often sense negative things that adults miss. The pennies it costs to run an electronic lightbulb overnight is a small price to pay for a child's peace of mind and restful sleep. Many future psychological problems can be preempted in this way. Most adults with Neg problems also had Neg problems as children, and they were often forced to sleep in the dark.

Houses suffering frequent Neg atmospheres often have bad areas that can be felt as cold or tingling spots by sensitives. During daytime, Negs will hide in the quietest, darkest areas of a house, such as vacant rooms, hallways, alcoves, basements and cellars, wardrobes, or attics. This causes a buildup of negative energy in those places. Many Neg problems can be solved by opening curtains and blinds during the day, by installing brighter lightbulbs or skylights, or by placing mirrors to reflect more light into dark areas. Increasing the light in these places will generally reduce Neg problems in a home.

SUNLIGHT

I have never encountered free-roaming Negs in direct sunlight. Sunlight is extremely detrimental to Negs and Neg attachments. Sunlight penetrates flesh and steadily reduces negative energies and attachments. In a way, attached Negs can be said to hide away from sunlight by moving deep inside the physical body.

Many people today suffer from a vitamin-D deficiency, even in sunny places like California and Australia. People spend too much time indoors, and sunscreen blocks the rays we need for good health. This deficiency weakens the immune system and causes all kinds of health problems. There is a relationship between immune-system health and natural anti-Neg shielding. What affects one affects the other.

I recommend a healthy, daily exposure of bare skin to the sun. Care should be taken, of course, not to get sunburned. Expose as much skin as possible so sunlight can penetrate deep into your body. In particular, make sure that areas of the body where Neg interference is frequently experienced are exposed to direct sunlight.

Good-quality sunlamps that produce healthy light frequencies can also be used, where natural sunlight is lacking.

ELECTRIC LIGHTS

Electric lights are a good general Neg deterrent. Simply turning on all the overhead lights can significantly reduce the intensity of Neg problems. Sleep with the main overhead lights on if necessary. Place a dark cloth over your eyes to help you sleep. Using brighter bulbs will increase the anti-Neg effect.

LED FLASHLIGHTS

LED (light-emitting diode) flashlights and small head lamps, such as those worn by cavers, can be used to counter Neg interference during sleep. These can be placed under the bedcovers, or taped to the skin over affected body areas. Typically, sharp pains in the feet and fluttering and tingling sensations in chakra areas are signs of Neg interference. LED-flashlight batteries can last hundreds of hours, making these flashlights ideal for this purpose.

Tiger Balm or tea tree oil should also be topically applied to affected areas of the skin, where flashlights are to be placed.

Magnets

Therapeutic magnets will help with Neg and attachment problems and as a general Neg deterrent. Magnets improve blood circulation and have many other health benefits. Magnetic mattress covers can be a good idea where regular Neg problems are being experienced.

Magnetic wraps are available for any area of the body. These have many health benefits, including the easement of pain in joints and spinal disks and improved general healing.

Magnets can be placed directly onto any area where Neg activity is being felt in the body. They can be combined with salt packs, light (LED flashlights), and Tiger Balm or tea tree oil.

A cheap source of magnets is old computer hard-disk drives. Dismantle the drives and remove the magnets. These are strong rare earth magnets, which are poisonous. They need to be wrapped in duct tape or plastic before being used on the skin.

Large, strong magnets can be used to sweep a building clear of Negs. The really heavy type of magnets needed for this countermeasure are found inside older types of commercial microwaves and in large audio speakers.

The Q-Link

There are many high-tech subtle-energy devices available today for protecting yourself against harmful electromagnetic frequencies and negative energies. I am most familiar with the Q-Link, which I wear myself. This is a small medallion that is worn around the neck or the wrist. It is like a modern-age talisman. I have recommended it to many people suffering serious Neg-related problems, and in all cases it has made a measurable difference. It is not a cure-all, but it helps. The Q-Link is marketed as EM protection, but experience tells me it also has an effect on countering more subtle negative energies. (See "Further References" and my website, Astral Dynamics, *www.astraldynamics.com.*)

Topical Ointments and Essential Oils

Many types of ointments, balms, perfumes, and essential oils will help with Neg problems when applied topically to the body. Anything with a strong smell will help, including concoctions containing camphor, cloves, menthol, and mint. The best all-rounders for general Neg problems are Tiger Balm and tea tree oil. Most supermarkets stock these. Various brands of mentholated chest ointments used for the treatment of colds and congestion will also help. Again, anything strong smelling will help.

Electric-Violet Fire

The use of imagination (also called visualization) is a valuable tool for countering psychic attacks and Neg-related problems. As introduced earlier, electric violet is a great color for treating negative energies and Neg-related problems. It can be used to burn away attachments, to treat a home atmosphere, and to generally convert toxic negative energies into positive energies.

If you cannot hold electric violet in your imagination, use purple, magenta, pink, or white. If you keep practicing, using electric violet gets easier.

Energy-Conversion Ball

Negative energy can be converted into positive energy using the following method.

Imagine a dark, murky, tennis-ball-sized piece of energy floating in the middle of the room. Make the ball spin counterclockwise. Concentrate on this spin. As it spins, see it sucking clumps of negative energy from your body and the surrounding area and growing larger. Move the spinning ball around the room like a vacuum cleaner, seeing it grow in size as it gathers up all the negative energy. Once it is the size of a large beach ball, reverse its direction and make it spin clockwise. Then imagine it changing color to brilliant white. Lastly, explode the ball and imagine its brilliant energy splattering everywhere, charging you and the room with positive energy.

Gemstones and Crystals

Gemstones, crystals, and stones have their own vibrations. They resonate with living energy. When worn, they change the frequency of a person's energy body and aura field. Certain gemstones, crystals, and stones have natural resonance properties that can offer protection against Neg interference and psychic attacks. These qualities can be increased if the stones are blessed or programmed with intentions.

To program a stone, relax and hold it in your hands. Imagine it vibrating at a high pitch. Imagine a field of light spreading out from the stone and enclosing your whole body. Holding this image in mind, program the stone with statements of intention. Express the desired qualities, such as repelling Negs, negative influences, and reflecting psychic attack, as we did earlier with programming a mental shield. Use positive statements, such as, "This stone protects me."

Once a stone is endowed with protective properties, maintain it by repeating the preceding programming method at regular intervals. Stones should be regularly washed under running water. Washing, blessing, and programming stones with statements of intention enhance the stones' effectiveness. When not being worn, protective stones should be recharged in sunlight and wrapped in clean cloth and kept in a small wooden box.

Which gemstones can be used for protection? Amethyst, amber, black onyx, black tourmaline, citrine, clear quartz, double-terminated crystal, hematite, iron ore, lapis lazuli, malachite, obsidian, pyrite, red jasper, ruby, rutilated quartz, selenite, smoky topaz, turquoise, tiger iron, tiger eye, petrified wood, and flint arrowheads all work. There are many others. Finding the right protective stones for you takes some research and experimentation.

Colors and Ambiance

The colors of walls and ceilings, drapes and floors, have a big effect on the ambiance and brightness of a room. The ambiance of rooms can be felt just by walking into them. Color generates energy, and Negs are repelled by bright, beautiful, balanced, and happy colors and light. Redecorating is advised if a home is rundown and dismal, and to generally refresh and brighten up a home. Redecorating is a good opportunity to impart some positive intention into your home.

Suicide

I am frequently asked about suicide. Many people are tempted to end their lives in the hope of sidestepping pain and problems, including serious Neg problems. However, suicide is not an effective approach to solving anything.

When persons die, the afterlife experience is shaped by their beliefs and their life experience. It is also affected by the traumas and emotional baggage they carry with them. People with enough pain to cause them to want to commit suicide will find their problems recreated in the afterlife. These problems (great life lessons) will be illusions, but they will seem just as real as they did in real life.

It can be difficult to tell the difference between the afterlife realms and real life. After death, most people do not realize they have died. There is some confusion for the first week or so, in the half-life fringe realm of ghosts, and then people move on into something more substantial. I have been a regular visitor to the spirit realms (also called heavens) for most of my life. It is difficult to tell that you are not still alive there. You can still get a cup of coffee or a beer, go out for a nice meal and a movie, read a book, walk on a beach, and hug a loved one. These experiences may be an illusion, but they are just as real as they are in real life.

The only things that give the afterlife realms away are the anomalies. The afterlife is full of anomalies. (This also applies to all levels of out-of-body experience and lucid dreaming—they are all full of anomalies.) Anomalies can include misplaced furniture, doors, items, and people. For example, your glass is never empty; you try to write, and your pen runs out of ink; you try to read, and the words jumble; you start walking to a destination, and suddenly you are there. I think these anomalies are programmed into all subtle environments (by the Great Programmer of life) to constantly demonstrate to us that these environs are outside the physical universe.

While people are alive, they are capable of processing and overcoming enormous problems in relatively short amounts of time. And through this process, huge leaps in spiritual growth are possible. People may experience months or years of suffering, but problems can eventually be resolved. Even if great problems are resolved just before death from old age, they are still resolved in a relatively short time. In the afterlife, however, problems take much, much longer to process. Life events are relived over and over until they are processed, resolved, and released. This processing can take hundreds of years of personal time. You have to genuinely let go and move on, to forgive and forget, to be free of serious baggage. So committing suicide is not a good way to avoid real-life problems and painful experiences.

As a mystic, I often connect with spirits and journey to afterlife realms. Suicides fare no differently from anyone else. They go to the same place everyone else goes to when they die. However, they generally have a lot more painful life experiences and baggage to process, so the afterlife can be more difficult for them. They do not go to any kind of hell that is not of their own making, nor do they go to any kind of special place for suicides. Religious beliefs form a part in shaping the early afterlife, but over time these fade away as they are outgrown. Opinions to the contrary on the question of suicide come largely from hearsay, dogma, and speculation, not from personal experience.

···◆···

So far we have absorbed a great deal of information concerning Negatives and anti-Neg countermeasures. Children deserve special consideration here, because their needs and issues are different from those of adults. The following chapter discusses children's Neg-related issues and provides specific advices and modifications to some procedures.

CHAPTER EIGHT

Children's Neg Problems

*Core Affirmation: "I am loved and I am worthy. I am
safe and I am free. I am powerfully protected. I am
master of my body and ruler of my mind."*

Children are more psychically and emotionally sensitive than adults.
They are, therefore, more open to negative energies, influences,
and attachments. Neg problems can begin at any age, including infancy.
Many adult problems stem from childhood Neg abuse. A major reason
for this sensitivity is that children's brainwaves are quite different from
those of adults.

When adults experience a brainwave state similar to those children
have naturally, it's called an altered state of consciousness, or a trance
state. During altered states, hypnotic suggestibility, psychic abilities, creativity, and sensitivity are greatly enhanced. This is why children, particularly before the age of six, will often see and hear and sense things
that adults don't. This does not mean that the things they sense are not
real, only that the typical adult brainwave state—the Beta state—filters
them out.

Here is a brief sketch of developmental brainwave states from birth to
adulthood:

> From birth to twenty-four months, the Delta state (0.5 to 4
> hertz) is prominent. Delta is experienced by adults only during
> the deep-sleep state.

From two to six years, the Theta state (4 to 8 hertz) is prominent. Theta is experienced by adults during deep meditation and for brief moments during presleep and awakening.

From six to twelve years, the Alpha state (8 to 13 hertz) is prominent. Alpha is experienced by adults during deep relaxation, light meditation, light hypnosis, and highway hypnosis.

From twelve years onwards, the Beta state (13 to 30 hertz) is prominent. Beta is the fully alert state. Adults spend most of their time in the Beta state.

The Delta and Theta brainwave states, in particular, greatly increase psychic and emotional receptivity. Children's minds constantly scan the environment on many levels. In a similar way, adults will sometimes connect with and feed Negs by reaching out and scanning with their senses to identify sources of Neg-related phenomena, as discussed in chapter 7.

Many adults disbelieve children when they complain of supernatural problems. "It's just your imagination" or "It's all in your head" are typical responses. Adults' closed minds when faced with the supernatural gives Negs free range and full access to children. No matter what terrible things Negs do to children, those children will not be truly believed. Children are frequently criticized or punished for complaining and worrying parents. Children soon learn to keep quiet about supernatural problems. But sometimes there actually are monsters under the bed.

There is a lot of natural fear involved in dealing with these types of supernatural problems. To accept that these problems are real is to realize that one is largely powerless and, hence, also vulnerable to unseen beings and forces. Denial is a far more palatable course of action for most people. Getting used to the reality of paranormal issues can be difficult.

I have questioned many spiritual teachers on the matter of children's Neg issues. I have been told that I should not interfere because children should be allowed to work out their own karma. Bad karma is said to result from bad deeds in past lives. This view blames children for their own Neg problems (a familiar story). I totally disagree with this view.

The only thing that stands between children and Negs are parents. Family lifestyle and associations, the home environment, and parenting have a great deal to do with how exposed children are to Neg-related problems. Few people really know what to do to help babies and children with Neg problems. Most start reaching for medication or fall back on karma as an excuse to do nothing. This book is all about doing something—anything—that can help. We don't know everything, but we know enough to make a difference.

Natural Defenses and Weaknesses of Children

Children are psychically sensitive, trusting, and easy to influence. These qualities make them highly susceptible to Neg influences. At night, children feel Neg activity and atmospheres intensely. Children are easily frightened, particularly by what is unknown. Neg phenomena can bring children to the point of mind-numbing terror. When this point is reached, natural defenses fall, and they are open to invasion, telepathic and hypnotic manipulation, energy-body attachments, and long-term conditioning and Neg abuse.

Children can be exposed to Negs in many ways, often through hereditary factors and circumstances beyond anyone's control. Children have little defense against hypnotic and psychological pressures, especially when they are tired. Negs can make sure that children are always sleep deprived.

When children play in a group, they develop a pack mentality. Individuals are psychologically exposed to other members of a group and to any Negs attached to those other members. This is one good reason to take care with the company that children keep.

When children have nothing to occupy them, they become bored and daydream, and their minds slow down. This increases their susceptibility to Neg influences. Television is a curse for some children because watching it causes them to enter a passive, trancelike mental state and, thus, become more susceptible to Neg influences. Playing computer games or reading are preferable to watching TV, as these activities require more active mental participation. Playing real games and sports is even better. Keeping children busy and active in healthy ways is important to reducing potential Neg problems.

The quality and activity of family life has a lot to do with Neg susceptibility. The company parents keep is also an important factor. Disreputable and psychologically unhealthy company should be avoided. Adults will often pick up Neg hitchhikers and carry them into the family home, exposing everyone there to Neg influences. Negs always make a beeline for children, because they are so accessible.

Some key signs to look for regarding Neg interference in children include sleep disturbances, night terrors, unexplainable tiredness, and behavioral changes.

Once a child is targeted by Negs, a predictable campaign begins to unfold. Negs are not good at adapting to change, and this is one of their major weakness. If Neg processes are interfered with for long enough, Negs will often just go away.

There are many things available in the modern world to help with children's health and Neg problems. These things include doctors, therapists, priests, naturopaths, bodyworkers, and healers.

Diet and health, including food quality, food additives, and food intolerances, are factors in Neg susceptibility. Electromagnetic-field exposure is also a factor in our modern world. For example, if the main power supply into the house is near a child's bedroom wall, it can cause problems. Computer equipment and TVs in or near a child's room can also cause problems. These things can be shielded or moved to reduce environmental stress. Some research and experimentation may be required to eliminate these stressors and improve a child's environment.

Advice from a Psychologist

Following are some observations and advice from a psychologist experienced with children's Neg-related problems, Benjamin Bruce.

"Childhood trauma can have very different effects upon different children, and as they develop into adults, there are infinite variables that compound this unpredictability. There are the effects of every child's individual personality differences, as well as biological, psychosocial, and environmental factors. The evidence given in this book also highlights the parapsychological domain. With an analysis of this variable, an X factor of unseen influences, or Negs, we can appreciate a whole other dimension to childhood developmental problems. The following are alternative hypothetical scenarios resulting from either acknowledging this X factor or ignoring it.

A child exhibiting Neg-related problems is told by his parents that it's all in his mind and that he should just be normal. Despite this "great advice," the Neg phenomena continues (while the child tries to sleep, for example) to the detriment of the child's physical and psychological health. There is also an interaction between the environment (the Neg interference) and the child's individuality, the thoughts and actions that are particular to him. The child will soon realize that his experiences are either real, if he is intelligent, perceptive, and trusts his senses, or fictitious, if he is unable to discriminate and has low self-esteem.

The former scenario (a sense of real experience) will promote a feeling of isolation within the child, and he will think that his life is *special* in some way. He may also lose respect for his parents and feel unloved, as they do nothing to protect him from the terrifying phenomena.

The latter scenario (a sense of fictitious experience) will cause the child to feel derogated and his reality undermined so that he starts to doubt his perceptual experiences. This doubt is worsened by the lack of quality sleep and Neg influences. Sensing that his experience is fictitious creates a schism in the psyche, where the child's private world becomes separated from the public world of consensus reality. The child can now start to believe he is abnormal and mentally deranged. This abnormality can be exacerbated with derogatory labels from his family and peers, such as "freak" or "weirdo," or with clinical labels, such as "schizophrenic," if he is introduced to a professional. This scenario will also be compounded with any antipsychotic or sedative medication (or other treatment) the child receives and by the side effects of this medication.

Over time, both scenarios may lead to a similar outcome of delinquency and aberrant or criminal behavior as the child/adult seeks to fit in and attract like-minded company: people with similar strange and erratic thoughts and behavior. The child/adult may even be institutionalized, especially if any aberrant and destructive urges are acted upon.

Conversely, when these experiences first begin, parents could be more sympathetic and investigative of the source of the problem. Indeed, it is possible that the child is suffering from mental illness or experiencing the negative effects of real-life problems, such as child abuse, but all possibilities should be explored. If parents are observant and open minded, any serious Neg interference should become noticeable, if it exists. This Neg interference often comes with multiple parasomnias (sleep and sleep-wake rhythm disorders), such as sleep paralysis, nightmares, night terrors, night sweating, open-eyed REM (rapid eye movement), sleepwalking, head banging, head rolling, body rocking, bedwetting, sleep talking, and tooth grinding.

Although parasomnias may exist as simple childhood disorders in their own right, they may be linked with Neg activity, especially if multiple parasomnias are linked with disturbing atmospheres, poltergeist phenomena, and other strange nocturnal manifestations. But one should be careful not to become paranoid or to develop a witch-hunt mentality. This line of investigation must be conducted with caution, in plain view of all the facts. Otherwise, a self-fulfilling prophecy could develop and come to fruition, which would counter the intention of genuinely helping suffering children.

If children are aware they are being taken seriously by an adult mind focused on problem resolution, there is less chance they will experience the previously described mental schism, and children will find their perceptions more trustworthy. Their self-esteem and self-respect will improve, as will their love and respect for their parents. They will feel more comfortable with, and connected to, reality, even if reality is extended to include paranormal events.

It is important to note that an apparently irrational person (child or adult) always has a reason for acting or thinking in such a way. In this sense, all thought and behavior is fundamentally rational—an effect resulting from a cause. Thus, a person who is apparently strange on the outside should be respected and given the benefit of the doubt. It should be kept in mind that the behavioral or thought disturbance has a cause, and that behavior is the person's way of reacting and coping. It is, thus, unconstructive and unhelpful to fob off the person as being irrational.

As well as having their experience validated, people must also be made accountable for their thoughts and actions, such as with the application of mental discipline, and help given accordingly. However, making people accountable for their thoughts and actions does not mean that one should blame the victims, especially children, for their Neg-related problems. But if this accountability does not occur, people will not take the necessary responsibility for their actions, and they may actually luxuriate or wallow in their problems and not face reality. Not facing problems or reality can lead to other psychological disturbances, from basic immaturity to complex personality disorders, later in life.

Regarding parental tactics, remember that children are generally braver and more open than most people think. They appreciate candor as much as adults. But too many details are counterproductive, needlessly frightening them. The truth can be desensationalized and honest explanations still given.

If Neg problems are apparent, tell children that something will be done about these problems. A good way of handling this discussion is to expand on the usual explanation that the problem is caused by their imagination. You can tell children that a person's imagination can sometimes cause problems for other people, and that sometimes other people's imaginations can cause scary things to happen. Point out that these things can only scare them and not cause them bodily harm.

Negs can be given a nonthreatening name, such as *Spooky* or *Ghostly*. Today, kids are fairly comfortable with the concept of harmless, but scary, cartoon monsters. If parents are matter-of-fact about this, children will respond positively. And keep in mind that explanations should be given only if Neg problems are noticeable.

Getting children involved with anti-Neg countermeasures and understanding how these countermeasures work helps distract them, which, in turn, helps demystify and desensationalize a frightening situation. And doing something positive about Neg problems promotes peace of mind for all concerned. A family united and grounded in truth is far stronger than a family split apart by denial.

The information children can provide is invaluable, and they should be encouraged to report anything that disturbs them. Encourage children with Neg-related problems to talk about their dreams and experiences, good and bad. Recurrent dreams can help identify core images and psychic attackers. Merely talking about bad dreams and nocturnal experiences and sharing them with loving parents, while being believed and supported, is beneficial to any child's psychological well-being."

Adequate Sleep: A Protective Measure

As any parent knows, a child's mind is a busy place. This mental activity is a natural defense against Neg influences. However, children's minds quickly weaken when they don't get enough sleep. The solution is to make very sure that children get enough rest.

If children experience frequent sleep disturbances or appear overly tired after getting adequate sleep, consult a healthcare professional. Keep in mind that sleep disturbances, nightmares and sleep terrors, listlessness and inability to focus, disassociation, and sudden behavioral changes are classic symptoms of child abuse. Neg abuse can cause identical symptoms.

Care must be taken when describing the source of a child's sleep disturbances to healthcare professionals. Some paraphrasing may be in order. For example, if you say to a doctor, "My son is not sleeping because he says there are monsters under his bed. I looked and found paranormal activity in his room. What do we do?" the doctor will be reaching for a prescription pad and writing *you* a referral to a therapist. Instead, say something more mundane and believable, like, "My son is not sleeping well. He has some problems at school, and we think he's watched some horror movies at a friend's home." This description may result in a referral to a child psychologist (a good thing) and some medication to help your child sleep (also a good thing).

Diagnosing Neg Problems with Children

Diagnosing Neg problems in children can be difficult. It's important to not leap to conclusions and think the worst just because children have behavioral or tiredness problems or are acting goofy and strange. Sometimes children are goofy and strange. Care must be taken not to develop self-fulfilling prophecies that will be detriments to children.

The golden rule: don't panic! We are all exposed to many different types of influences, good and bad. Children are no different. Dealing with these influences is a part of life and growing up.

Communicating with Children About Neg Problems

When Neg problems surface, children often have no idea what to do or how to ask for help. Typically, parents are also very frightened. They go into denial, get angry, and insist children are making it all up. Children are often coerced into pretending their problems are not happening (even if they are) and into keeping things to themselves so as to not worry parents. For sleep disturbances, children are usually told to *think happy thoughts,* and they are often blamed for not doing so correctly if they still cannot sleep. This is understandable, but not very helpful. It's hard to think happy thoughts when a Neg manifestation is taking place in your bedroom. Parental denial only drives Neg problems underground and forces children to suffer in silence, which can be psychologically damaging in the long term.

Children greatly appreciate anything that is done to ease their fears. If done intelligently and in a matter-of-fact way, the basic countermeasures given in this book will not upset children. Turning on the overhead light and a radio, smudging with white sage, rubbing Tiger Balm or tea tree oil into a child's feet, and placing some incense and a few slices of garlic around a child's room (to keep away bad dreams) will not trouble their imagination. Taking a child outside and walking him/her over a hose gushing water on the ground, or taking him/her to the bathroom for an extra shower (saying this shower will wash away bad dreams) are positive actions. A child's feelings of security are always reinforced by positive adult actions.

Repetitive nightmares and night terrors, as well as sudden behavioral changes, can be symptoms of Neg interference, as will be discussed later in this chapter.

Psychic Attacks on Children

The youngest child I have seen under direct psychic attack was nine months old. At the time, several adults were in the house, but no one sensed anything out of the ordinary. The child had been having screaming fits and not slept well for several days. Numerous visits to a children's hospital and a diagnosis of colic was no help. The colic came on only at night.

The attack began soon after the child and his parents arrived at my home in the early evening. The baby was sleeping peacefully when he suddenly started screaming—face red, eyes screwed shut, fists clenched, body spasming. I vaguely sensed *something* and, with the mother's permission, picked up the baby. The child was rigid. A mild wave of tingling and light cramps in my upper back suggested Neg attack.

Everyone else in the house thought I was wrong, that the child was clearly suffering from a medical condition. Fortunately, the parents gave me the benefit of the doubt and allowed me to take action.

With the mother in tow, I took the infant outside and turned on the garden hose, gushing water on the ground. I held him by his arms and carried him across the running water, dangling him like a stiff puppet, his little feet brushing through the cool water. The *instant* we crossed the running water, he stopped screaming and went limp. I lifted a happy, yawning baby into my arms. He fell asleep within seconds, and I returned him to his mother. He slept till noon the next day, and the problem did not return. His colic problem also disappeared.

A long sleep after a Neg release is not uncommon. I have seen adults sleep for a few days after a release. Children recuperate more quickly.

I have used this running-water countermeasure many times with children and babies under direct Neg attack, always with good results. Relief is obtained the exact moment running water is crossed. Many other people have used this method on their children with similar good results.

It is worth mentioning that this baby had been *carried* across running water many times prior to what I did. The family had to walk across a water-main pipe to cross the street and enter my house. Trips to the hospital would involve numerous similar crossings in a motor vehicle. I think the ineffectiveness of those water crossings stemmed from the child being insulated by the vehicle and the mother, who was holding and nursing the child constantly. While carrying her baby to my house, for example, she held him at least three feet above the ground. .

The child's physical body must be close to the ground and/or the running water for Negs to be removed. The Neg attachment with this child was quite advanced, and he needed to physically touch the running water and thus receive strong electrical grounding for the Neg to be removed. Physically paddling through running water, as I did with this child, is more effective than just stepping over running water.

Night Terrors and Nightmares

Nightmares and night terrors are indicators that Neg-related events may be occurring. Many children experience patches of these, usually before the age of six. They can happen at later ages, but that is less common.

Nightmares: Twenty percent of children and 10 percent of adults experience nightmares. After nightmares, children should be gently questioned as to the nature of the bad dreams. They will usually involve nothing more than frightening images from movies or books, but these things could relate to core images. Rapid eye movement (REM) is always present during true nightmares, showing that the dream mind is active. The eyes are usually, *but not always,* closed during REM. The eyelids will be seen twitching rapidly. Children can be easily wakened from nightmares and will usually remember the details

Night Terrors: Also called sleep terrors, night terrors are different from nightmares. Five percent of children and 1 percent of adults suffer night terrors. With night terrors, no REM activity is present, indicating the dream mind is probably not the cause. Children may cry out, but are difficult to wake. When awakened, they are often distraught, bathed in sweat, and have a rapid heartbeat. The cause of night terrors is never remembered. While the cause of night terrors is unknown, they are often hereditary.

Incubus Nightmare: Children can experience the classic incubus nightmare, which involves sleep paralysis, great fear, difficulty in breathing, and the sense of a heavy weight on the chest. During an incubus nightmare, they will often whimper or cry out. Children should always be awakened to break the disturbance. If they cannot be easily wakened, the water-crossing countermeasure should be used. A tepid shower or bath can also be used. (According to the latest studies, it is generally safe to wake people from any sleep disturbance, including sleepwalking.)

Children should not sleep alone when they are having episodes of nightmares or night terrors. If Negs are involved, having children sleep between the parents is the best way to protect the children. If disturbances continue even in these circumstances, parents should take turns watching for a sleep disturbance and waking the child whenever one happens. Countermeasures should also be applied. Increasing lighting, burning incense, playing music, putting Tiger Balm on feet, using essential oils, and sleeping earthed are advised. Setting up the bed so it is electrically earthed is also advised. A power extension cord should also be laid around and under the bed. These countermeasures will make it easier for everyone to sleep.

Sleep Deprivation: After Neg-related bouts of nightmares and night terrors, a process of sleep deprivation will often begin. I learned what happens during this process by observing and questioning many children. I also draw on my own childhood experiences with this sleep-deprivation phenomenon.

Negs will hold children in a trancelike state throughout the night. The children's bodies appear to rest quietly, but their minds are held awake and active. During this time, they are shown a string of animated visions. Children's eyes will often be open and moving rapidly during this process (open-eyed REM). Rapid eye movement indicates dream activity, but there is more to this process than just bad dreams. Children are difficult to wake during the open-eyed REM state. They are often sweaty and have a rapid pulse. Minor phenomena, such as a creepy, heavy atmosphere, tiny pings of flashing lights, and taps on the walls and fittings and furniture, may also be noted in the room.

This sleep-deprivation process appears to be similar to military brainwashing methods, where persons are denied sleep until their minds weaken and they become highly suggestible. They can then be hypnotically reprogrammed. False memories, obsessions, and beliefs can be implanted. Personalities and behaviors can be drastically altered in a very short time.

It is wise to check children's eyes regularly during and after bouts of nightmares and night terrors. Use a small flashlight to see if their eyes are open, starting one hour after children fall asleep. If the eyes are open, children should be awakened and walked over running water or gently showered. Other countermeasures should be applied as necessary. Children should also be gently questioned about their nightmares or night terrors after being wakened, as they may remember important details concerning core images.

Even if symptoms of night terrors have not been noticed, it's a good idea to check children's eyes periodically as they sleep. Checking their eyes is especially important if there have been behavioral changes, or if children are tired and listless during the day. If children appear to be getting plenty of sleep, but are tired during the day, something is wrong. A medical checkup is also recommended to eliminate physical problems.

Head Banging and Rolling: Some children experiencing Neg problems will repeatedly bang their heads into their pillows before sleep. They lay face down and bang their foreheads into the pillows over and over. This can go on for hours. When caught doing this, children are often confused and sweaty, with a rapid pulse. Children have told me that the head banging helps stop voices, noises, and other unpleasant symptoms. Children may also roll their heads from side to side on the pillows for the same reason. Music and headphones can be a big help with this particular problem. It is also advisable to take children into your own bed and use other countermeasures as necessary when this happens.

Miscellaneous Symptoms: Night sweats, fever or coldness during sleep, bouts of frequent belching and passing gas, frequent need to urinate after bedtime, regular difficulties settling down to sleep, insomnia, oversleeping.

Implementation of Neg Controls

If the process of Neg-induced night terrors, nightmares, and sleep deprivation is successful, Negs will begin to coexist with children. This coexistence can involve intermittent overshadowing. Children will often be aware of Negs around them, seeing the Negs and/or hearing them. Negs will try to gain children's confidence by pretending to care about them while also tormenting them. This is very confusing for children.

Negs use rewards and punishments to condition children to respond to their prompting. This is the same basic conditioning Negs use on adults. Children are made to feel bad when they disobey Neg-related compulsions and to feel good when they obey. Children quickly learn to keep these things to themselves. Adults do not understand and often punish children for making up disturbing stories. Negs will continually get children into trouble by influencing them to misbehave.

Invisible Playmates

Some invisible playmates are imaginary and harmless. However, sometimes Negs will pretend to be invisible playmates, often pretending to be a child of a similar age. Whether an invisible playmate is innocent or a Neg is something for parents to ascertain. Invisible playmates should be judged by what effect they have upon children. Care is urged here as convincing children to turn away from invisible playmates can be difficult. It is like forcing children to dump playmates they like and can drive Neg problems underground. Parents are always in a better position to influence their own children than are Negs. Good parenting can do a great deal to circumvent problems that might arise from this type of association.

Behavioral Changes and Patterns to Watch For

Any sudden changes in child behavior are warning signs that something is wrong. Some Negs, once successfully attached to a child, will back off until after the child reaches puberty or adulthood. Other types of Negs will begin the process of integrating with a child's personality. When this happens, Negs can begin forming a darker side of a child's personality. Behavior will fluctuate between good and bad, and children will become more controlling and manipulative.

Children can be influenced by many sources—TV, movies, music, books, computer games, schoolmates, friends, and other family members. Dealing with these sources is a typical parenting issue. But if no reason can be found for a child's sudden behavioral changes, others causes should be explored.

Children with Neg-related problems can exhibit a wide variety of physical and behavioral problems. These problems may include the child becoming tired, listless, and withdrawn and frequently daydreaming. Children may also become cruel, selfish, emotionally demanding, manipulative, aggressive, and even violent. They may also show signs of obsessive-compulsive disorder (OCD) and a variety of other psychological problems, including depression, attention deficit, and hyperactivity disorders.

It's not the behavior in itself, but the sudden changes that can indicate Neg problems. If a normally kind child suddenly becomes cruel, or if a normally placid, cooperative child suddenly becomes hyperactive and stubborn, this behavior may indicate Neg influences.

Children exhibiting adult behavior—using adult language, exhibiting adult reactions and behaviors that are too sophisticated for their age—is a strong indicator of Neg influences.

One of the most common Neg-related symptoms (for adults and for children) is the urge to control others. Children under Neg influences often become bossy, controlling, and critical of others. They will often prefer to play with younger children, because these children are easy to manipulate.

Children's ability to withstand pain and punishment can increase dramatically under Neg influences. Their willingness to risk facing serious consequences for their behavior can also increase. They may have only a limited sense of right and wrong, honesty and dishonesty. It becomes more a matter of what they can get away with.

While the above symptoms can all have natural causes, they are also indicators of possible Neg interference. If some of the above-given symptoms, including nightmares, come on suddenly, a well-known psychological profile can begin to appear. These are the classic symptoms of child abuse, but in this case, the abusers are Negs. Psychological pressures and abuses from any source have well-known consequences for children.

Once children's Neg problems have been identified, you will begin to notice patterns of behavior. The children will experience mood swings and behavioral changes at predictable times. Prime times are when children are getting ready for something, such as school, bedtime, mealtimes, or outings. It is almost as though children are deliberately trying to cause unhappy, stressful situations by making parents late. Children may also throw tantrums over particular things or at particular times. This is attention-getting behavior and also behavioral training of the parents.

I have seen hungry children fall into trance, change personality, and completely lose their appetites within moments of sitting down to dinner.

I have seen children throw hysterical tantrums around the same time every night. Eventually, everyone tippy-toes around children, trying not to trigger more episodes. The atmosphere is tense, and the children seem to look for reasons to explode. When they do, they can rage and cry inconsolably for hours until they fall asleep. Their rooms are often trashed, and they will blame everyone else for it being that way.

Such children seem to have an excuse for everything. "You made me do it!" is a common excuse. The world is against them, and anything that happens to them is always someone else's fault. Doing simple things, like getting dressed, brushing teeth, going to bed, and doing homework, can become inordinately difficult.

If a child under Neg influence has a chore, like washing dishes, getting him or her to do it can be a nightmare for parents. The child may literally take hours to do a simple load of dishes that should take no more than ten minutes. He or she will cry and complain and cause arguments and break things—anything to make the experience painful for the parents. If parents leave the room, the child will cheat by piling unwashed dishes onto the draining board, or just walk away. Eventually, the parents stop asking the child to do anything because it is just too much trouble. The child wins, and parents are trained. Taken to extremes, this training can lead to children becoming totally uncontrollable. When such children grow into adults, their abnormal behavior will often continue.

I have seen cases where children sleep only in front of the TV, eat only fast food, never brush their teeth, and rarely shower or wear clean clothes. If a desired food is not provided, they will often go without food for many days, to punish parents and get what they want. Parents give into their children's demands in cases like this because they are frightened by their children's behavior (their ability to go without food). Such children will do *anything* to exert control and get what they want. Normal parenting tactics will not work in this situation, because parents are not dealing with normal children. An adult-minded Neg in control of a child is an extremely disturbing situation.

These types of problems are usually minor to start with, but will escalate and become habitual if left unattended. Consistent, intelligent parenting can do a lot to turn around bad situations. A long-term approach is best. Children cannot be allowed to win a battle of wills with parents. It is also wise to seek the help of a good child psychologist, if only to witness and validate that what is happening is abnormal.

Overshadowing in Children

Children undergoing Neg-related abuse and sleep deprivation are particularly vulnerable to overshadowing. Overshadowing is most likely to happen when children are mentally inactive and/or tired. It will often happen while they are watching TV or eating dinner, both of which are activities requiring little mental activity. Family dinners also provide an audience, which overshadowing Negs seem to like.

When episodes of overshadowing start, children go suddenly quiet as they slide into a trancelike state. Their eyes and facial muscles droop, and they stare fixedly for a short time. Then they take a deep breath and straighten up, as if waking themselves. Their facial aspects alter slightly, their eye color darkens, and an indefinable shadow falls over their faces. From this moment on, such children are capable of anything, because they are no longer in full control. They may move, walk, talk, and respond very differently from normal.

When parents recognize the symptoms of approaching overshadowing, they can intervene and stop it before it takes hold. Swift action is needed. Make sudden loud noises to get the child's attention, leap up and tickle them, drag them into a shower—do anything that will break the overshadowing. In a way, children fall asleep when they are overshadowed, so this action is to wake them up and keep them awake.

It is important that parents do not abuse their children during or after overshadowing episodes. Children are innocent. It is also wise never to let Negs know that their presence is known. If Negs know that they have been detected, then the gloves can come off, and the situation can get a whole lot worse.

It should be kept in mind that if Negs can overshadow children while children are awake, they are most certainly doing much more while children are in bed or asleep. So it is wise to use appropriate countermeasures in children's bedrooms to make life as difficult as possible for Negs.

Neg-Abuse and Overshadowing Example

I witnessed a classic case of overshadowing and child abuse by a Neg while helping a family. Their five-year-old son had recently been through the whole spectrum of Neg invasion and conditioning symptoms—night terrors, presleep problems, sleep deprivation, open-eyed REM, head banging, mood swings, sleepwalking, behavioral changes. He had a history of paranormal activity happening around him. I had known this family for a couple of years and witnessed some major poltergeist activity at times while I was in the family's house.

The child was very sweet, but he made my skin crawl whenever he came near me. The parents admitted to feeling the same. (A sensitive's skin will often prickle with revulsion when a Neg-controlled child moves close to him/her. This reaction can also happen between parent and child. This problem may come and go according to the strength of a Neg presence at the time.)

The boy had developed some dangerous habits. He would pour his drinks into electrical appliances when no one was watching, and he would suck on the ends of power extension cords. No matter where he was, he would find something electrical to mess with. He had destroyed many appliances and had received several electric shocks as a result. It was a miracle he had not killed himself. At night, he had to be locked in his room with a security screen on the window. All power outlets in his room were disabled. This may sound extreme, and illegal, but there were no other options.

The boy's father knew there was a paranormal problem, which is why he asked for my help. He had been trying to break his son of these dangerous habits with consistent discipline. All reasoning and positive reinforcement methods had failed, as had other consequences. Every time the boy interfered with an electrical device or sucked on a power cord, his father told him off and smacked him. But this punishment was not working. His parents had run out of solutions.

While I was there, the boy was caught red-handed, sucking on the end of a power extension cord. The father yelled at him, took the power cord away, and smacked him hard on the back of his hand. The father forcefully explained, once again, how dangerous chewing on power cords was to the boy. But before his father had left the room, the boy had the end of the cord back in his mouth and was giggling and grinning defiantly at his father. I saw the back of the boy's hand glowing red from the smack, so I know it must have hurt. His father repeated the warning and smacked the boy even harder. This happened several times in a row, until the boy's forearm and hand were all red with the smacking.

Finally, the father stood over the boy, hand raised, and glared at him with full fatherly force and volume. It was then I witnessed the clearest case of overshadowing I have ever seen. A titanic battle raged within the boy. His eyes, facial aspects, and expression changed every few seconds.

He switched from a scared little boy nursing a hurt arm to something that glared at his father with a sickening grin as it reached for the power cord again. But before he could touch it, he would change back and retract his hand, tears gushing. He changed back and forth a dozen times or more, battling the Neg influence.

Finally, the human side of the boy won the battle, folded his arms, and cried profusely. His father, sensing what had happened, picked him up and cuddled him. A short time later, the body was playing happily as if nothing had happened. He did not remember the confrontation or why his arm hurt.

The next episode of overshadowing I witnessed with this boy came a few days later at dinner. We had all just sat down to a dinner of spaghetti bolognaise (the boy's favorite) when it happened. I watched as the boy's head drooped and his eyes flickered, and his face darkened as he was quickly overshadowed. He then took a deep breath and glared at his father with a defiant grin. With deliberate actions, he picked up and upended his plate of spaghetti over his own head and rubbed it into himself. He then threw handfuls of spaghetti at his father, making a loud, guttural noise with each throw. On my advice, the father responded by holding his son under a cold shower, clothes and all. This countermeasure worked and not long after, the boy was happily watching TV and eating a spaghetti sandwich. I questioned the boy, and he had no memory of what had happened. He thought we were joking with him. He was well behaved for the rest of the evening.

Another typical overshadowing behavior exhibited by this boy was that he spied on his parents. He would eavesdrop, peek through keyholes and windows, and listen at doors to adult conversations. If he heard anyone talking about him, he would sometimes fly into a rage and start throwing things. While I was at the family's house late one evening, talking with his parents, we heard a noise. The boy was hiding underneath the nearby dining table, listening to us. When he was dragged out from under the table, he was disoriented and sleepy. His parents said he had invaded their adult privacy many times. He had even been caught spying on them from outside their bedroom window late at night. This was part of the reason why they locked him in his room at night.

I would like to say that the above situation is rare, but I have encountered many similar cases over the years since then. The description of my work with this family continues in the next chapter.

Mystery Maladies

Children's mystery maladies are common Neg-related conditions. These apparently serious medical conditions suddenly arise in the middle of the night, but disappear while the child and his/her parents are on the way to hospital. Most parents are familiar with this scenario: A child wakes at 2 a.m., screaming in pain, often with a high fever. Parents rush the child to a hospital, only to find themselves presenting a healthy, sleepy child to the emergency-room doctor.

Mystery maladies can present a variety of severe symptoms—earaches, stomachaches, sore throats, headaches, asthma attacks, toothaches, colic, croup—any of which may be accompanied by fevers high enough to panic any parent. If a condition disappears rapidly when the child is on the way to hospital, it's a fair indicator that the child is being interfered with by Negs during sleep, and appropriate action should be considered.

The main reason mystery maladies disappear so quickly is that water-main pipes get crossed many times along the way to the hospital. As established earlier, crossing water-main pipes in this way removes lightly attached Negs and/or disrupts whatever energy body interference is causing the child's illness symptoms. I have witnessed this phenomenon countless times over the years. I have also seen my own children go through it many times.

The first few times this happened to my son, we quickly dosed him with pain-and-fever reducing medication and rushed him to the hospital, only to find ourselves presenting a healthy child to the emergency-room doctor. This happened a few times. It was not long before I realized what was really happening, and after I did, I used running-water countermeasures before giving my son medication or driving to the hospital. Every time, without exception, the symptoms—earaches, croup, stomachaches—stopped instantly, and the fevers disappeared within a few minutes.

Croup is a particularly strange malady. It is technically caused by an upper-airway virus, but it mainly occurs at night. Croup causes raspy breathing and a cough that sounds like a seal barking. It will normally last several days. Many times I have seen croup disappear after the child has crossed running water; with the croup symptoms last only minutes. Any malady that heals this rapidly after exposure to running water is likely to be Neg related.

I am not suggesting parents delay seeking necessary medical attention for their children. But I do recommend parents walk or carry children over running water (a water main or garden hose gushing water on the ground) on the way to the car and that they then recheck their child's condition before leaving for the hospital. Alternatively, give the child a quick lukewarm shower first. A shower will do the same thing as a garden hose, as well as helping to reduce a child's fever.

Electromagnetic pollution can also contribute to children's mystery maladies. It is wise to check the positioning of electronic equipment and electrical fittings to see if these are causing problems. Rearranging a child's bedroom and moving the bed to a new position may help.

COUNTERING NEG-RELATED BEHAVIORAL PATTERNS

When Neg-related behavior patterns are identified, aim to counter them as soon as possible. While the countermeasures will help, behavioral retraining takes time, effort, and consistent parenting.

A good start is to identify problem times and situations, and to plan in advance how to make things go smoothly. For example, prepare dinner half an hour earlier than usual, and set aside more time to supervise children getting ready for school and outings. Change bedtimes and procedures so that everything goes well and there is plenty of time, so that potential problems are lessened.

Keep children busy and engaged. Get them involved in the running of the home and family life, as opposed to using TV and computer games as babysitters. Being engaged in conversation with adults has a powerful effect on children. When children are engaged in positive ways, Neg influences are less likely to happen.

Mealtimes are important for family communication and bonding. Turn off the TV and radio while you eat as a family. Use this time to talk, exchange stories, and share as a family. Take turns around the table to talk and share news. For some, the evening meal is the only time when family can be together. Take advantage of this opportunity to improve family connections.

Watching a lot of TV can allow Neg influences to thrive, because it is a passive activity that does not require much mental activity. Many people, adults and children, slip into trancelike states while watching TV. Watching TV has become a socially acceptable excuse to ignore everyone else. If Neg influences are at work, overshadowing and behavioral problems can result. The TV problem is easily fixed. Turn off the TV and put on music the children like. Dance and sing and play with them. Read them stories, go for walks, play games, get some energy going that requires family activity and togetherness. Stimulate children's minds in positive ways. Mental stimulation and activity helps a great deal.

Bedtime is a big deal for children. Get some art and craft supplies, and have each child make a fancy bedtime clock with movable hands. Then hang the clocks high on the wall in the main family area. Work out a system where stars are given for good behavior, for doing chores and being nice—all the things children need to do every day. If the children earn enough stars, bedtimes can be extended in five-minute increments up to a half an hour. The reverse would also apply, and bad behavior means an earlier bedtime. Have other rewards available that children can work towards. I have seen this system work many times, and children love it. Parents just need to be consistent. Children like to know their boundaries. It makes them feel safe. And it's nice to be rewarded for being good.

Children are children only for a very short time. Spending more quality time with them is worth the effort. They will all too soon become teenagers with infinite knowledge and then adults with their own families.

Ideally, no harsh words or arguments should ever happen inside the family home. This generates negative energy. Go outside to settle disputes.

I have used these simple methods in families with serious Neg problems. These actions lift the home atmosphere and improve harmony. The positive, loving atmosphere of a home builds up and provides a natural family shield. These things will not in themselves completely solve Neg problems, but they will help a great deal and reduce the damage that Negs might otherwise cause.

Neg-Affected Children

Neg issues seem to be a natural part of the human condition. Neg-human interactions and relationships have always existed. What can happen when children are exposed to Neg interference is difficult to predict. This depends on so many factors, including parenting, family lifestyle, and the child's natural strengths and weaknesses. Everyone is different, and while typical patterns can be observed, every situation unfolds differently. Some children will grow and fight their way out of these types of problems and grow stronger, and some do not do so well.

Negs can form a dark side to anyone's personality. This dark side is, in turn, opposed by the many positive influences to which people are exposed. More than anything, good parenting and parent-child communications can do much to counter the effects of Neg abuse and interference. Parents are in much stronger positions than Negs are to influence the development of their children.

A good analogy here is to imagine that children have little angels on their right shoulders (whispering encouragement and right action) and little devils on their left shoulders (whispering discouragement and wrong action). With wise, consistent parenting in support, these opposing influences will at least create a balance. The struggle between positive and negative forces is the natural way of things. The interaction between these forces cause change and growth to occur.

The advice and countermeasures given in this book can do a lot to ease and even remove children's Neg-related problems. Breaking the initial attachment process, such as when night terrors and sleep deprivation begin, is the most effective way to help children grow up Neg free. Negs have a window of opportunity, a few years while children are vulnerable. If Neg activities are recognized and countered early, Neg attachment will not take place. It is much more difficult for Negs to invade and attach to them as adults.

It is commonly believed that if people live good lives, they are invulnerable to Neg problems and influences. However, the evidence contradicts this belief. Like may attract like, but opposites also attract. Saints and holy persons are well known to frequently experience serious Neg attacks. Spiritual development and purity can attract negative forces and entities. This testing provides natural resistance to spiritual progress.

Diagnosis of Neg problems is difficult, and you should never jump to conclusions. Most especially, never blame children for Neg-related problems. Children have no control over these matters. Children change as they grow, and they will experiment with changes in personality and behavior. But if you know your child, you will know what is normal and what is unusual. Trust your parental instincts to fill in the gaps.

Countermeasures for Children

All the countermeasures given earlier for adults can be used with children. However, there are a few modifications and some additional countermeasures particular to children's needs. Some of these modified and additional countermeasures can also be applied to adult problems.

RUNNING WATER AND GROUNDING

Running-water and electrical-grounding methods are the main lines of defense. Use these immediately if you suspect a Neg problem. These methods are totally safe. They should be employed first while other countermeasures are considered. Negs are weakest when they first arrive on the scene, and the powerful effects of running water and electrical grounding will remove them.

Some people cannot accept that something as simple as running water and electrical grounding can help. Others are afraid of the implications of accepting supernatural possibilities. To overcome these resistances and get help for children with Neg problems, I have often told people that children can develop excess static electricity in their bodies and that walking children through running water removes it. These statements are at least partly truthful. I also say that exposing children to running water and simple electrical grounding often cures night terrors and other sleep-related problems for the same reason. I have been praised by parents for this explanation. These same parents would never accept the idea of Neg problems.

Babies can be carried over running water. A garden hose gushing water along the ground is all that is required. When using the hose method, I dangle babies and very small children by the arms and walk them through the running water itself, touching their feet in the water as I carry them across it. If the weather makes using a garden hose difficult, this running-water method can be done in a bathtub or shower, with the taps running warm water. Remember, the greater the volume and velocity of running water, the bigger the anti-Neg effect. So if the method fails at first, increase the water volume and exposure time.

The shower plus imagination method given earlier can be adapted for children and babies, as can the use of a garden hose coiled multiple times. Parents can perform the visualization after placing children among the loops of coiled hose, under the shower, or in the running water of bathtub taps. If children are old enough to understand, try to get them to help with imagining the electric-violet light. (Use another color if electric violet is too difficult for them to imagine.) Make a game of it. Children love imagination games.

Normally, a direct Neg attack will cease the instant running water is crossed. Remember that the Neg may wait on the other side of the hose.

Throwing a loop of hose over the place where the child crossed the hose can trap the Neg and allow safe passage back into the home. (A Neg will always be opposite its intended target and will follow its target up and down the hose length.) The hose can be closed and gushed with water to demanifest the Neg afterwards.

Some innovation is required to trap and demanifest Negs in a bathroom. Find some way of placing a hose of running water across the bathroom door, so that when the child steps over it, the Neg will be left behind. The bathroom can then be sprayed with water, or buckets of water sloshed over the floor to demanifest the trapped Neg.

If Neg attachments are firmly entrenched within children over a long time, the attachment moves beyond the point where simple exposure to running water and grounding will work. In this case, a setup for sleeping earthed will be required to drain the Neg away. The strongest setup would be to have children sleep within a fine-mesh Faraday cage, on electrically grounded bedding, surrounded by moist air; a humidifier will help. Given time, this setup will remove just about anything, but other countermeasures will need to be employed as necessary.

Some Neg controlled children will not allow themselves to be exposed to running-water and electrical-grounding countermeasures. Some parental cunning and trickery may be required to enforce this exposure.

Placing children between the parents in their bed is a strong countermeasure for most nocturnal Neg problems. The energy bodies of the parents enfold the children, and Negs have to go through the parents to get at the children. The family bond also causes energy bodies to connect and flow together, which is strengthening and shielding. Some Negs may continue an attack under these unfavorable conditions, but this is rare. Most parents can handle a few cold shivers and a negative atmosphere, which is preferable to having a child face them alone.

If disturbance continues, use other countermeasures as necessary, like turning on overhead lights, burning incense, playing soft music, rubbing Tiger Balm on everyone's feet, and placing garlic and saltwater around the bed. These countermeasures will ease the atmosphere considerably.

If Neg activity continues, it is time for everyone to cross a garden hose or take showers, and then to have late-night snacks, while the bedroom is fumigated with lots of incense. Eating will help. If the room is still too creepy, sleep in the living room with the TV on and playing something happy, such as Disney cartoon movies.

Detaching a Neg completely so it does not return may take weeks or months, depending on the situation, so please give the countermeasures time to work. When countering Negs, there is no single solution. Every situation is different. Combinations of countermeasures and tactics are needed.

To reduce fear levels, parents need to be positive and matter of fact. Remember, your energy goes where your attention goes; you don't want to feed Negs and make them stronger. Facing scary things together as a family and supporting each other will help considerably with the level of fear involved. Most of the fear stems from dealing with the unknown and the supernatural. When you get used to these things, however, they are more annoying than scary. Being annoyed is preferable to being scared.

In my home, the slightest negative atmosphere, chill, or phenomenon is immediately countered with the lighting of several sticks of incense and the playing of spiritual music. If the atmosphere survives these countermeasures, we break out the censer and essential-oil misting sprays. Affirmations, commands, electric violet fire, and banishments soon follow. It is rare that a Neg atmosphere will survive this process for long.

LIGHT, MUSIC, AND NOISE

Many Neg-related children's problems can be overcome using light, music, and noise.

Leave on overhead lights or bedside lamps if children want them. Modern electronic bulbs are cheap to run, and nightlights are generally too dim to be of much help reducing the scare factor.

Noise-making devices will help break up negative atmospheres in children's rooms. Drums and cymbals, trumpets, sports whistles, even pots and pans banged together—anything that makes loud noises—will help. This approach should be used with bright light whenever a Neg atmosphere is first noticed, to break it up and reduce its creepy effects. Employing sounds and light is a positive action that parents can take and that children will see and appreciate. It should be explained to children that these things help drive scary things away. Do not be surprised, though, if at times you are woken by your children doing these things for themselves in the middle of the night. Being woken up is a small price to pay for peace of mind.

You can play music softly through the night. Pick something children like, such as soundtracks from animated children's movies, like *The Hunchback of*

Notre Dame, The Little Mermaid, and *The Lion King.* Playing the soundtrack of a cartoon movie children know and love will transport their minds into the theme of the movie, keeping children's minds occupied and away from paranormal phenomena. A full audio recording of a movie, including dialogue and not just the songs, is the best for this purpose.

If a child still senses a bad atmosphere or hears disturbing noises, place the source of music closer to him or her. Pillow speakers, ear buds, or headphones are good for this. MP3 CD players are another good option. Many children (and adults) overcome serious Neg problems in this way.

Get your children to alert you if they have a spooky problem and are too scared to get out of bed. Give them flashlights, whistles, or bells with which to call for help. A baby monitor can also help them communicate with you. Just knowing they can talk to Mom and Dad at any time will help children feel safe and sleep better.

MAKING CHANGES TO A CHILD'S ROOM

When decorating a child's room, a bright, harmonious, nonfrightening ambience should be the goal. There should be no dark corners. Some children think it's cool to have pictures of monsters on their walls, but these can trigger negative mental associations and cause nightmares, which Negs can use. Be firm and say no to these. Find some nice, positive pictures instead.

Use bright pastel colors. Keep the room clean and tidy. This is no easy task, knowing children, but it's worth the effort to counter potential Neg problems.

Place pictures of angels, unicorns, and other positive things around the child's room. Tell the child these things will help ward off bad dreams. Children generally love having these items around them. If children are worried what their friends might think, these pictures can be put away before visitors arrive.

BEDTIME AFFIRMATIONS AND PRAYERS

Teach children to do affirmations and to pray aloud for protection at bedtime. Explain that prayers help keep them safe. The prayers can be very simple, like writing a wish list to God. If your family is religious, using something you believe in will help.

The Core Affirmation is suitable for children and should also be used. Get children to memorize it and advise them to repeat it—verbally, if possible—whenever they are frightened: "I am loved and I am worthy.

I am safe and I am free. I am powerfully protected. I am master of my body and ruler of my mind."

Like incense, prayers and affirmations have residual effects. They sink into the environment and the mind with frequent use.

Get children to decide what they want to dream about and to state their desires before sleep: "I choose to dream about horses." "I choose to dream about flying." Children love doing this, and it will affect their dreams. Teach children to use commands and to take control of their mind's eye imagery, to remove scary images and thoughts from their minds: "I choose not to see that." "I choose to see unicorns."

Mind and Memories

On the unconscious level, the human mind never forgets anything. Conscious recallable memory may fade with time, but the unconscious mind remembers everything. Every moment of life is recorded. Every image and word and experience is recalled perfectly. Everything you put into your mind stays in your mind.

Your memory is a big part of who you are. So ideally, you only want to store high-quality experiences in your memory. Fear-inducing, unsavory, and poor-quality experience memories should be actively avoided. It might seem like fun to watch an occasional coarse movie with violence and cussing, but would you choose for the movie's harsh images and words to become a part of you?

In particular, what you see, hear, read, and experience immediately before sleep has a big effect on your sleeping and dreaming. Reading half a page of uplifting prose or verse, or listening to or watching something amazing, will affect your dreams that night. This factor is particularly important for children, who are far more impressionable than adults.

Helping Infants

It can be difficult to tell if infants are suffering Neg abuse, because they cannot communicate with words. The usual symptoms are sudden screaming, babies' bodies going rigid and not responding well to feeding, diaper changing, or cuddling. In this case, exposing the baby to grounded running water as soon as possible is advised. If this has no effect, then you know you have a physical problem and can take appropriate action.

Remember, the water needs to be electrically grounded for best effect. A running tap provides grounding through the water pipe.

Babies can be effectively grounded by holding their feet under a tap running water. A garden hose gushing water on the ground is even more effective for removing Negs. When the hose is crossed and the baby's feet touch to the water, the Neg is left on the other side of the hose. It can then be trapped by throwing a loop of hose over it and demanifested by gushing water into the loop.

Again, the above can be done in an apartment bathroom, but you will need a garden hose. You can get hand shower hose attachments—the type that allow you to wash your hair in a sink—that will fit over a standard tap. A garden hose attached to this fitting can then be used. It will then be possible to carry out running-water methods in a bathroom. Remember, hoses should be empty before babies are placed into looped hose areas or over many coils. Once the babies are in place, you can turn on the tap and run water through the hose and out into a drain. (Make sure the outer coils of the hose fill first.)

Disturbed infant sleep can indicate Neg interference. Babies are very psychically and emotionally sensitive. They do not settle well if there are negative atmospheres around them. Just being around upset parents can cause babies to be unsettled and to not sleep well. A strong Neg presence is unsettling for adults; however, if a Neg presence is *focused* on a baby, parents may sense nothing unusual.

Dietary intolerances can be another symptom of Neg interference; children may stop eating or develop allergies or peculiar tastes. Sudden pain that results in screaming fits; strange infections that come on quickly; repeated jerking and/or sudden frequent waking, as if the baby were being jabbed or pricked; and head banging and rolling are other symptoms.

If you suspect Neg interference, immediately employ appropriate countermeasures— grounded running water, light, incense, salt. Before using Tiger Balm or other ointments on a baby, test them on a small area of baby's foot, in case there is a bad reaction. Tiger Balm and ointments can be diluted with petroleum jelly or baby oil. Camphor and fresh herbs can also be put in a cloth bag and placed near a baby's feet. A string of sandalwood beads will also help, but it should be placed under the crib sheets, so the beads cannot be swallowed accidentally.

If babies show any signs of being disturbed—even if they only have gas, are teething, or are generally unsettled—it does not hurt to expose them to running water and grounding just to be sure. This is a good test. Trust your intuition and always err on the safe side. It is wise to not take chances and to use countermeasures as a matter of course. A setup for sleeping earthed, frequent exposure to grounded running water, Neg-deterrent herbs and scents, potpourris, music, light, ointment on the feet, sleeping with Mom—all of these will do no harm and can make all the difference. This approach will stop Neg problems before they can take hold.

Parents need to be careful not to jump to conclusions and see Neg problems where there are none, which can create a self-fulfilling prophecy and a lot of needless worry.

Negs and Family Life

The advice I offer here is fundamental to all Neg problems, psychic influences, and attacks involving groups of people. However, it mainly applies to families with Neg problems.

A family is like a closed environment. Neg influences and activities are magnified within it. But because they are magnified, Neg strategies can also be more easily recognized. Families are interconnected with strong emotional bonds and subtle energy links. Nonverbal communications flow through these links. Negs use these links to manipulate family members and to turn them against one another, creating widespread disharmony and unhappiness, often out of nothing. This disharmony and unhappiness will affect everyone and generate negative energy. The home atmosphere needs to be nurtured. Positive energy can be generated through laughter and expressions of love and compassion.

If Negs succeed in attaching to one family member, they will try to spread their influences to others. Everyone in a family is vulnerable. Everyone sleeps. Following is a typical example of how this works.

Take one happy family just before dinnertime. Some people call this "Acid Hour" because it stings. This is when arguments and upsets are most likely to break out.

Mom is busy preparing dinner, Dad is trying to watch the news on TV and the children are hungry and squabbling. This is a recipe for disaster.

The Negs start with the weakest links: the children. Two children start fighting loudly. Mom's busy cooking, but tuned into what's happening.

She starts to get annoyed. The Neg switches to Mom, pushing her to over-react. The father tries to quiet things down, already annoyed at having his peace interrupted. The Neg switches to him and pushes him to overreact. He yells at the children. The mother, protecting her children, turns on her husband while dinner burns on the stove. The Neg has played the family like puppets, one against the other, creating the worst possible domestic argument.

The evening is ruined for everyone. Everyone is upset, even the dog. The children have bad dreams, and the parents sleep apart. It may take weeks for a loving family home atmosphere to be restored. Just imagine what happens to a family where this kind of thing is a daily event. This atmosphere creates a living hell that often ends in divorce and heartbreak for all.

I have watched Neg-besieged families go through scenarios like this many times. I have seen clouds of dark dots (like swarms of flies—a typical Neg manifestation) moving from person to person, spreading discord wherever they touch. If these energies are allowed to proceed unchecked, creepier and more serious Neg-related phenomena will often follow, including multiple overshadowing.

"United we stand and divided we fall." A family must communicate and work together to overcome Neg influences. Everyone must agree and cooperate in countering Neg influences. Family connections can be made to work for the family unit instead of against it. Family members need to work together, recognizing and countering Neg influences as they arise, and regrouping quickly after a problem. Forgiveness and compassion and contrition are key. Family members should watch over and warn each other of behavioral changes, and there should be agreed-upon procedures and workarounds ready for dealing with situations before problems escalate. A positive change should be made as soon as bad behavior is noticed in anyone. One child misbehaving is a warning beacon that parents need to notice. Immediate action and change will stop this misbehavior spreading.

When children have Neg problems, adults should realize that they will also be influenced. Adults need to observe their own behavior and moods carefully. Parents, especially, need to work together and monitor each other's behaviors.

Anyone who believes they are above Neg influences is kidding themselves. Neg influences are subtle and insidious. They are rarely noticed when they start. It is only in hindsight that odd behavior will be seen as odd. It can also be difficult to admit that one has behaved badly. Honesty, contrition, and openness are powerful anti-Neg weapons.

Family interactions are fairly predictable, and Negs use this predictability to plan ahead and create stressful situations. Negs are not good at adapting to change, so it pays to be spontaneous and a little on the crazy side when countering Neg influences. For example, Dad can turn off the TV and pay attention to the children, occupying them by chatting and playing with them ("Okay kids, who wants to learn how to play poker?"). Or Dad could finish cooking dinner while Mom plays with the children. One parent could take the children out for a game of ball or to walk the dog—crossing many underground water-main pipes in the process.

Do Something Else

One simple Neg countermeasure is to watch less TV. Watching TV is generally bad for family harmony when Negs are around. Television turns a family unit into a loose-knit collection of preoccupied, semientranced individuals. In this state, family members are more exposed to Neg influences. A family that is active and engaged with each other, even if they are just playing cards or board games, is far less exposed.

I have yet to see Negs bring down a strong, happy family atmosphere where this advice is being actively applied. A strong positive atmosphere full of spontaneity and humor can overcome any negative influence. If you can generate and spread happiness and laughter among children, something like a humorous exorcism takes place, effectively driving Negs away. Keep it up, and they will eventually stay away.

Limit Discussion of Negs

Most Negs can understand human speech and thoughts, so it is generally wise not to discuss Neg problems and countermeasures when one might be overheard. Go for a walk or a drive to have discussions about these matters. Walking or driving also involves crossing many water-main pipes (running water), and this will make things difficult for any Negs that might be trying to follow and eavesdrop.

When you must mention Neg problems in the home, paraphrase. Instead of calling them *Negs,* refer to them by alternate names you have agreed upon, like "the bad neighbors" or "the gribblies." Change the terms regularly in case Negs catch on. For example, say, "The bad neighbors are noisy tonight. Let's take the kids for a drive and get sodas until the house smells better." This means: "Negs are active. Let's fumigate the house while we go for a drive."

With all Neg-related stuff, be very careful with whom you share information. Some people will pretend interest and sincerity, only to ridicule you later. I have known many families to develop social problems because they weren't cautious about talking to others about Neg experiences. Some have been reported to child-welfare departments and police for alleged child abuse. Some have had to move and change schools. They had to take such drastic measures because other people were concerned about what seemed like crazy, outlandish ideas and dangerous, cultlike religious beliefs. Most so-called normal people cannot handle real supernatural problems.

WHOLESOME FAMILY LIFESTYLE
The home and family lifestyle, as well as the family's visitors and associates, play a part in whether or not Neg-related problems will arise. Consider your children's friends and playmates. Children's exposure to Neg-carrying people is a common cause of Neg problems. As any parent knows, bad company equals bad influences. Children quickly pick up bad traits and habits—and Neg influences—from other children.

Allowing children to associate with badly behaved, unsavory, and undisciplined children is an easy way for them to pick up Neg hitchhikers. Bad associations can be countered by good parental advice. Discourage bad associations and encourage good ones, and teach children to discern the difference for themselves.

People with lifestyle problems, such as substance abuse, personality disorders, and mental illness, should also be avoided. Protect the family home from anyone that might bring negativity into it.

Again, never allow arguments inside your home; go outside to settle disputes. Cultivate the home as a spiritual haven, free of disharmony and strife, as a sanctuary for children and parents alike. This sounds like a tall order, but can be done if everyone works together.

Core-Image Work for Children

Children of language age can be guided through core-image work. This work can be desensationalized by being explained in a nonfrightening way. All children are great with imagination, so explain that the images they might see are not real, but of their imagination. Tell them that getting rid of these images will help get rid of bad pieces of their own imagination that might be causing them to experience creepy atmospheres and bad dreams.

By gently talking children through the core-image treatment process, you, as a parent, can direct the flow of events and boost your child's courage until he or she feels confident enough to do the process solo. Introducing them to the process gives children tools with which they can help themselves when you are not around. Children usually want something a little more elaborate than a mere sword and a blowtorch. Laser swords, rocket launchers, and fire-breathing dragons—whatever makes them happy will work.

First, talk with children and make a list of potential core-image scenarios. These should relate to any bad real-life experiences, as well as bad dreams or disturbing thoughts and fantasies the children have been having. Next, talk them through a basic relaxation process with their eyes closed. Have them take several slow, deep breaths, while they focus on *feeling* the rise and fall of their stomachs as they breathe. When they are settled, continue with the following core-image treatment process.

Describe one of the scenarios that you took note of earlier. Pick something small for starters—say, a schoolyard argument. Get them to relive the experience. Get them to shrink this scenario to postcard size and then grab it with their body-awareness hands and turn it over. Get them to chop this postcard scenario up with a sword, then burn away the pieces with electric-violet fire or other suitable color. Get them to repeat the Core Affirmation. Then gently bring them back to full wakefulness. (Encourage children to memorize the Core Affirmation and use it whenever they are disturbed by bad thoughts, feelings or dreams.)

It can help if children act out the shrinking and turning of the postcard-sized image physically, with their eyes closed. Get them to reach out wide with their real arms, shrink the image, and then turn it over. (Adults can also do this if they have problems with body-awareness actions.)

CHILD CORE-IMAGE CASE HISTORY
A mother was concerned about her eight-year-old son's behavioral problems. She had been learning meditation and practicing core-image work on herself, and she wanted to use these things to help her son.

While he was taking a nap on her lap, she focused on him, visualizing his image with all the thoughts and emotions she felt about him. As the image of her son appeared in her mind, she attempted to shrink and turn this image over to see what was behind his behavioral problems. The image would not budge, so she tried another method, tearing strips away from the surface of the image. After several minutes of effort, the image of her son vanished, and a startlingly clear vision of a beer bottle appeared. The mother was shocked, as the image showed her regular brand of beer.

At this moment, she had an epiphany. She realized that she had a drinking problem and that this was what was causing her son's problems. She attacked the image with the cleansing technique given earlier in the book. She then sought professional help and set about changing her life. In time, her son's behavioral problems were resolved.

The moral of the above real-life story is that some things are not what they seem. Often, we are the cause of our own problems. Also keep in mind that your higher self will work through whatever means are available. Core-image work provides an opening for this help to manifest. The saying "God helps those who help themselves" is very apt here.

In this chapter we have taken a good look at Neg-related problems and how they can affect children and the home environment. In the next chapter, we look more deeply into overshadowing and possession.

CHAPTER NINE

Possession and Release

Core Affirmation: "I am loved and I am worthy. I am safe and I am free. I am powerfully protected. I am master of my body and ruler of my mind"

Our modern, materialistic world does not recognize possession for what it is. It is mostly written off as mental illness or personality disorder. But this dark malady is a fairly common part of the human condition. It has always has been. A person can be controlled or *possessed* by a nonphysical personality or by another living person. The term *possession* carries a lot of ugly baggage and is poorly understood. It sparks images of red-eyed lunatics running amok, but possession itself does not mean insanity or total loss of control. Possessed people are usually not insane, and they behave normally most of the time.

Possessing entities can be ex-human ghosts, hereditary attachments, or nonhuman Negs. (Possessing nonphysical personalities can also include positive spirits, even angels, but these are beyond the focus of this book.) Possession is just the mechanism of control. There are many degrees of this control, ranging from influence to obsession to full control and personality replacement.

Typically, possession involves a progressive implementation of Neg controls over a period of time. Most people have natural resistance and shielding against this implementation. Negs are attracted to psychically and emotionally sensitive people with poor or damaged shielding. Negs have to overcome natural defenses in order to implement attachments and controls. The length of time this takes depends on the strength and experience of the Neg and the strengths and weaknesses of the person involved. A typical Neg can take months or years to establish significant levels of control. Stronger and more experienced Negs can possess people far more quickly.

Neg influences will fluctuate, and their manifestations will seem like the darker side of a personality. These manifestations are often diagnosed as bad moods or personality disorders, which are accurate enough descriptions. Personality changes that occur while someone is under the influence of alcohol or drugs are also included here. Possessing Negs are often at the root of addictions.

Negs may exert influences only at certain times, only in certain situations, or continually. Possessing Negs will often cause depression, anxiety, and personality disorders. These conditions may be inherent to the nature of the Neg concerned or side effects of its presence. Conditions will worsen if Negs are threatened or if they do not get what they want.

By and large, possessing Negs will not normally take full control of people. Full control by a Neg does happen, but it is rare. Most possessing Negs are content to sit back and enjoy the human ride, to share human lives and pleasures and to exert hefty influences. Possessing Negs usually cannot function unaided in human society. They need human minds and memories to take care of all the little details of life, such as travel, work, socializing, relationships, and hygiene.

It is common for possessed people to become overshadowed and react aggressively when the status of their possessing Negs become threatened. These reactions usually happen when the Negs are faced with some form of exorcism or demanifestation. When Negs are threatened with exorcism, the situation can become unpredictable and dangerous.

Generally, possessing Negs will actively hide their presence. Consequently, most possessed people are not even aware they are being controlled. If victims suspected they were under Negs' control, they would actively seek outside help that could hinder or remove possessing Negs. This help includes medical and psychological support, as well as exorcism.

If possessing Negs are communicated with, typically a network of lies, half-truths, and misdirections will emerge. A possessing Neg will try to deflect questions and gain sympathy by presenting itself as a lost earthbound spirit, often a child. Alternatively, it may present itself as something sinister in order to induce fear. Exactly what it says will depend on the situation and on its nature and intentions.

Negs possess people by infiltrating their chakras and autonomous nervous systems. The autonomous nervous system controls things like heartbeat, cell repair, digestion, and breathing. Breathing is a good comparison for how the mechanism of possession works. Breathing is largely automatic, controlled by the autonomous nervous system and unconscious mind. But you can also take direct control over your breathing whenever you want to, holding your breath, panting, or breathing differently.

Try this now. Take conscious control and feel yourself breathing, taking deeper breaths, and blowing out. You will notice that you feel no different, whether you take control of your breathing or leave it on automatic. If you take control, a few seconds later, you forget to stay in control, and your breathing goes back on automatic. My point here is that you are unaware of any change, whether you have conscious control or not. Possession works in very much the same way. A Neg personality may similarly shift in and out of a person without its host (the possessed person) realizing it.

Being Neg influenced or overshadowed is similar to how you might sometimes raid the refrigerator and eat things that you have previously decided not to eat. You might, for example, eat a lot of ice cream or chocolate, even though you are on a diet. When this happens, it is like half your brain has switched itself off and someone else has temporarily taken control. You know you should not be eating this way, but you do it anyway. Then afterwards, you are kicking yourself for breaking your diet.

Typically, once a possessing Neg attaches to a person, it will begin the process of learning how to operate the person's body—how to move arms and legs, how to walk and speak. There will be intermittent losses of control of body parts during this process, as body parts do things on their own, outside the person's conscious control.

There will also be blackouts, where persons do not remember what happened for certain lengths of time. Incidences of loss of body control and blackouts will become progressively more frequent. Eventually the Neg will become capable of subduing the original personality and taking full control. If this happens, the person then becomes a powerless observer, with no control for the duration of full possession episodes.

When a possessing Neg invades a person, there will be an incident where the main attachment is inserted. This event will often involve some kind of traumatic Neg attack, which can include scary nocturnal atmospheres, presleep terrors, nightmares, supernatural phenomena, and obsessive thoughts and urges. During this event, one area of the body will be particularly affected with pain and/or swelling. Over the next few days or weeks, this area will turn into a granuloma, a gristly lump. This granuloma can be under the skin and visible, or deeper inside the body and invisible. If it is inside the body, it could cause a slipped disk, a hernia, or an infection. A visible granuloma lump is the classic Stigmata Diabolis—the physical evidence sought by Inquisition witch hunters to indict people as witches (see chapter 6).

In one case I observed, a young man disgraced an older colleague during a violent altercation. The disgraced older man was already possessed, so a revenge attack ensued on the younger man. In the coming weeks, the young man experienced all the symptoms of Neg attack, and a granuloma the size of a walnut appeared on his leg. This was a classic Stigmata Diabolis. We broke the possession using the methods given in this book, including electrical grounding, crossing running water, drawing blue ballpoint-pen symbols on the granuloma, energy work, salt baths, and healing. The granuloma burst at the exact moment of release. This was a relatively easy case, because the attack was fresh and there was no strong level of permission involved. More well-established cases take more time and effort to achieve release. Negs that have been with adults since early childhood can be even more difficult to move—sometimes impossible.

I have worked with many people suffering this dark malady. There are many types of Negs and many ways this condition can progress. My own experience with possession and release is a fairly dramatic example.

The Classic Possession Event

For a nonphysical personality to possess a living person in a short time indicates great strength and experience on its part. Negs of this caliber are uncommon. Many factors are involved, especially the degree of permission that has been given. High-level Negs do not attack at random. There are always reasons, but sometimes these reasons are unfathomable.

A Neg with this intention will try to create an opportunity where the act of possession can occur. Rapid overshadowing can happen to most people, but possession itself does not happen at random. An event and an opportunity, permission and a reason, are always involved.

The classic formula for possession involves a person who wants something very badly. He/she may obsessively want a promotion, a particular lover, a pile of money, a new car. In desperation he/she *passionately* states something like, "I will give *anything* to have this!" A voice is then heard to say something like, "I can give you this!" or "Would you give your soul for this?" The person may be frightened, but if he/she wants this badly enough, he/she may then say "*Yes.* I will give anything!" Then they will hear something like, "The deal is done!" or "It is yours for three years!" This is the classic act of *selling your soul to the devil.* Exactly how this exchange transpires depends on how theatrical the Neg involved is.

After such an event, the Neg attachment will be inserted, unless it already exists. The person will get exactly what he/she asked for. The "gift" will, however, always be hollow. It will never be what the person thought it would be like. The new car, for example, may be a lemon or drive the person into bankruptcy. The new job may be a nightmare of stress. The new lover may be hateful and unfaithful. The pile of money may be an insurance payout after a painful accident.

The Neg that possessed me orchestrated a situation where I would voluntarily give it direct permission. This denotes intelligent planning. I did not hear a voice, but the situation fits the classic possession formula. I offered a deal by saying, "Take me and leave the child," fully knowing that I was talking to a demon. I did not realize that it could hear my thoughts or that it could actually accept the deal, but I said the words and meant them. Ignorance is no excuse, apparently. I would never do this again. I barely survived.

(Again, for those people with compulsions: When words or thoughts are loosely said, no matter how passionately or obsessively, please trust that your higher self knows your true intentions. It will not allow possession to occur if your intentions are not sincere. Pretending to be sincere does not work. You cannot fool your higher self.)

While the possessing Neg was conditioning me and learning how to use my body, I made some interesting observations. The occasional involuntary actions I experienced were fast, smooth, and precise. They were not spasms or muscular twitches. For example, my hand and arm would suddenly reach out, pick up something, then throw it. My controlled arm and hand did not just lash out crudely and knock something over.

During episodes of personality replacement, my mind disassociated from my physical body. There was a great feeling of pressure and a slight falling sensation, and then I floated in a surreal, dreamlike world. I felt my physical arms and legs moving on their own accord. I had zero control over any part of my physical body. My mind felt weak and tired. It was very quiet, and the world outside seemed at a distance. I was a powerless observer.

In this situation, it would be easy to think, "This is a dream," and just fall asleep. You are aware of your physical body, but it feels distant. You know when it is walking, but you feel like the walking is being done on huge fluffy pillows. If your body picks up something, you are aware it is doing so, but cannot really feel what is in your hand. You can feel pleasure and pain, but these emotions are vague and blunted.

My best advice to anyone experiencing personality replacement is to stay calm and focus. Don't fall into the trap of believing it's a dream. Fight it with every ounce of courage and mental strength you have. Never give in! Fighting weakens the possessing Neg's grip.

Fighting personality replacement is similar to fighting sleep paralysis. During an episode, you may feel powerless to move, but you are still in touch with your body. It will feel numb, vague, and unresponsive, even though it may be moving of its own accord. But it is still your body, and *you can regain control.* The best way to recover control is the same way to break out of sleep paralysis: concentrate on moving a big toe or an index finger, or try breathing heavily. Try all three ways. The instant you move a big toe or index finger or take a deep breath, you will regain full control over your body. Then it is time for a long shower and a serious think about applying other countermeasures.

For some reason, breathing, big toes, and index fingers are the easiest things to reanimate during both sleep paralysis and personality replacement. The underlying subtle mechanisms involved in these two conditions are likely related.

My Possession and Release

In my early thirties, I thought I had seen just about everything. As a veteran healer and mystic, I had worked on any number of spiritual problems, including psychic attacks, poltergeists, and hauntings. Back then, I only had a very basic idea of how these things worked. I just followed my instincts and did my best, which usually helped. At this time, however, life saw fit to initiate me into the greater reality and begin a different type of education. Here's the short version of what happened to me.

I had been working with a family on and off for a couple of years, trying to free a small boy from what appeared to be possession. (This is the same boy mentioned in the last chapter—the one with the obsession with sucking the ends of power extension cords.) I had witnessed some amazing phenomena around this boy. Nothing I did had worked with him because, as he admitted, he kept calling the entity back. He believed it was his friend, and he was lonely without it. Nothing anyone said or did could shake this belief.

Then one night, with his mother in attendance, I spent two hours trying everything I knew to release him. In exasperation, without knowing the gravity of what I was about to do, I mentally offered myself in exchange for the boy. I remember seeing this done in the movie *The Exorcist*, just before the priest jumped out of the window. I thought that I would have a better chance of dealing with this Neg than the boy did. In my mind I literally said, "Take me and leave the child." And the possessing Neg did take me, instantly.

The Neg struck the exact moment I gave permission. It hit me in the mouth like a boxer and paralyzed my body. My lower lip swelled up and bled as if I had been physically punched. I realized at this moment that I had been set up and tricked into doing this. I was paralyzed and in great pain and distress for several minutes before I collapsed out of my chair and onto the floor.

I was badly shaken, but pulled myself together as best I could. The swelling in my lip grew into a granuloma the size of a shelled almond over the next few days. A powerful Neg attachment had been inserted into me.

A few days later, I started losing control of my body, one part at a time. The first episode came while I was reading a magazine. My arm moved on its own, picked up a book, and threw it across the room. This action shocked me, but I still felt okay. A few hours later, my foot shot out and kicked my beloved dog, Blueboy.

I did not sense anything evil in me or around me. But the loss-of-control episodes became steadily more frequent. Within two weeks, I knew that if I did not do something quickly my life would be over. My self-confidence was shattered, and I did not trust myself. I did not want to think about what this Neg might do if it gained full control over my body.

I did not hear voices or have insane thoughts, but I could feel these in the background. I tried everything I knew to heal and free myself, but nothing worked. There is very little practical information available on possession. I visited several spiritual healers and teachers, but nothing they did helped. Some of these people got very annoyed with me. I felt judged and blamed for something that was not my fault.

The senses of shame, sadness, and isolation I had at this point were extreme. No one could relate to what I was going through, not even my own mother. Everyone thought I should see a doctor and get medicated. So I deeply sympathize with anyone who is suffering this darkest of all maladies.

I had a good, long think about my situation. I was faced with two logical choices: I could turn myself into a mental hospital, or I could kill myself. Neither choice was appealing. Then I came up with a third option. I could surrender to the divine and let it lead me out of the darkness. This surrender would probably kill me, but I had nothing to lose. I chose this third option, figuring I could always feed myself to the sharks later.

I had only the vaguest notion of what to do. I knew I had to get in touch with my higher self, but I did not know how. I had no time to wait or to think about it. I had to do something right away, or I would die. I decided to dive in and just wing it.

Everything I knew and believed in told me that my higher self would try to get a message to me. I had come so far in life; I could not believe that it was all over now. There must be a cure, a way out of my dilemma. Seizing the moment, trying to work with my intuition, I went out for a walk with the firm intention that I would find a message from God. And no matter how crazy the message was, I promised myself that I would follow the instructions to the letter. I had nothing to lose.

The weather outside was dark and unseasonably stormy, and I slogged through the rain-drenched scrub. I cleared my mind and held my intention firmly, trying to open myself to the all-important message on which my life depended. Everything I believed in told me this message would come. I could not allow myself to not believe this.

After an hour of walking in the wet darkness, I was soaked and freezing. I jogged to keep warm, but ran into a tree and almost knocked myself out. I rebounded into a muddy ditch. Clawing my way out, I regained my footing and rubbed my head. As I brushed myself down, lightning flashed, and I saw a piece of muddy newspaper stuck to my leg. Hope surged in me. This was it—the divine message!

Back at home, I gleefully spread out the wet newspaper on the table. It was mostly torn and blackened. I dabbed it clean with tissues. I could only make out a few words from an advertisement: "Come to . . . garden nursery . . . Jarrahdale . . . nestled in the hills . . . open 7 days . . . potted Kangaroo Paws $2.95!" I knew where these hills were—a few hours drive away in some rough bush (the Australian wilderness).

I had no option but to follow the message. So I dressed rough and packed a bundle: a couple of blankets, a groundsheet, some warm clothes, a couple of canteens, a big water bag, an old kettle, and some billy tea. I took no food, as I was not going for a holiday.

My *very* worried wife drove me through the hills of Jarrahdale as I searched for the next omen. I saw a flash of light from the top of a hill about a mile off the road. We stopped there, and I started out. Several hours later, almost dead with exhaustion, I found a soda can on a rock and knew that it had caused the flash of light. Sounds crazy, but the omen was true, and I was actually on the right path.

I spent several days and nights wandering those hills, looking for signs and omens. I had a lot of amazing experiences. This is rough land with almost no groundwater. The day temperature was around 100 degrees Fahrenheit, and I froze at night. At times I thought I was going mad, almost dying of thirst and exposure, starving, dodging snakes and wild pigs, wandering aimlessly during the day, sleeping on the ground at night. I had vowed to free myself or die. There was no way I was taking this thing back home to my family.

On the second-to-last day of my quest, I awoke at predawn light. I was weak from hunger and half expecting to die soon. But I was not afraid. For all this, I was in good humor. My decision to stay and rid myself of this thing or die in the process was massively liberating. I figured, "If I die, I win by default."

I got up and walked to the precious little spring near my camp for water. About halfway, there was a sudden impact in my mouth as the gristly tumor in my lip burst. At the same moment, a huge weight lifted from me. I suddenly felt wonderful, even though I was spitting blood and bits of gristle. The lump was completely gone, leaving a gaping hole inside my lower lip. I was free at last.

Only seconds after the lump had burst, I experienced the most violent Neg attack of my life. I dropped screaming to the ground. My body felt like it was tearing itself apart from the inside, all my muscles working against themselves. This attack lasted for about twenty seconds and then stopped as suddenly as it began, just as the first rays of the dawning sun peeked over the hills. I staggered the rest of the way to the spring. I fell into it and cleaned myself up. I had some painful torn muscles, hernias, and a ripped lip to contend with, but I felt wonderful. The dark thing inside me was gone.

For two days after this release, I lived in what I can only describe as a state of grace. No insects landed on me—no flies or mosquitoes—and no wild animals ran from me. They seemed to sense that I was no threat. I could hug kangaroos and emus and pick up wild rabbits and snakes and play with them. This state of grace left me the day I returned home, but the Neg never came back.

In hindsight, the deciding factor in my release was that, for my last few days in the hills, I was sleeping directly above an underground stream. When I walked down to the water that last morning, I walked over an area of much stronger flow. Crossing this running water was what I think weakened and finally evicted the possessing Neg. The dawning sunlight may also have played a part in demanifesting the Neg.

The vicious attack I experienced during my release is typical of a Neg during eviction. They are cruel and vengeful creatures. They do not like to lose. I expect it was demanifested.

Even though the Neg had taken me up on my offer to "take me and leave the child," it had not actually left the child. It may or may not have vacated the child during the few weeks I was possessed by it. (I was too preoccupied with my own survival at the time to notice.) Higher-level Negs (demons) seem to have the ability to make multiple copies of themselves. It may have been a copy that possessed me and could have been destroyed during my release, while the original remained with the child.

This child is now an adult in his mid-twenties at the time of this writing. His Neg problems continue today. He has had a troubled life. Further direct work with him is not possible. On the surface, his problems appear to have lessened. He now has more self-control. But on occasions when I see him, the same Neg briefly overshadows him and smiles at me, to let me know it is still there and in control. I consider this case to be a work in progress.

Possession Issues

All the symptoms of Neg attachment given earlier in the book can be involved in possession. There are also some conditions and issues specific to possession and worthy of discussion.

The classic symptoms of possession are unpredictable behavior, mood swings, threatening atmospheres, tendencies towards violence, lust, perversion, greed, a need to control and manipulate, and unnatural powers of persuasion. These symptoms can be progressive and/or episodic.

The unusual *power* of persuasion comes from persons being possessed by a spirit personality that has a stronger mind. This type of being has an atmosphere of power and authority far stronger than the best salesperson or politician could ever produce.

In most cases, people are not aware they are possessed, especially if this condition has existed since childhood. People become acclimatized to Neg controls. Possessing influences will often come and go. People often explain away these influences as mood fluctuations or as a bipolar disorder. Other symptoms involved in possession can include the entire range of mental and psychological disorders.

Possession can be related to hereditary attachments. A Neg may come down through family lines and possess susceptible family members.

Behavioral Training

Neg-affected people are rewarded for obedience and punished for disobedience to Neg urges. Reward often entails endorphin releases, adrenaline rushes, heightened arousal, and feelings of comfort and well-being. Punishment entails feelings of pressure, confusion, obsessive thoughts, depression, or anxiety. Punishment can include loss of control of bodily functions, loss of libido, and pain and disability.

Neg-pressured addicts are rewarded with endorphin surges and feelings of well-being. The psychological pressures exerted by Negs are far stronger than those caused by chemical addiction alone.

Involuntary and Patterned Movements

A sure sign of trouble is when one's body begins performing actions independently. For example, your hand might reach out and break something, or your foot may kick something for no apparent reason. This type of involuntary action can indicate that progressive possession is underway or already established.

With some types of possession, rhythmic movements can occur. People might circle their hands in particular ways, pick at the air, make repetitive patterns or gestures, or feel compelled to dance or walk in circles or compelled to hop on one foot. Repetitive sounds and words can also be involved.

Sexual Issues

Unusual sexual arousal and urges can be involved with some cases of possession. These urges can be guilt-inducing or reward-and-punishment devices. Permission can also be involved, because each time urges are given into, Neg controls are reinforced. Most Neg types will use sex in some way or other, because sex is a great weakness in some people.

Neg-induced sexual fantasies are reinforced with direct stimulation of the genital energy center, which is extremely powerful. Over time, sexuality can even be altered by Negs. They reinforce particular types of sexual fantasies and weaken others. Natural sexual inclination and orientation can, in this way, be compromised.

Hearing Voices

The phenomenon of hearing disembodied voices can have many potential sources, both positive and negative. A common phenomenon is to hear one's name called. What effect this has depends on one's beliefs. It can be fear inducing, intriguing, or just odd.

Logically, if Negs have opportunities to make people hear their voices, they would not just calmly and politely speak a name, but would say something nasty or intimidating. In my experience, when people hear only their names being spoken, a Neg is not involved. A benevolent spirit or one's higher self can be responsible. This contact is usually to bring your attention to something important.

Hearing disembodied voices is a symptom more commonly believed to be related to mental illness than the supernatural. Schizophrenia can involve auditory, tactile, or visual hallucinations, or combinations of these. Neg problems can involve these same symptoms.

Neg problems can cause mental illness, but mental illness can also open one to Neg problems. Hearing disembodied voices is a common symptom of possession. But hearing voices in itself does not always indicate possession. Possession can occur without any voices being heard. While I have experienced objective voice phenomena on many occasions, I did not hear voices at any time while I was possessed.

There are two distinct types of voice phenomena: subjective and objective. The subjective voice is heard inside the head, while the objective voice is heard with the ears as a normal voice or noise.

I reference a study on schizophrenia voice phenomena (see bibliography), where functional MRI (magnetic resonance imaging) is used to map the brains of subjects. The study found that the same auditory pathways in the brain activated whether the subject heard a real sound or a disembodied voice.

Based on my own experiences and observations concerning auditory phenomena, it is clear that in some cases, when an objective voice is heard, the parotid gland (the gland beneath the ear) vibrates. This vibration spreads through the mastoid bone behind the ear, where it can be felt with the fingertips, much like the vibrations given off by audio speakers. The mastoid vibrates in tune with the voice being heard, transferring vibrations into the ear canal and making the eardrum vibrate to produce a real voice sound. This type of objective voice experience results from energy-body manipulation by spirits. Mastoid-vibration-modulated voices are not uncommon, but they are generally not recognized for what they are.

Sleep

Sleep is essential for good health. Neg and possession problems frequently involve insomnia and other parasomnias. A few days without sleep, and natural defenses fall, and the gates to the mind are wide open.

If you are having disturbed sleep and insomnia, see a healthcare professional and get some help. If Neg problems are suspected, getting professional help should be a high priority.

Alternatively, some types of Neg problems will cause extreme fatigue, necessitating long hours of sleep. In this case, some form of energy draining is likely in progress. Appropriate countermeasures, including medical advice, should be employed to counteract this drain of vitality.

Dream Signs

Neg interference and conditioning will cause noticeable changes in sleeping and dreaming. Nightmares, night terrors, audio, visual and tactile hallucinations, and presleep visions are common for possessed people.

Dreams and astral-sight visions containing abnormal or frightening content—for example, dreams of spiders and snakes, of being pursued and in danger, or of seeing or engaging in violent or perverted activities—indicate that something is wrong. They can indicate the presence of Negs, Neg dream manipulation, and core-image creation. These dreams can also contain metaphorical content, depicting what is happening in the local nonphysical environment. This content can contain advice from your higher self.

It is useful to keep a journal of nocturnal activity, including visions and dreams. This record can help you identify core images and sources of psychic attacks.

Changes in Eye Color and Facial Aspects

Eye color and facial aspects can darken and change in response to strong Neg presences. During episodes of overshadowing and personality replacement, these changes can happen in a few seconds.

My eyes are normally a light blue-gray. During the few weeks of progressive possession I experienced, my eyes changed to a medium-dark gray. After my release, they immediately turned a light, clear sky blue and stayed this color for several days before reverting to their normal light blue-gray.

Physical changes can occur during episodes of overshadowing and possession. A shadow seen falling over the victim's face is common. During such times, the aspects of the face can appear to transfigure as facial muscles contort to try to match the face and facial expressions of the possessing Neg.

In extreme cases, the face and other body parts of the victim can become clouded over by a thick, murky-green ectoplasmic discharge. When this happens, the Neg's true face and eyes will be seen superimposed over the physical face. The eyes may turn completely black or red. The face may be nonhuman. I have seen this several times with possessed people that I have worked with over the years. This is a very disturbing thing to observe. If this happens, my best advice is to move quickly away. This can be a very dangerous situation, because it indicates the Neg is in full control of the victim. And a Neg in full control is capable of anything. Do not wait to find out what it will do.

When Negs are in full control of a human body, they are not able to move or react quickly as a normal person can. Movements are generally slow and deliberate, particularly when the Negs are negotiating obstacles, such as locked doors, gates, and furniture. They would not be able to catch a ball or run nimbly around a house. Knowing this makes it easier to run away from them, which is advisable. Pushing over chairs and other things to delay any pursuit is also advised.

In this circumstance, performing a pentagram banishment (see the next chapter) and/or exposing the possessed victim to lots of electrically grounded running water are the best options for banishing the possessing Neg.

It should be kept in mind that fully possessed, Neg-controlled people can develop superhuman strength, so they are extremely dangerous. For example, a Neg could enable a possessed person to easily pluck a brick or chunk of concrete from a wall with his or her fingers.

Hair and Skin Symbols

Attachments by powerful spirit personalities, positive and negative, can cause patterns to appear on the skin or in the hair, or even in an eye. These patterns will form a symbol or a diagram (a sigil).

If this sigil is on the skin, the area can be the color of a mole or nevus, or it can appear pale from a lack of pigmentation, as if it had been bleached. These sigils can include some types of birthmarks, which indicate where attachments were made before birth.

If this symbol or diagram is on the head, there may be no mark on the skin, but the hair growing through the affected area can be bleached white. If the hair is cut short, the symbol will be clearly seen; otherwise, the hair will appear to be streaked.

This phenomenon is uncommon. I have only encountered a handful of people with skin or hair or eye symbols. All were psychically gifted, with histories of Neg-related problems.

Peculiar Medical Problems

Strange infections can flare up suddenly and strongly during Neg invasions. Neg-related infections tend to be virulent. Medical attention should be sought sooner rather than later, if these infections do not respond normally to home treatment. It is wise to keep a first-aid kit and iodine on hand for treating infections, if you are countering Neg problems.

Severe headaches and other violent pains are common symptoms of strong Neg attack and possession. Pain will often come and go in episodes minutes or hours apart. Pain can be widespread or localized to only a small area. The sudden onset of allergies and dietary intolerances can also be side effects of Neg overshadowing. These intolerances can be likened to moods, as they will tend to come and go.

It is the on-and-off nature of these medical problems that identifies them as possibly having supernatural causes. Imagine needles being inserted into and removed from a Voodoo doll, and the doll being pushed in and out of flames or dunked in iced water. The sensations the doll would feel if it were alive equate to sharp pains, hot flushes, and cold shivering a human experiences during a Neg attack.

CRAMPS AND HERNIAS

Muscular cramps and torn muscles can be caused by Neg manipulation of the physical body. Muscles are made to pull against themselves, resulting in muscle tearing.

This type of internal attack usually happens suddenly. It is most likely to occur at night. It can be very painful and cause physical damage. One might, for example, get a cramp in a bicep; a calf; a shin; a small area of the chest, back, or face; the stomach; or a single toe—anywhere on the body.

Sudden, painful tears in muscle and tissue may occur for no apparent reason. For example, a back muscle might suddenly cramp and tear itself while one is resting or sleeping. Herniated spinal disks can also occur, as can damage to internal tissue and organs. These injuries are traumatic and can be life threatening, requiring urgent medical attention.

Some of these conditions are medically impossible events. I have seen such conditions happen to others and experienced them myself. It is generally pointless explaining the spontaneous occurrence of such things to doctors. No offense to doctors, but this kind of thing is way outside their training, beliefs, and experience.

A woman I know collapsed with acute abdominal pain while talking on the phone. She had no history of cramps of any kind. The surgeon who saved her life a few hours later said it was like she had been hit with an axe on the inside.

My calf muscle tore so badly one morning while I was resting in bed that I was in a wheelchair and on crutches for weeks. I also have a clearly visible twelve-inch tear where my outer abdominal muscles tore clean through in the shape of a numeral seven. This tear happened while I was resting in bed. Fortunately, the inner layer of abdominal muscles remains intact.

STOMACH AND BOWEL PROBLEMS

Nausea, vomiting, stomach and bowel cramps, diarrhea, and unexplainable bouts of flatulence and belching can all be caused by Negs. These types of problems can flare up suddenly when resident Negs feel threatened. These symptoms can also be used as punishment devices.

I once gave contact healing to a woman who began belching loudly the moment I touched her. This belching continued every ten seconds or so for over half an hour with no letup. She had eaten nothing unusual and had no history of anything like this ever happening before. A medical explanation is possible, but unlikely given the timing and circumstances.

I have also known people who were forced to obey possessing Negs through loss of bladder and bowel control. One such man, who used to be an engineer, has lived on the streets for years because of this. His possessing Neg makes him do silly things, or he is punished. For example, he will be forced to walk a city block and touch the right taillight of every parked car, or his bowels will empty themselves.

Healing Yourself of Possession

You can heal yourself of possession. Doing so takes consistent time and effort, but it can be done. Achieving release always involves a spiritual quest and growth. The details of how one approaches this depends on circumstances and personal choices. Following are some tips and guidelines that might help.

To begin with, take some time out for yourself. You will need time to think and plan. Apply all of the countermeasures and advice given earlier, as necessary. Start invoking the help of your higher self, while using other countermeasures to make your body and your mind an uncomfortable place for Negs. This includes saying affirmations, sleeping electrically grounded, using the blue ballpoint-pen ink method on skin blemishes and suspected attachment points, taking mega salt baths, burning incense, using Tiger Balm and/or magnets—everything. These countermeasures need to be taken seriously and applied consistently.

Actively seek outside help, including energy workers, healers, and bodyworkers. You may need to visit several before you find someone with whom you are compatible. Attend spiritual workshops and seminars, and increase your knowledge and experience.

Your higher self holds all the keys. The saying "God helps those who help themselves" applies here most strongly. Possessing Negs will do everything they can to discourage, distract, and scare you into stopping your quest for a release. Do not be afraid of this. Freedom is something worth fighting for. Consistent effort and focused intention are needed to achieve release. Be positive and do not doubt your ability to achieve release.

Affirmations are the most powerful tool you have to help yourself. Verbal affirmations are many times more powerful than silent affirmations. The spoken word activates your throat chakra and projects your words onto the astral level. Your higher self is more receptive and proactive on the astral level.

Verbally repeat the Core Affirmation—"I am loved and I am worthy. I am safe and I am free. I am powerfully protected. I am master of my body and ruler of my mind."—for several hours per day or as often as you possibly can. Driving time and alone time are good times for repeating it strongly and at length. Make good use of such times. The Core Affirmation petitions the higher self. It is designed to evict Neg personality controls and restore natural shielding. The more you use this affirmation, the stronger its effect will be. Also use silent affirmations while resting or meditating, and especially while falling asleep, so they continue in your mind during sleep. Record the Core Affirmation, and play this recording on repeat during the day and at a barely audible level during sleep.

Once you start using affirmations, you will need to be vigilant for synchronicities and coincidences, signs and omens, which contain guidance from your higher self. Then you will need to take action on this information. This guidance will lead you to the information and help that is needed.

Electrically ground yourself during sleep and as much as you can during the day. Ground your bed to a water pipe. Use conductive cloth next to bare skin. Computer antistatic wrist straps will also help with grounding. Stay grounded. Set up grounding wires with clips in multiple locations in your home—at your bed, TV, computer. Clip yourself to these wires as much as possible during the daytime. Carry a grounding wrist strap with a cable and alligator clips and a metal tent peg with you whenever you leave your home. Use these to ground yourself as much as possible. Get some leather-soled shoes or shoes with brass studs to improve grounding. Walk barefoot on wet grass and sand and paddle in water whenever you can.

Wear a Q-Link or similar device for electromagnetic-field (EMF) protection (see "Further References" in the back of this book). These devices will help keep you focused and will reduce Neg-related effects.

Take mega salt baths regularly, and as often as necessary, to reduce Neg effects. Soak your feet in a bucket of electrically grounded saltwater every day. Take frequent long showers while performing the electric-violet-visualization cleansing exercise.

Mark skin blemishes with symbols drawn in blue ballpoint-pen ink. Replenish the symbols as they fade or wash away.

Apply Tiger Balm often to your feet and always before sleep.

Spring clean and declutter your home. Make it as beautiful as you can and keep it clean and tidy, to improve positive energy in your home. Burn incense and essential oils.

Eat a healthy diet with lots of raw, organic food.

Pray to the power(s) you believe in, in whatever way appeals to you. Perform the pentagram banishment in the morning and at night (see the next chapter).

Get some therapy! Everyone living in our modern world can benefit greatly from the help of a loving psychologist.

Avoid alcohol and recreational drugs. You need to be sober and in control. If addictions are a problem, including addictions to food, caffeine, nicotine, and sugar, target these with affirmations and seek professional help.

Get plenty of sleep. This is the first priority if you are under attack.

Accept full responsibility for your condition. Do not give your power away by blaming others or by blaming life for being unkind. Take your power back. Own this experience! If you take control, then you have the power to heal yourself. Be determined. Keep up your regime of countermeasures for as long as it takes to release the Neg. This is a war. Plan to win more battles than you lose.

At some point, the main Neg attachment point will begin to rupture. The physical indicator of this attachment may be an external lump or mark you know about, or it may be an internal one of which you are unaware. You will know when this rupture happens, as there will be change at the attachment location. This change may involve pain and/or swelling. You may, for example, herniate a disk while sleeping, or get an infection—anything.

If the pressure eases, do not let your guard down. Continue applying countermeasures. The Neg will attempt to reconnect and reinsert its controls. Nightmares and phenomena will escalate during reattachment attempts. These attempts will continue until your body and mind heal and your natural shields are repaired, or until the Neg is demanifested. Then and only then will Neg attack be over.

With regular exposure to electrical grounding, running water, and other countermeasures, Negs will eventually break away and desist. It is advisable to continue grounded-sleeping practices in the long term, to prevent further Neg attachments.

In this chapter, we have explored the dark malady of possession and what can be done about it. The next chapter teaches how to banish negative energies and Negs more directly.

CHAPTER TEN

Pentagram Banishment

Core Affirmation: "I am loved and I am worthy. I am safe and I am free. I am powerfully protected. I am master of my body and ruler of my mind."

The pentagram banishment and cleansing rituals given here are cut-down versions of the full Lesser Banishment Ritual of the Pentagram (LBRP). This versatile and effective banishment ritual is an absolute lifesaver if you have serious Neg problems. The most powerful way to perform this banishment is with hand signs and verbal commands. The voice should be vibrated and deepened, and a commanding tone and attitude used.

The sacred names given here for banishment can be varied, so the ritual can be customized to suit any religious belief or tradition. The names of angels and deities can be substituted. If you do not have a strong religious preference, though, I suggest the Kabalistic version I give here be used, because this is a proven formula.

As a mystic, I have a personal relationship with the divine and do not follow any particular religion or tradition. To me, rituals and sacred names are tools. I keep using the banishment method given here because it works. It has never let me down, even in many extreme situations.

The essence of a banishment pentagram involves signing a hand action while giving a direct and authoritative command in the name of the divine (a sacred name).

The Pentagram

The pentagram symbol represents humanity and the five elements: earth, air, fire, water, and akasha (also called aether). When one point of a pentagram is on top, the pentagram represents light and goodness, but when two points are on top, its meaning is reversed.

The function of a pentagram is determined by how it is created and used. Starting at the bottom left point and signing it clockwise renders an earth banishment pentagram. Figure 13 is a diagram of a pentagram; 1. is Earth, 4 is Air, 5 is Water, 3 is Fire. A clockwise hand action is banishing. An anticlockwise hand action is invoking. The starting point defines the function. So to banish Earth element, we start and finish at 1, and the hand moves clockwise.

The Earth banishment pentagram is the most widely used, as Earth and earthbound spirit types are by far the most troublesome.

Sacred Names

All Negs are repelled by ancient sacred names. The sacred names used for a banishment pentagram are traditionally Kabalistic God names.

The primary Kabalistic God name is *YHVH* (pronounced *Yude-Heh-Vahv-Heh*). (There are multiple ways to pronounce God names.) Other sacred God names suitable for banishment are Adonai *(Ah-Doh-Nye)*, Agla (Ah-Glah), Eheih *(Eh-Heh-Yeh)*, and Shaddi *(Shadday)*. For best results, vibrate these names in the base of the throat and deepen your voice as you speak.

Other sacred names can be substituted for the primary Kabalistic God name. Use sacred names from your own religion or tradition. For example, you may like to refer to God as *Allah, Brahman, the Buddha, God, the Goddess, Jehovah, Shakti, Shiva, the Great White Spirit.*

Names of archangels and angels can also be used with a banishment pentagram—for example, *Michael, Gabriel, Uriel, Raphael, Azrael, Ariel, Metatron, Sandalphon, Zadkiel.* (The first four archangel names above are used in the full LBRP.)

The Banishment Hand Sign

To perform the earth element banishment hand sign, stand and point the index and middle fingers of your right hand, then reach across your body

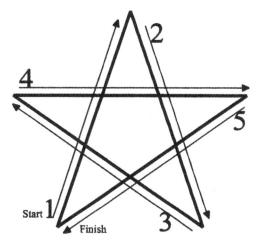

Figure 13: Drawing the banishment pentagram

and touch them to your left hip. With sweeping moves of your arm, trace the pentagram symbol in front of you with your pointing fingers. While you do this, imagine a blue streak, like a gas flame, trailing from your fingers. Imagine the blue lines hanging in the air as you form the symbol. When you have completed the symbol, imagine the pentagram remaining in place where you signed it.

Again, start from your left hip (touching your left hip with your fingers). Ascend your arm in a straight line to a point in the air above your head (as far as you can comfortably reach), then sweep down to your right hip, then diagonally up and left (to a point adjacent your left shoulder), then horizontally across to your right (to a point adjacent your right shoulder), and then diagonally down to finish back at your left hip (see figure 13).

Practice the hand action until you can do it smoothly with a confident, sweeping action. Once you have learned this action, add the words while you sign the pentagram.

Banishment Words

Banishment words should always be spoken in a deep and commanding voice. Spoken words are *vastly* more effective than just thinking words silently. The voice activates the throat chakra and projects spoken words onto the astral level. Your higher self (your direct connection with the divine) is far more receptive and proactive on the astral level.

The banishment pentagram ritual works because the combination of a command with sacred names and the banishment pentagram evokes a particular aspect of the divine, triggering a surge of banishment energy.

Direct Banishment Action

A direct banishment action is used to banish a presence, a manifestation, or a direct attack. To perform a direct banishment action, face the disturbance. Sign a banishment pentagram with hand gestures. As you do so, commandingly say: **"I banish you in the name of Almighty God, *Yude-Heh-Vahv-Heh, Ah-Doh-Nye, Ah-Glah, Eh-Heh-Yeh, Shadday!*"**

Repeat the above sequence as necessary. If you cannot ascertain the direction of the disturbance, turn and repeat this ritual in each of the four compass points around you, starting in the east.

While learning this procedure, you might find it easier to use only one sacred name, YHVH *(Yude-Heh-Vahv-Heh).* Add other names as you can remember them. The primary God name should come first in a banishment ritual. The order of the other names used is not important. Write the names on a card and hold the card in your free hand or tape the card to a wall to help you remember the sequence. It is okay if you mix up the names or forget some while learning. Just do the best you can.

This banishment can be used to dispel any kind of Neg manifestation, disturbance, or atmosphere. It can also be done while you are lying in bed, to repel nocturnal attacks and interference. Aim the pentagram at the disturbance or where you feel it as emanating from most strongly. Imagine the gas-blue pentagram forming above you as you sign it. Imagine this pentagram growing to fill the ceiling area above you. Repeat as necessary.

A direct banishment can also be performed on a body part. If, for example, you have a lot of negative activity in a foot or a leg, you can perform a banishment on it. This will help to stop or reduce activity. Repeat the banishment as often as necessary.

The banishment action can be imagined and the words spoken only mentally, if necessary, but remember that performing the banishment action only in the mind greatly reduces its effectiveness. It should be done mentally only if you find yourself paralyzed, or if the situation is inappropriate for spoken words. Repeat as necessary.

Banishment words can also be whispered quietly, while the words are still vibrated in the base of the throat.

Clearing Spaces

The following extends on the above direct banishment action, but is still a simplified version of the full LBRP. The full version is far more powerful, but also significantly more complex. (See Donald Kraig's book *Modern Magick*, listed in the bibliography, and the Wikipedia article "Lesser Ritual of the Pentagram," listed in "Further References" for more details.)

First, use a compass to ascertain true east. Stand in the center of the room or space to be cleared and face east. Relax for a few moments and center yourself, holding in mind the intention of what you are about to do: banish all negative spirits and influences.

Perform the first pentagram banishment facing east. Hold the image of the blue-fire pentagram and imagine it hanging in the air. Touch its center with your pointing fingers to activate it and hold that position. Pause a moment to reinforce the image in your mind, and then turn clockwise ninety degrees to face south, imagining you are trailing a line of blue fire to the next quadrant.

Imagine a line of blue fire flowing from your fingertips, connecting the center of the first pentagram to the center of where the next will be signed. Perform the banishment in the south.

Touch the second pentagram in the center, pause a moment to reinforce the image, and then turn ninety degrees clockwise to face the west, trailing blue fire from your fingertips to touch the center of where you will sign your next pentagram. Perform the banishment in the west.

Touch the third pentagram in the center, pause a moment to reinforce the image, and then turn ninety degrees clockwise to face the north, trailing blue fire from your fingertips to touch the center of where you will sign your next pentagram. Perform the banishment in the north.

After drawing the final banishment pentagram, complete the circle by turning clockwise to face the east again, trailing blue fire as you move your pointing fingers back to the middle of the first pentagram to complete the circle of blue fire.

Concentrate and imagine the four pentagrams hanging in the air around you, connected by the line of blue fire touching each pentagram's center. Imagine the pentagrams growing in size and perfection and expanding out and filling and sealing the four quadrants of the room. Imagine them forming a wall of protection around you.

A full banishment ritual (all four quadrants) should be done in every room and open area of a house that is being cleared and protected, including garage and basement areas. You cannot overdo the banishment space-clearing procedure. It will grow in power the more practiced at it you become.

During serious and ongoing Neg problems, a full home banishment should be performed twice per day, morning and evening, for best results. With a little practice, this full banishment does not take long to accomplish. At the very least, perform it in your bedroom morning and night. Other countermeasures, including incense, electric-violet fire, affirmations, running water, and electrical grounding, should be applied as necessary.

The pentagram banishment method can also be applied to the core-image removal procedure given earlier. It can also be used during lucid dreams and astral projections, where it is even more powerful.

A Few Last Words

Core Affirmation: "I am loved and I am worthy. I am
safe and I am free. I am powerfully protected. I am
master of my body and ruler of my mind."

The subject matter of this book is something I would much rather have
never had to think about, let alone experience. However, life has led me
to where I am today and given me great personal experience and understanding of these matters. I hope my experiences might spare you some
of the painful mistakes I have made on my own journey, and make your
life a whole lot smoother.

This book is written as a practical guide to combating negative forces.
I have done my best to communicate this information in a matter-of-fact
way, to deemphasize the fearful emotional impact inherent to the subject
matter of this book. My work in the field of negative-entity and -ener-
gy research is ongoing. Please see my website community for the latest
updates in procedures, new countermeasures, and discoveries.

As I look back on my life and everything that has happened to me, good
and bad, I can see how these experiences have crafted me into who I am
today. I would never have chosen for parts of my life to happen the way
they did—that would be crazy—but now I would not change a thing. I
am in total awe of this amazing evolutionary process we call life.

We have come a long way together. I sincerely hope you never have
need for any of the advice I have given here in my book. But you are now

equipped with the knowledge needed to seriously hinder the activities of unseen negative forces that plague our world today. The more people who resist and overthrow Neg influences, and the more children who grow up Neg free, the better this world will become.

Removing influential Negs from your life requires real personal change and growth as a human being. The end result of a serious Neg encounter can involve profound contact with your higher self. When this happens, life will never be quite the same for you again. May the light of grace shine upon you always.

Bibliography

Ashley, Leonard R. N. *The Complete Book of Ghosts and Poltergeists*. Fort Lee, N.J.: Barricade Books, 2000.

Barlow, David, and V. Mark Durand. *Abnormal Psychology: An Integrative Approach*. 2nd ed. Pacific Grove: Brooks Cole, 1995.

Belanger, Michelle. *The Ghost Hunter's Survival Guide: Protection Techniques for Encounters with the Paranormal*. Woodbury, MN: Llewellyn Worldwide, 2009.

Boucsein, Wolfram. *Electrodermal Activity*. New York: Springer-Verlag. 1992

_____ . *The Psychic Vampire Codex: A Manual of Magick and Energy Work*. Boston: Weiser Books, 2004.

Bruce, Robert. *Astral Dynamics*. Charlottesville, VA: Hampton Roads, 2009.

_____ . *Energy Work: The Secret of Healing and Spiritual Development*. Charlottesville, VA: Hampton Roads, 2002.

_____ . *Practical Psychic Self-Defense*. Charlottesville, VA: Hampton Roads, 2002.

Cacioppo, John T. *Handbook of Psychophysiology*. Cambridge, UK: Cambridge University Press, 2007.

Chajes, J. H. *Between Worlds: Dybbuks, Exorcists, and Early Modern Judaism*. Philadelphia: University of Pennsylvania Press, 2003.

Cunningham, Scott. *Cunningham's Encyclopedia of Magical Herbs*. St. Paul, MN: Llewellyn, 2000.

Denning, Melita, and Osborne Phillips. *Practical Guide to Psychic Self-Defense and Well-Being*. St. Paul, MN: Llewellyn, 1980.

Fortune, Dion. *Psychic Self-Defense.* Wellingborough, UK: Aquarian Press, 1988.

Guirdham, Arthur. *Obsession: Psychic Forces and Evil in the Causation of Disease.* London: Neville Spearman, 1972.

Horne, James A. "Sleep and Its Disorders in Children." *Journal of Child Psychology & Psychiatry & Allied Disciplines* 33 (1992): 473–487.

Kraig, Donald Michael. *Modern Magick: Eleven Lessons on the High Magical Arts.* St. Paul: Llewellyn, 2000.

Lennox B. R., S. B. Park, I. Medley, P. G. Morris, and P. B. Jones. "The Functional Anatomy of Auditory Hallucinations in Schizophrenia." Department of Psychiatry, University of Cambridge. *Psychiatry Research* 100 (November 20, 2000):13–20.

Mackay. Christopher. S. *Malleus Maleficarum.* Cambridge, UK: Cambridge University Press, 2009.

Moore, Arthur Dearth, ed. *Electrostatics and Its Applications.* New York: John Wiley & Sons, 1973.

Oschman, James L. *Energy Medicine.* London: Churchill Livingstone, 2000.

Preston, Michael D. *Hypnosis: Medicine of the Mind.* Tempe, AZ: Tiger Maple Press, 2005.

Reilly, Harold J., Ruth Hagy Brod: *The Edgar Cayce Handbook for Health through Drugless Therapy* – 3 revised edition. A.R.E. Press. VA. 2008

Robbins, Hope Rossel. *The Encyclopedia of Witchcraft and Demonology.* New York: Crown, 1959.

Sambhava, Padma. *The Tibetan Book of the Dead.* Translated by Robert A. Thurman. New York: Bantam Doubleday Dell, 1994.

Turner, John T. *Medicine, Miracles, and Manifestations.* Franklin Lakes: NJ: Career Press, 2009.

Further References

General

Baldwin, William J. *Spirit Releasement Therapy*. Terra Alta, WV: Headline Books, 1995.

Ellis, Melissa Martin. *The Everything Ghost Hunting Book*. Cincinnati, OH: Adams Media, 2009.

Fiore, Edith. *The Unquiet Dead: A Psychologist Treats Spirit Possession*. New York: Ballantine, 1995.

Hummel, Christian. *Do It Yourself Space Clearing Kit*. Oceanside, CA: One Source Publications, 2004.

John of God: João de Deus—The Miracle Man of Brazil *(www.johnofgod. com)*; website for the healer and clinic.

"Lesser Banishment Ritual of the Pentagram," Wikipedia: The Free Encyclopedia *(en.wikipedia.org)*.

Martin, Malachi. *Hostage to the Devil: The Possession and Exorcism of Five Americans*. San Francisco: Harper San Francisco, 1992.

The Modern Mystery School. *http://www.modernmysteryschool.com/*

Q-Link: Clarus *(www.clarus.com)*—manufacturers and suppliers of Q-Link products.

"Sulfur: the Chemical Element," Wikipedia: The Free Encyclopedia *(en. wikipedia.org)*.

Tolle, Eckhart. *The Power of Now: A Guide to Spiritual Enlightenment*. New World Library. Novato, CA. 1999.

Electrical Grounding

Barefoot Health, Inc. *(www.barefoothealth.com)*. Information and research on personal biological grounding and earthing technology. (This is an example reference. There are many websites offering information and products on EMF protection and grounding.)

Ober, Clinton. Stephen Sinatra, and Martin Zucker. *Earthing: The Most Important Health Discovery Ever.* Laguna Beach, CA: Basic Health Publications, 2010.

Also see Dr. Sinatra's website and blog *(www.drsinatra.com)* and his newsletter issue on earthing at *www.equilibrauk.com/Sinatra_Review.pdf.*

Running-Water-EM-Field Demonstrations and Physics

Valone, Thomas. *Harnessing the Wheelwork of Nature: Tesla's Science of Energy.* Kempton, IL: Adventures Unlimited Press, 2002.

Vanderkooy, John. "An Electrostatic Experiment of Lord Kelvin with Running Water." *Phys 13 news* (January 1984). Department of Physics. University of Waterloo, ON, Canada.

Online Video References

Please check the author's website, Astral Dynamics *(www.astraldynamics.com)* for updates to the following links and other related links to this subject area.

"Walter Lewin Makes a Battery Out of Cans and Water." YouTube *(www.youtube.com)*. Online video of a physics demonstration by MIT physics professor Walter Lewin. Posted by Free Science Lectures *(www.freesciencelectures.com)*.

"Static Electricity." MetaCafe *(www.metacafe.com)*. Online video demonstration of the comb-and-running-water experiment described in chapter 7.

Meerman, Ruben (the Surfing Scientist). "Science Tricks: Electric Water Bender." Australian Broadcasting Corporation (ABC) *(www.abc.net.au)*. Online video demonstration of the comb-and-running-water experiment described in chapter 7.

"Stream of Water and Static Electricity." Newton BBS: Ask a Scientist Service (archive). *(www.newton.dep.anl.gov)*. February 1, 2005. Scientists' written response to a question about why a stream of running water will bend toward a charged rod.

Index

challenging, 115
description of, 1–2
hitchhiking, 137–138
indications of presence of, 47–50
motivations of, 22–23
plumbing and, 13–14
problems caused by, 27–31
profile of, 10–13
psychic attacks and, 26–27
source identification and, 113–114
types of, 14–21
Neg-draining water method, 140–141
night terrors
children and, 174–176
core images and, 84
hereditary attachments and, 14
nightmares
children and, 174–176
core images and, 84
hereditary attachments and, 14
noises
children and, 189–190
as countermeasure, 13, 128–130
Negs and, 54–55
spirit, 48
see also music

OBE. see out-of-body experience
objects
contaminated, 66
secondhand, 66–67
obsessive behavior, 29
obsessive thoughts, 90
occult dabbling, risks of, 62–64
oils
essential, xii, 12, 150, 151, 160–161
on feet, xi
protective, 155–156
ointments, 160–161
Ouija boards, 63
out-of-body experience, 9
overshadowing, 43–45, 180–182
see also channeling; possession

pains
astral wildlife and, 18
Neg-related, 214
panic attacks, 11
paranormal phenomena, 28
parasomnias, children and, 169–170
see also sleep

parenting, 184–186
see also children; family environment
pentagram banishment
banishment words and, 221–222
clearing spaces, 223–224
direct banishment action and, 222
hand sign and, 220–221
overview of, 219
pentagram and, 220, 221
sacred names and, 220
percussion, 129
see also noises
permission
channeling and, 46–47
children and, 63
dangers of, 64
higher self and, 116–118
possession and, 202–203, 205
revoking, 118
seduction and, 57
permission issues, 4
personal artifacts, 67–68
personality replacement, 203–204
see also possession
pets
health problems of, 42
psychic sensitivity of, 52
pine, 156
Pingala, 5
pings, 49
plumbing
ghosts and, 16
Neg concentrations and,
13–14
poltergeists and, 20
see also running water
poltergeists
activity of, 48–49
description of, 19–20
positive thinking, effect of, 123
possession
author and, 204–208
behavioral training and, 209
of body parts, 58
classic formula for, 202–203
description of, 199–202
dreams and, 211–212
example of, 203–204
granulomas and, 98–99
healing of, 215–218
hearing voices and, 210–211

About the Author

Robert Bruce is a true spiritual pioneer of our times. Author of several groundbreaking books, he has dedicated his life to exploring the dynamics of all things spiritual and paranormal and to testing the boundaries of the greater reality. This particularly involves exploring the mysteries of the human energy body, which is the foundation of physical existence and spiritual incarnation. The depth and scope of Robert's experiential knowledge is remarkable. His other fields of experience include out-of-body experiences (OBEs), kundalini, mind's eye vision, spiritual and psychic development, metaphysics, psychic security, the afterlife process, and manifestation.

Robert is a man who lives in the greater reality and asks others to join him. He lectures internationally and currently resides in Australia. You can find him on the web at his online community *www.Astral Dynamics.com,* where you will find a wealth of information and products. Robert also conducts online workshops, teaching energy work and astral projection.

Robert began having OBEs at the age of four and taught himself to write after raising his kundalini in his early thirties. He describes his life before kundalini as a series of necessary educational experiences, leading to his spiritual rebirth in the Australian wilderness. His experiential approach to life has resulted in profound contact with his higher self that continues to grow.

When not writing or lecturing, Robert is often found diving enchanted coral reefs, seeking new guests for his saltwater aquarium, or exploring wild and lonely places in the Australian outback.

Robert Bruce has a thriving online community website, forums, and blog at his website, Astral Dynamics *(www.astraldynamics.com)*. Here you will find the latest information and updates on the author's work, including:

Psychic Security Section—with updates and private support forums.

Astral Dynamics Forums—covering Robert's main topics and more.

Conversations With a Mystic—Robert's fabulous blog and podcast.

The Hall of Learning Online Workshops
    Energy Work
    Astral Projection
    Spiritual Development

Quality Products
    Q-Links
    CDs
    DVDs
    Autographed books

Free tutorials, articles, audios, and videos on
    Psychic Security
    Astral Projection
    Energy Work
    Manifestation
    Healing
    Kundalini

www.astraldynamics.com

Hampton Roads Publishing Company
... for the evolving human spirit

Hampton Roads Publishing Company
publishes books on a variety of subjects,
including spirituality, health, and other
related topics.

For a copy of our latest trade catalog,
call 978-465-0504 or visit our website at www.hrpub.com